D1294886

GREATEST MOMENTS IN
Iowa Hawkeyes
Football History

By Mark Dukes and Gus Schrader

Edited by Francis J. Fitzgerald

From the Sports Pages of

TRIUMPH
BOOKS
CHICAGO

Joe Hladky, *President and Publisher*
Ken Slaughter, *Vice President/Treasure*
Dale Larson, *General Manager*
Mark Bowden, *Managing Editor*
Mark Dukes, *Sports Editor*
Terry Bergen, *Promotions and Public Affairs Manager*

Acknowledgements

RESEARCH ASSISTANCE
Phil Haddy, Steve Roe, Traci Howard,
Theresa Walenta, Matt Ellison,
Mark Dukes, George Wine and Al Grady.

All Iowa game stories featured in this book were originally published in *The Gazette*. Reprinted by permission of the Cedar Rapids Gazette, Inc. All rights reserved.

ISBN   1-57243-261-6

COVER AND BOOK DESIGN
by Chris Kozlowski

PHOTO IMAGING
Imagine Color, Detroit, MI

PUBLISHED BY
Triumph Books
644 South Clark Street
Chicago, IL 60605
(312) 939-3330

For other sports publications in the Triumph library, call toll-free 1 (800) 335-5323.

"Iowa football reflects the ...
greater community which is all
of Iowa."

— *Loren Hickerson*

Contents

Iowa Football Is Rallying Cry For The Entire State

By Al Grady
....

The year was 1900.

The Spanish-American War was over. Lamplighters were familiar figures in cities and towns throughout America.

George M. Cohan had yet to give his regards to Broadway. The Iron Horse was rolling across the prairies, spitting smoke and soot, frightening man and beast, and winning the West. A guy named Henry Ford was wondering if he could mass produce something called an automobile. It had the power of several horses, and didn't eat as much.

In Iowa City, a small college town of some 8,000 persons nestled on the banks of the Iowa River, it was an exciting autumn. In December of the previous year Iowa had been invited to join the Intercollegiate Conference of Faculty Representatives, later to become the Big Ten. Over the summer $1,500 worth of improvements had been made at Athletic Park, formerly Sullivan's Pasture and later to become Iowa Field, on the east bank of the river just west of the present university library.

The football team was outstanding. The football team was great. It would win the conference championship in its very

first season of membership. Now, on successive weekends, it had gone to Chicago and beaten Amos Alonzo Stagg's wonderful team, and to Detroit (not Ann Arbor) and beaten Hurry Up Yost's marvelous Michigan machine. When word of the latter victory reached Iowa City by Western Union at mid-afternoon on that November Saturday, the town went wild.

Crowds invaded the campus and downtown areas. Bands played ragtime music and a massive bonfire was built.

Several students pulled University President George MacLean and other faculty members out of their buggies and paraded with them around the fire so that the president's hair and beard were singed. The heat became so intense that plate-glass windows cracked in several downtown buildings and, for a time, flames were threatening an entire block of the downtown business district as horse-drawn firewagons were called to stand by.

Hysteria remained at a fever pitch throughout Sunday and into Monday morning, when the team arrived home from Detroit. Iowa's university band, two city bands and more than 2,000 people crowded the railroad platform on the south edge of the city between Clinton and Dubuque streets, hoisting each of the 23 players to their shoulders as each stepped off the train.

Thus began a love affair with University of Iowa Hawk-

In 1919, Iowa football was beginning its ascent with Howard Jones as head coach. Jones would lead undefeated teams in 1921 and 1922, including memorable wins over Notre Dame and Yale.

eye football among citizens of Iowa City and the state of Iowa that is still as much alive today as it was then as, we near a new century and a new millenium.

Old Iowa Field ... Duke Slater ... Howard Jones ... Aubrey Devine ... A new stadium ... The Depression, and depressing days ... Nile Kinnick and the Ironmen ... Dr. Eddie Anderson ... Forest Evashevski ... The Rose Bowl ... More bad years ... Feuds within the athletic department ... Hayden Fry ... Bowl games galore.

Games played in sweltering September heat ... on painted autumn afternoons ... amid some showers ... in downpours ... on cold days ... on windy days ... in blizzards.

The flying wedge ... leather helmets ... canvas pants ... mouth guards ... face masks ... the drop kick ... shoulder pads ... knee pads ... the hip pad connected to the thigh pad ... the T-formation ... the single wing ... the Notre Dame box

... the fullhouse backfield ... the belly series ... the winged-T ... the Split-T ... the veer ... the option ... the I-formation ... the pro set ... the tight end ... the split end ... the flanker ... wide-outs ... the two-point conversion ... overtime.

Tailgating ... Oh, the traffic ... cheerleaders ... pom-pon girls ... the marching bands ... the fight songs ... pep rallies ... Homecoming parade ... Homecoming badges ... the corn monument ... Floyd of Rosedale ... Herky the Hawk ... Iowa Fights ... Go Hawks!

The years roll by. Seasons of triumph and autumns of despair. But there is one constant if you are a Hawkeye football fan. September can't come too soon.

The Roaring 20's began with a roar as far as Iowa football was concerned, and ended with a crash.

Howard Harding Jones had been named as the 11th official head coach of Iowa football in December of 1915, but

World War I delayed the Yale graduate's timetable for Hawkeye greatness. But he got there in 1921 and '22. From midway through the 1920 season until early in 1923, Iowa thundered through 20 straight games unbeaten, winning two Big Ten championships and a mythical national championship.

One of the stars of those teams was Fred (Duke) Slater, a giant of a man by 1920 standards who played tackle, often played without a helmet, and became the first black from Iowa to receive All-America honors. One of his teammates was quarterback Aubrey Devine, who ran, passed, punted and place-kicked and became the first Iowan ever to make Walter Camp's All-America team. Fullback Gordon Locke also made Camp's All- America team in 1922.

A couple of memorable moments from that season must be told. For one, Iowa traveled east to meet Yale, a football power for 40 years, in New Haven, Conn. The game matched the coaching wits of Howard Jones against his younger brother Tad. When Iowa stunned the Bulldogs 6-0, The Chicago Tribune headlined it on the front page of its Sunday editions. Never before had Yale lost at home to a team from "the West."

A month later, when Iowa played Minnesota in Iowa City, some 26,000 fans showed up to see Iowa stymie the Gophers, 28-24, despite a heavy rain during the game. Irving Weber, the late Iowa City historian, recalled in one of his books, "The dirt roads in all directions from Iowa City became quagmires.

"Five hundred cars were stuck between Iowa City and Cedar Rapids and 1,500 fans were forced to sleep in their cars or seek shelter on the floors of the homes of friendly farmers.

"On Sunday and Monday, farmers with teams of horses pulled the cars out of the mud."

One other game comes to mind from the storied days of Old Iowa

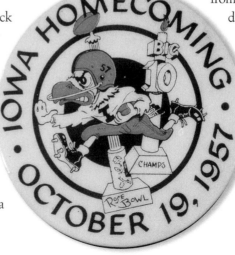

Field. It was in 1925. Howard Jones had moved on to become head coach at Southern California, where he built a dynasty with his Thundering Herds. The new coach was Burt Ingwersen and it was in 1925 that the great Red Grange of Illinois, the Galloping Ghost, Old No. 77, brought his show to Iowa City. A record crowd of 27,712 overflowed the stands beside the river. Grange did not disappoint, returning the opening kickoff 89 yards for a touchdown. But Iowa rallied behind the tremendous play of running back Nick (Cowboy) Kutsch, who kicked two field goals and rammed in for the winning touchdown in the final minute as Iowa upset the Illini, 12-10, and set off another wild celebration.

No one knew it at the time, of course, but football celebrations in salute of the Hawkeyes were to be few, and far between, for the next 15 years.

In the meantime, in 1929, a new stadium was constructed, seating 42,184 fans in the east and west stands.

But two other things happened in that same year, and both were bad — very bad. The Big Ten suspended Iowa from membership, effective Jan. 1, 1930, "for losing faculty control of its athletic department." Although the actual suspension lasted only 31 days, until Feb. l, 1930, it was a paralyzing blow to the athletic department. And when, in the same year, the stock market crashed on Wall Street and the Great Depression began, it was a double whammy from which Iowa would not recover for a decade.

Although the 1930's were mostly dismal days — the team scored seven points in 1931 — there were some historical highlights.

One had to do with the birth of Floyd of Rosedale. The center of the controversy which produced Floyd as the most prized trophy in Hawkeye athletics was Ozzie Simmons, a black Iowa halfback from Fort Worth, Texas.

In 1929, a jam-packed crowd of 42,184 turned out to watch the first game played at the newly constructed Iowa Stadium. The Hawkeyes tied Illinois, 7-7.

As a sophomore, Simmons leaped into headlines quickly when he led Iowa to a 20-7 win over Northwestern early in the season by rushing for 304 yards, an unheard of total in those days.

When Minnesota's national-championship Golden Gophers came to town later in the season they humiliated the Hawks, piling up a 34-0 halftime lead and gaining 595 yards to Iowa's 70. Simmons had to be helped from the field three times as the result of vicious hits and Iowa fans thought the Gophers roughed him up because of his color.

When the Gophers returned to Iowa City again the next year, Iowa fans were ready for mayhem. Iowa Governor Clyde Herring issued a statement saying, among other things, "If the officials stand for any rough tactics like Minnesota used last year, I'm sure the crowd won't."

To all this, Governor Floyd B. Olson of Minnesota sent Herring a telegram saying, "... If you seriously think Iowa has any chance to win, I will bet you a Minnesota prize hog against an Iowa prize hog that Minnesota wins today. The loser must deliver the hog to the winner in person. You are getting odds because Minnesota raises better hogs than Iowa."

A record crowd of 53,000 fans turned out to see the blood battle. The Hawks played gallantly against the heavily favored Gophers, losing only 13-6, Simmons played hard and well and was unhurt, and the Iowa fans were relatively civil. A few days later, a pedigreed porker named Floyd of Rosedale was delivered to the governor's office in St. Paul. Governor Olson presented it to the University of Minnesota but, in the meantime, commissioned an artist to make a bronze statue of the likeness of the pig.

As another historical highlight, Iowa is quite probably the only major football school in the country to have had a future president announce its games. The man was Ronald

Iowa hasn't had to run far to find success on the gridiron. But they did have their lean years, especially in the 1930's. During this period, from 1930-38, the Hawkeyes posted a record of 22-28.

(Dutch) Reagan, who worked for WHO radio in Des Moines before Jim Zabel was heard, or heard of, which goes back a ways. Reagan auditioned and was accepted in 1932, working Iowa games through the 1936 season.

The man who would become the 40th president of the United States wrote in an *Illustrated Preview* of the 1936 season: "... One broadcast fault acquired (in my first Iowa game) is still with me. The inability to be impartial when Iowa takes the field. A fighting courage, good for sixty minutes of every game, made me an Iowan that first day and that same courage has been typical of every Iowa team in the four years since."

Too bad for Dutch he didn't get to see the Hawks at their best. Still, they say he did OK after leaving Iowa.

As noted, the 1930's were chiefly days of despair for the Iowa football program. From 1930 through 1938 Iowa won only 22 of 50 games, and the wins were mostly against the likes of Bradley Tech, South Dakota and Carleton College. During five of the nine seasons Iowa failed to win a Big Ten game and only once did it win more than one conference game.

So it was understandable that absolutely no one was ready for the 1939 season — the miracle of miracles in Iowa football, and a season almost unlike that ever had by any college team.

The team had a new coach, Dr. Eddie Anderson, a native of Mason City, who had played for the hallowed Knute Rockne at Notre Dame. It had a returning halfback named Nile Kinnick who had shown some promise the previous two seasons. But it seemingly had little else. Bill Osmanski, a star player under Anderson at Holy Cross, had come out to Iowa City to help with spring practice in 1939 and upon his return home to Worcester, Mass., told that city's Daily Telegram, "Of 5,000 male students at the University of Iowa,

Iowa fans celebrated Rose Bowl titles in 1956 and 1958. The Hawkeyes went to the Rose Bowl in 1981, '85 and '90, but lost each time.

there are only five real football players."

Osmansksi was wrong. There turned out to be about 15, and what they accomplished was unbelievable. In several games eight men played the full 60 minutes, and 15 was about the average number of players used, earning the team the nickname of "the Ironmen."

When they opened against traditional patsy South Dakota, winning 41-0, the crowd was 16,000. The next week, when Iowa beat Indiana for its first Big Ten win at home in six years, the crowd was 20,000. By the time of the next home game, a month later, 46,000 turned out to see the 4-1 Hawkeyes face unbeaten Notre Dame, ranked No. 1 in the nation.

Iowa won, 7-6, with Nile Kinnick scoring the game's only touchdown on a play devised in the huddle by first-year quarterback Al Couppee. Kinnick also dropkicked the winning extra point and punted beautifully throughout the afternoon, including a 68-yarder that pinned the Irish back on their own 6-yard line with less than two minutes to play.

The next week, when hated rival Minnesota came to town, 50,000 customers paid to get in. They weren't disappointed as Iowa, beaten into virtual submission by the bigger, and deeper, Gophers through three bruising quarters, rallied to win, 13-9, on a pair of Kinnick touchdown pass-

es in the final nine minutes.

The state had an orgasm, so to speak. The Hawkeyes hadn't beaten those damn Gophers for a decade, and now it was done. The team that couldn't, did. Back-to-back wins over Notre Dame and Minnesota had made the Ironmen the darlings of the football world, coast to coast. Forgotten, at least momentarily, were the bread lines and the foreclosures and the crop disasters. The state had something to be proud of!

The Des Moines Register declared: "Iowa City was wild with joy Saturday night. Hundreds of nearly hysterical men and women were skipping, running or lurching through the streets of downtown Iowa City. Long years of hunger in the wilderness of monotonous football defeats seemed to have stored some sort of an explosive that broke loose when Iowa arrived in the promised land of midwest gridiron supremacy."

When the season was over, Kinnick won every major college football award of the year, including the famed Heisman Trophy. Anderson was named college coach of the year.

Alas, along came World War II to send Iowa football into the doldrums again. And that same war snuffed out the life of Kinnick, Iowa's greatest football hero. On June 2, 1943, while bringing his Naval fighter plane in for a practice landing on an aircraft carrier in the Gulf of Paria off the coast of Venezuela the plane crashed into the sea and Nile was gone. Almost 30 years later, in 1972, Iowa Stadium was renamed and dedicated in his honor as Kinnick Stadium.

The glory years didn't return again until the early 1950's when a tough, determined young man from Michigan by way of Washington State became Iowa's head coach. Forest Evashevski started in 1952 and retired to the athletic directorship in 1961. But in those nine years he made an indelible mark on the game.

His very first team scored college football's upset of the year by beating Ohio State in Iowa City as Buckeye coach Woody Hayes raged on the sidelines. A year later, Iowa had to accept a tie at Notre Dame in the "Fainting Irish" episode.

In 1956 Iowa went to the Rose Bowl, and won. It did so again in 1958. And fought for the national championship in 1960.

When Evy moved up to the athletic directorship in 1961,

The Iowa football team has its rabid followers. The love affair goes back to the turn of the century.

having said he "didn't want to grow old in coaching," his Hawkeye teams had gained the distinction of being rated among the top three teams in the nation in three of five consecutive years and in the top five in four of the five.

Then the bad times again. Through four coaches and 17 years, 1962 through 1978, Iowa did not have a winning record and Iowa football again became the butt of many jokes.

But another miracle worker arrived. This one Hayden Fry, from Texas. Saying his teams would "scratch where it itches," Fry set out to remove everything negative from the Iowa football scene, and succeeded, handsomely and suddenly.

His third team, in 1981, not only broke the string of 19 successive nonwinning seasons, longest in college history at that time, but tied for the Big Ten title and went to the Rose Bowl. The Hawkeyes went to Pasadena, Calif., again after the 1985 season and again in 1990. They didn't win any of the three, but each time the trip set the state agog as West Coast writers could not believe the number of Iowans who descended on Pasadena to party and call the Hawks.

As this is written, Fry has taken Hawkeye teams to 13 bowl games in 18 seasons with more in sight. Rose, Peach, Gator, Freedom, Rose, Holiday, Holiday, Peach, Rose, Holiday, Alamo, Sun, Alamo.

If we're dreaming, don't wake us!

What is it about Hawkeye football that demands such a big place in our hearts, and in our state's history?

Perhaps it was written best more than 40 years ago by the late Loren Hickerson, the first executive director of the University of Iowa Alumni Association, when he said: "Iowa football reflects the mores of a greater community which is all of Iowa. There are striking similarities between the uphill fight of the Hawkeyes to win football recognition among the toughest foes, and the uphill fight of the university itself to win a higher place of honor, respect and proud support among its own people, and the uphill fight of the state itself to become a positive factor among the community of states. ..."

Thus Iowa football has often been a rallying point for the entire state and will no doubt continue to be as we look ahead to the 21st century.

Iowa Ends Notre

Iowa defeated a Notre Dame team, coached by the legendary
Knute Rockne, which had not lost in three seasons. Iowa finished
with its first undefeated, untied season.

Dame's Rule, 10-7

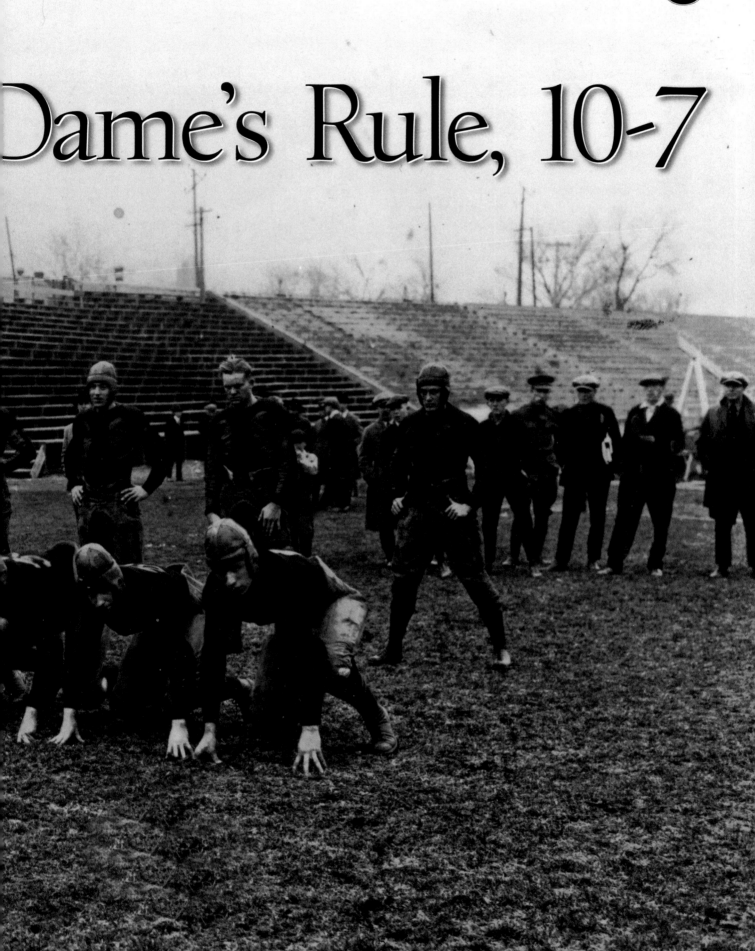

Iowa ended Notre Dame's span of years of triumph with a 10-7 victory over the Catholics in a game of bitter intensity. The bruising contest was played over a gridiron pelted by a snow and hail flurry, and was marked for crushing tackling and hard charging.

When the closing whistle blew, several men of both teams limped off the field, aided by their mates and admirers, but the two Hawkeyes who made all the points, Aubrey Devine and fullback Gordon Locke, were the heroes.

Locke was a battered athlete, who had to be taken out in the third quarter, but came back in critical moments in the fourth, only to be hurt again.

Iowa crammed its scoring into the first period. The backs early found the vaunted "Irish" line to their liking, with Devine, Locke, and Johnny Miller carrying the ball for varying distances, from 2 to 20 yards. Stopped momentarily on the 1-yard zone, Locke bucked across and Devine added the extra point.

The crowd of 8,000, which had been a maelstrom of joy, changed in a few minutes, however, when Johnny Mohardt, Chet Wynne, and Dan Coughlin bucked Iowa's line for 50 yards, but the Hawks braced, and Devine and

Iowa's line opened hole after hole against the Notre Dame defense. Fullback Gordon Locke scored the decisive touchdown on a 1-yard run in the first quarter.

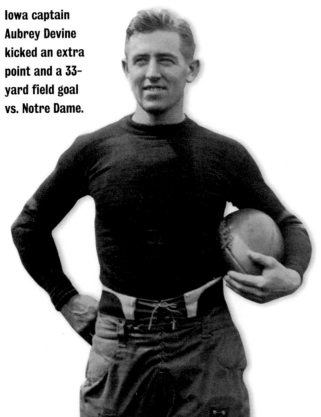

Iowa captain Aubrey Devine kicked an extra point and a 33-yard field goal vs. Notre Dame.

SCORE BY QUARTERS
Iowa City, Oct. 8, 1921

NOTRE DAME	0	7	0	0	— 7
IOWA	10	0	0	0	— 10

Locke led a reverse march to Notre Dame's 33-yard region, where the Hawkeye captain booted a drop kick for the points that decided the game.

Finding the locals' line sturdier after this score, Notre Dame's strategy veered to the aerial, and Johnny Mohardt tossed forward pass after pass to Roger Kiley and Chet Grant, many registering gains. Even two interceptions at critical stages by Iowa failed to stop the passes, and Mohardt finally completed a long one to Ed Kelley, who ran 30 yards to a touchdown. Buck Shaw kicked the extra point.

Iowa hit the line hard enough for Devine and Locke to gain slowly, but surely, in the third quarter, and advanced to Notre Dame's 5-yard line, but Notre Dame held desperately, and Locke was hurt. Then the Catholics rammed and slashed to Iowa's 5-yard line, where the third quarter ended.

Iowa held again, and Mohardt tried a 40-yard drop kick to tie the count, but failed, just as more passes did. Gus Desch went in near the end of the game and used his fresh speed in a final effort, which, with a successful pass to Eddie Anderson, planted the ball on Iowa's 7-yard line, but the Hawkeyes staved off this final threat, and the game ended in midfield.

DUKE SLATER

Helmetless Star Tackle Was an All-American On, Off Field

By Gus Schrader

One of the greatest photographs in Iowa football history shows Fred (Duke) Slater, playing as usual without a helmet, blocking out three Notre Dame players as fullback Gordon Locke comes charging through the hole in a 10-7 upset scored by the Hawkeyes in 1921.

His teammates always insisted the picture was not a bit unusual. They said it was typical of the way Slater played in his four years at tackle. He was just as effective on defense, a huge factor in helping Iowa record its first unbeaten, untied season and an outright Big Ten championship.

Small wonder that Slater became one of the first black players to win All-America honors. He also was installed at tackle on Iowa's all-time honor team and was inducted into the Halls of Fame by the National Football Foundation and the Helms Athletic Foundation.

Fred Slater was born Dec. 19, 1898, in Normal, Ill., the son of a Methodist minister. His mother died when he was 11, and two years later his father married again. His stepmother was a kind, understanding woman who came to mean a great deal to Fred.

The family Fred had — four sisters and a brother — moved to Clinton, Iowa, in 1911, and the Rev. Mr. Slater became pastor of the Methodist Church.

The elder Slater disapproved when he discovered his strapping young son was playing football on the vacant lots.

Duke's father forbade him to go out for football at Clinton High because he didn't want him to be injured in the rough sport. Duke did anyway, but his dad discovered it when he saw his wife sewing up the rips in the ragged uniform that had been issued to Duke.

A football career would have ended right there, but brokenhearted Duke went on a hunger strike for several days. Finally his father yielded to the pleas of Duke and his stepmother, and he reluctantly acquiesced with the condition that his son must be careful to avoid injury. Every time Duke came home with bumps and bruises, he was careful not to limp or complain around his dad.

Each player had to provide his own football shoes and helmet. His father said he could not afford to buy the helmet and shoes, so the tall, 144-pound Duke decided he needed shoes the most. He played his entire career at Clinton High and all but a few games as a senior at Iowa without a headgear.

Another star on the Clinton team was Burt Ingwersen. The two were classmates, played in the line together and became close friends. Ingwersen went to Illinois, Slater to Iowa. They played against each other four years (2-2 standoff). Ingwersen became head coach at Iowa (1924-34) after Howard Jones left for Southern California.

Ingwersen later said his former Clinton teammate was one of the best linemen he had ever played with or against.

Duke's father heard neighbors saying complimentary things about Duke's football ability. For the first time, he attended practice and then went to see his initial football game. He became so enthused that he attended every game he could when Duke played.

Fred got his nickname "Duke" as a boy. He had a dog

named that, and somehow his family and friends transferred the nickname to him. He also became famous for big feet. Special shoes — size 12 — were a bit snug and had to be ordered from Chicago for him.

Clinton Osborne, hailed as one of the finest high school mentors, in the land, left Clinton High to coach at Northwestern College in 1914. His former assistants, Peterson and Craig (first names not available), replaced him.

Clinton did so well in 1914 that it was chosen to face West Des Moines for the state championship on Thanksgiving Day. The contest ended 13-13. The star of the other team was quarterback Aubrey Devine, who became Slater's teammate at Iowa for four seasons. Both would end up as All-Americans and Hall of Fame members.

"We were on Clinton's 10-yard line with a few seconds to go," recalled Devine. "I tried to forward pass but never was able to get rid of the ball as a big boy wrapped his arms around me and smothered me to the ground. That was my first taste, so to speak, of Duke Slater. In later years he was on my side, which made the going much easier."

Slater and Devine played four seasons at Iowa (1918-1921). Their coach was Howard Jones, who had a 40-17-2 record in eight seasons before going to Southern California, and later made the Hall of Fame.

After Slater's freshman season, he was named to the state all-star team by The Des Moines Register. Team pictures of Clinton High and Iowa show Slater was the only black man on either squad.

Iowa finished 6-2-1 in 1918, losing to a strong Navy team from Great Lakes and Illinois, and tying Camp Dodge.

After a disputed 9-6 loss to Illinois in 1919, Walter Eckersall wrote in The Chicago Tribune: "Iowa's line outplayed the Illinois forwards while Les Belding was a stone wall for Iowa on his end. Slater, the giant (215 pounds) tackle, was strong throughout. He broke up Illinois plays time after time and frequently followed around behind the line and caught the runners from behind."

The Hawkeyes had a 5-2 record that season, the only other loss being to Chicago. This time, Eckersall wrote: "In Slater, Iowa has one of the best forwards in the country. This man

Duke Slater was one of Iowa's first All-Americans. His father initially didn't want him to play football.

is one of the most powerful players seen since the days of Joe Curtis of Michigan, Walker of Minnesota and Buck of Wisconsin. He is so powerful that one man cannot handle him, and opposing teams have found it necessary to send two men against him every time a play was sent off his side of the line."

Fritz Crisler, later to be a Hall of Fame coach (and athletic director) at Michigan, was an end who played against Slater in the 9-6 Illinois victory over Iowa. He commented: "Duke Slater was the best tackle I ever played against. I tried to block him throughout my college career, but never once did I impede his progress to the ball carrier."

Iowa lost only to Illinois and Chicago in 1920, and Slater was named on many All-Western teams. That set the stage for the 7-0 1921 campaign, with victories over Knox, Notre Dame, Illinois, Purdue, Minnesota, Indiana and Northwestern.

It was in the 10-7 shocker over the Irish that Slater, for the first time, wore a helmet in a game, reportedly because it was so rough playing against Hunk Anderson, Notre Dame's guard.

Following a 14-2 victory over Illinois, Jim McMillen, later an Illini All-American, said: "It became apparent the Duke was feeling sorry for our awkward and futile efforts. He began picking the Illinois boys up and sending them back with a friendly pat on the back and words of encouragement. This was my introduction to Duke Slater, All-America gentleman."

After that season Devine was selected on Walter Camp's All-America team. Slater made two other first teams, but was on Camp's second unit. Slater went on to play pro football with the Chicago Cardinals, and he still found time to earn his law degree at Iowa. He became a prominent lawyer and judge in Chicago. He helped encourage numerous Chicago-area players to attend Iowa. The most famous was Ozzie Simmons, the talented ball carrier in the middle 1930's.

Jones, a hard coach to satisfy, never addressed Slater as Duke (always Fred). The two had a reunion years later.

"Well, Coach, I played a lot of football for you," Slater said.

"Yes, Fred," replied Jones, "but you could have played much better."

Hawks' Coach Jones Gets Best of Brother's Yale Elis

Special to The New York Times

SCORE BY QUARTERS					
New Haven, Conn., Oct. 14, 1922					
IOWA	0	6	0	0 —	6
YALE	0	0	0	0 —	0

Brother Howard from Iowa had much the better of the Jones family quarrel in the Yale Bowl this afternoon. His husky corn-fed football team from the Midwest gave Brother Tad's Yale warriors a beating that will linger long in memory. The margin was only one touchdown — 6 to 0 — but the size of the score does not begin to tell the difference between the teams.

As far as the final result was concerned, this important intersectional battle might as well have been stopped in the first part of the second quarter. By then it belonged to Iowa, who, behind superb interference, swept over the Yale goal line for the only touchdown of the afternoon. The game was over after that.

Yale then decided to lock and bolt the stable doors.

In the first two quarters the Elis had played such miserable football that Iowa should have scored more than once. But between the halves Yale decided to brace up and play determined football. But it was too late.

After watching the Elis play sharp, hard football in the second and third periods, Yale fans undoubtedly left the big bowl wondering why their team had not played that way in the big moments of the game.

Yale looked soft and feeble against the big-boned Iowans, who showed a crisp attack, a superb interference, lots of speed and plenty of weight behind the speed.

Leland Parkin, the quarterback of the Hawkeyes, showed why he is one of the best backfield men of this

Iowa's 1922 squad, which went on to finish undefeated and win the Big Ten, dominated Yale in the first half. Leland Parkin scored for Iowa on a 9-yard run.

year or any year. Parkin, who hails from Waterloo, Ia., played Wellington to Yale's Napoleon today.

It was Parkin who skirted Yale's left end in the second quarter, flung himself past a bevy of tackles and half fell, half crawled across the goal line. He was the player of the game which was fast in action and briskly played. Except for punting, he was the entire Iowa backfield. He threw passes, bucked the line, flew around the ends, dodged tacklers, twisted and writhed like a dancing dervish.

The Iowan looked much like Glenn Killinger, the Penn State hero of the gridiron. He has the same tricky ability to pivot rapidly, twisting like a corkscrew, offering to the opposing tackle.

He is the successor to Aubrey Devine, the great triple-threat back who led the Hawkeyes last season. Parkin stands out as a quarterback that the East will find hard to match.

A crowd of nearly 35,000 saw the battle between these teams from the East and the West, the first Yale has played since 1914. The Yale Bowl was only half filled, with the east and west stands along the full length of the field jammed to capacity, but the end zones were a yawning vacuum. Several hundred Iowans were on hand to cheer for their team.

The contest was the first East vs. West battle of the season. It was to prove everything about the comparative merits of the sections, but, in reality it proved nothing. Nothing, except, this — that on Oct. 14 Iowa knew more football, played better football, was further advanced and better coached than Yale. The Elis in the first half played as if they had started practice last Monday.

Yale realized what it was up against late in the first quarter when Iowa launched its attack. After receiving a punt at midfield and aided by a penalty against Yale, a galvanized Iowa started upfield.

After a 3-yard gain, Parkin broke loose, running almost laterally behind the line, then reached the Yale right end and turned the corner behind his blockers. Squirming and slipping, the Iowa star picked up 12 yards — and went down just 30 yards from the Yale goal.

Parkin added 3 yards. He then called upon Capt. Gordon Locke, a giant in stature and a line-plunger of repute. But Locke fumbled and lost 5 yards.

Taking the initiative, Parkin, the 168-lbs. quarterback, dropped back and winged a pass to Glenn Miller for 8 yards. Next, he hurtled through the line and made a first down near the 19-yard line.

Afterward, the whistle blew to end the first quarter.

With the attack shifting to Locke, the Iowa captain picked up 3 yards through the middle, and then picked up a first down with a diving lunge.

But it was made by the smallest of margins, with the linesman bringing out their yardsticks to measure the distance. As the tape was tightened and stretched, the players gathered around. It would take the referee two careful inspections before he was convinced that Iowa had made the needed distance.

Yale's troubles began to pile up in leaps and bounds.

Parkin pierced the line again and reached the Yale 5-yard line. He added another yard on the next play.

Parkin was stopped at the 3 on the next play, but the Hawkeyes were penalized 5 yards for being offsides. Every one of the referee's five strides seemed to indicate Iowa would now fail.

With the ball on the 9 and fourth down, only Parkin

could have done it right.

And he did it at the very moment Yale was getting ready to unleash a deafening roar.

Taking the pass from center, Parkin went around right end, moving fast and ahead of his blockers, he saw an opening directly ahead, and cut like a frightened rabbit making for his hole. A Yale tackler lunged but missed. Parkin moved sideways, and lurching from his own twisting momentum, fell toward the white chalk line. He was a foot short, but crawled and clawed his way over the remainder just as an Eli defender jumped on him in a belated leap. The point-after attempt failed, yet Iowa led, 6-0.

Yale was too late. If the Eli tackler had pinned him to the turf the touchdown might have been avoided. But he didn't and that was Yale's greatest mistake of the afternoon.

Yale played great football in the second half and had two opportunities to even up the score, once in the third period and later in the fourth, but was unable to rally.

In the third quarter, Yale blocked an Iowa punt on the Hawkeyes' 30-yard line and the ball sputtered 13 yards to the 43. The Elis moved the ball up to the 20 and the Yale cheering section was in an agony of anticipation.

But all good things must come to an end, including a Yale offensive. A bad pass from center that lost 6 yards killed a promising drive, when Locke threw himself on the bouncing ball.

Yale later missed a drop-kick from the 30.

Yale's second golden opportunity occurred with the afternoon's shadows falling over the field.

Driving from their own 30-yard line, the Elis uncorked four straight first downs to the Iowa 17. A tough Hawkeyes defense and a failed pass attempt eventually ended the Elis' last hope with less than a minute remaining.

Iowa Students Wildly Celebrate Victory Over Yale

By The Gazette Staff

One of the greatest celebrations ever staged at the end of an Iowa triumph took place Saturday from the time the last victory flash came over the wires until nearly midnight. Three special wires besides the radio announcements brought the glad tidings to the thousands of students and townspeople who gathered to hear the game — the next best thing to seeing it. The game was hardly over before long lines of students were snake dancing up the long hill; the lines winding around until the dancers nearly dropped from exhaustion. Nobody on Clinton or Washington streets, later in the evening, could tell whether or not there were any street lights. The lurid flames from mammoth bonfires and the shooting colored lights from thousands of rock-

ets and Roman candles dimmed the best that electricity could do and painted the skies with new colors.

Nearly 7,000 students and townspeople paraded the streets of the city, chiefly in the business district, as soon as darkness fell. The university band, which did not accompany the Iowa team to Yale, but sent a cheerleader in its place, at its own expense, led the Herculean procession Saturday night and the yelling, cheering, singing multitude followed as crazed a New York City New Year's eve army at Broadway and 42nd Street.

Oratory was blended with music and salvos, in honor of of the Iowa victors nearly 1,500 miles away.

A large gathering is expected to meet Howard Jones and the Iowa team upon its return at the train station.

Nearly 7,000 gathered in Iowa City's downtown for a New Year's Eve-type celebration following word of the Hawkeyes' 6-0 victory over Yale.

HOWARD JONES

Hawkeyes Coach Brought Program to a Higher Level

By Mark Dukes

....

Before he made his mark and his moniker on the West Coast, Howard Jones began earning his reputation — taskmaster, fundamentalist and sound strategist — at the University of Iowa. Jones eventually stamped himself as one of the greatest college football coaches, leading the Southern California "Thundering Herd" to two national championships and five Rose Bowl victories. But it was at Iowa that Jones essentially got his start on stardom.

Until it hired Jones for the 1916 season, Iowa never had made such a large commitment to the football program. He signed a five-year contract at $4,500 annually — the longest commitment and most money given to a coach at the U of I.

Not everyone was convinced it was the wisest move, especially with someone of Jones' meager experience. Since graduating from Yale in 1908, Jones had been in and out of coaching. He had jobs right out of college as head coach at Syracuse, Yale and Ohio State, went into business for two years, went back to his alma mater as head coach in 1913, then returned to the private sector for another two years.

Jones might not have landed the Hawkeye job without the urging of Reed Lane, a

Howard Jones, left, and his brother, Tad, both became college coaches.

Davenport businessman who was on the U of I Athletic Board. Lane and Jones had spent a year at Exeter, a Yale preparatory school. While they went their separate ways — Lane to Iowa and Jones to Yale — Lane kept in contact with Jones and had followed his playing and coaching career.

The board, after discussing the football position and overall status of athletics with Jones, approved his appointment by a unanimous vote.

Success did not come quickly for Jones' Hawkeye teams, but there were circumstances that impeded the process.

Fred Becker, an All-American as a sophomore in 1916 and described as "unparalleled in Iowa football annals," was killed in World War I. He enlisted a month after the war started and, 10 months later, the Waterloo native was killed. Becker undoubtedly would have been a star on Jones' second and third Iowa teams, in 1917 and 1918.

Jones took on the added duties of athletic director in 1917, as Fred Kellogg left the post for military service. It became a trying season for the Hawkeyes, who finished 3-5 with losses of 47-0 to Nebraska, 10-0 to Grinnell and 20-0 to Wisconsin in successive games.

But Jones began to turn things around the next three years, leading the team to 6-2-1, 5-2 and 5-2 records. The climate changed in 1918, as the Big Ten Conference threw out eligibility requirements. Players did not lose a year of competition, because of several players' commitment to the war effort. The conference reverted to the former eligibility rules the next winter.

As the decade of the 20's neared, Jones' recruiting efforts were paying off and his philosophy was sinking in. While Jones occasionally enjoyed golf or bridge, he had a one-track mind toward football. He tried to allocate responsibilities to coaches, but always had the last word.

That is essentially how he later earned the nickname "The Man," courtesy of Southern California historian Al Wesson.

"Howard lived and breathed football," Wesson recalled. "If it were not for football he would have starved to death — couldn't possibly have made a living in business. His assistants tried to get him to organize the practices and let them do most of the heavy work. He'd promise to do it but after 15 minutes on the field, he'd be down on the ground showing them personally how to block, following every play on the dead run, and acting as though he were still playing end at Yale. He just couldn't relax and let others do the heavy work."

Players at Iowa had similar recollections.

"He liked clean, hard football. He never would stand for anything out of line," said William Kelly, captain of the 1920 Hawkeye team. "He never was known to swear. He was a terrific disciplinarian. For him to 'go after' one of his players was something never to be forgotten. He was a hard man to get close to. During most of the years, he was athletic director as well as coach. Many times, he actually was selling tickets up to within an hour or so of game time."

Although he was a heavy smoker, Jones was sold on superior conditioning. While at Iowa, he wrote a book on conditioning and conduct for players.

"I prohibit the boys from hanging around poolrooms,

Howard Jones prohibited his players from going to poolrooms and dance halls, but he didn't mind them listening to music.

because the air in such places is usually bad and his associates are not always the best," Jones wrote.

"There are always a certain number of men hanging around such places who think it their duty to offer suggestions about various phases of the work done on the practice field and these men can often do more harm in one hour than the coach can do good in three or four practice periods. A boy playing football does not need the exercise afforded by pool or billiard playing, which is a waste of time."

Jones prevented his players from dancing but welcomed them playing music.

"The objections I have against dancing are: first, it breaks in upon sleeping and eating; second, it is a different form of exercise than the boy is used to and is tiring; third, there is the danger of getting heated up and then cooling off too quickly; fourth, a midnight lunch is usually partaken of, mostly because of the obligations to the girl; fifth, the boy usually does not feel like getting up for breakfast."

Music, Jones enjoyed.

"I like to hear a squad singing popular songs after a hard practice and while dressing. I know then that most of the men will leave in good spirits, that they will have forgotten the unpleasant, unimportant occurrences of the practice by the time they were dressed."

With a new five-year contract to start the 1920 season, Jones took the Hawkeyes on a tremendous ride at the start of the decade. The 1920 season started quietly enough, as Iowa split its first four games. But victories over Northwestern, Chicago and Iowa State to finish the campaign opened wide the door to two incredible campaigns.

The 1920 finish began a string of 20 straight victories, two conference championships and a national title for Jones' Hawkeyes. It was achieved in unique Jones style, and with the talents of such players as Duke Slater, Aubrey Devine and Gordon Locke, each an All-American.

A big hurdle in the streak was overcome in the second game of 1921, at home against Knute Rockne's mighty Notre Dame squad. The Fighting Irish had not been defeated in three seasons and it was the sternest test yet for Jones' troops.

In the first quarter, Locke scored a touchdown and Devine booted a field goal to give the Hawkeyes a 10-0 lead. The Irish scored in the second quarter, but Iowa repeatedly turned them away the rest of the game. It was a monumental, 10-7 victory.

Jones had five more meetings against Rockne's Irish when he was coaching Southern California, and Rockne won four of them, including a 27-0 triumph in Rockne's last game in 1930. Ironically, Rockne considered accepting the Iowa coaching position after Jones resigned in 1924.

Later, a Southern California-Notre Dame game provided Jones with his biggest victory and, indeed, one of the most legendary in Trojan football history. Rockne had died in March 1931 in a plane crash in Kansas, leaving the Irish reins to Hunk Anderson, but the death of his friend was on Jones' mind.

In South Bend in 1931, the national championship and Notre Dame's 26-game undefeated streak was on the line when Southern Cal visited. The Irish bolted to a 14-0 lead and held it going into the fourth period. Southern Cal responded with 16 unanswered points, the final three on a 23-yard field goal by guard Johnny Baker.

As luck would have it, Metro-Goldwyn-Mayer had a crew covering the game and the film was made into a full-length feature. Southern Cal historian Braven Dyer did the voice-over.

"They rushed the film down to Loew's State Theater, then the top movie house in downtown Los Angeles," Dyer said in a book written by Tim Cohane in 1973. "When the twin bill first went on, the football game was one half of a double feature. After the first day, business was so good and everybody admitted it was the football game that lured them to the theater, that the manager jerked the second feature and ran the gridiron picture over and over. It broke all house records at Loew's State."

After the victory over Notre Dame in 1921, Iowa dispatched five more opponents, allowing only 22 points in those games, and the Hawkeyes had their first undefeated and untied season in school history. A claim to the national championship was well grounded. Iowa also received an invitation to play California in the Rose Bowl but didn't participate because the Iowa Board in Control opposed postseason play and the Big Ten Conference prevented it.

How could Jones possibly repeat such a tremendous season, especially since Devine, Slater and Lester Belding would not return in 1922?

Again, the second game of the season provided a showcase. Iowa had opened the 1922 campaign by trouncing Knox College, 61-0, setting up a meeting with eastern power Yale at the Yale Bowl. Coincidentally, Yale was being coached by Howard Jones' younger brother, Tad, who won 72 percent of his games in 11 seasons. In their only previous meeting, Howard's Yale squad — unbeaten and unscored upon in 10 games — beat Tad's Syracuse club, 15-0, in 1909.

Relying on superb defense, Iowa toppled Yale, 6-0, a result trumpeted in a banner headline in the Chicago Sunday Tribune and across the land. Walter Camp later noted that Iowa's use of a huddle to give signals — which was

"If it were not for football (Jones) would have starved to death."

Southern California historian Al Wesson

Iowa Coach Howard Jones had a one-track mind toward football. He often tried to allocate responsibilities to his assistant coaches, but always had the last word.

becoming more and more popular in the Midwest — had some effect on the outcome.

Iowa completed another 7-0 season and the Hawkeye victory streak grew to 17 games by the close of 1922. Faced with a relatively inexperienced team in 1923, Jones stretched the winning streak to 20 games before a sophomore named Red Grange led Illinois to a 9-6 victory in Iowa City. The Hawkeyes won only two games the rest of the way, finishing 5-3. In his final game as Iowa coach, Jones defeated

Northwestern, 17-14.

After much wrangling with himself and the Iowa board, Jones resigned in February 1924. He actually had written his resignation three months earlier but had been persuaded to reconsider. Jones had had a prolonged run-in with board member B.J. Lambert, who wanted to strengthen academic requirements for athletes. And Jones had wrestled with his wife's dislike of Iowa City.

Thus closed a great chapter in Iowa football history, but not the final word in Jones' coaching career. He went directly to Duke University, then known as Trinity, but only for a year before Southern California hired him.

In the glitter of Los Angeles, Jones became not only a storied coach, but a veritable celebrity.

Movie stars and celebrities embraced the Trojans, even attending some practices. Wesson, the USC publicist, collaborated on a book with Jones in which they answered questions from such stars as Gary Cooper, Mary Pickford, Douglas Fairbanks Sr. and Oliver Hardy.

Jones, who accumulated a 116-36-13 record at Southern California, held the upper hand on almost every coaching legend he faced except his best friend, Rockne. In the five Rose Bowl victories, he topped the likes of Bob Neyland, Bernie Bierman, Jock Sutherland and Wallace Wade.

Jones' biggest rival, in the West or anywhere, was the imaginative and innovative Pop Warner of Stanford. Warner defeated Jones' USC teams in their first two meetings in 1925 and 1926, 13-9 and 13-12, and their teams tied in the third encounter. But Jones' teams, conquering Warner's double-wing attack, then won five straight games, contributing greatly to Warner's leaving Stanford in 1933.

"Howard had great respect for Pop Warner," Wesson said. "He always worked the hardest to get his teams ready for Stanford."

Southern California teams won Rose Bowls in 1930, 1932 and 1933. The Trojans experienced a four-year slump in the middle of the decade, going 17-19-6, but Jones rebounded. He directed Southern Cal to an 8-2 record in 1938, then back-to-back Rose Bowl berths in 1939 and '40.

When Jones died of a heart attack in 1941 at age 56, his closest associates were convinced his preoccupation with football contributed. Ironically, it was the same work ethic and strong convictions that vaulted Jones to coaching greatness.

Kinnick's TD Pass Caps 1st Win vs. Badgers since '33

By Tait Cummins, The Gazette

SCORE BY QUARTERS						
Madison, Wis., Oct. 28, 1939						
IOWA	0	6	6	7	—	19
WISCONSIN	7	0	6	0	—	13

Nile Kinnick, by long odds the finest ball player on Camp Randall's historic sod here Saturday afternoon, trotted out Iowa's famed aerial circus and on lightning overhead thrusts to Bill Green, Al Couppee and Dick Evans — plus a drop kick conversion — personally conducted the amazing Hawks to a 19-13 victory over the scarlet clad Badgers of Wisconsin.

It was the first Iowa victory at Madison in 10 years and for heart-stopping thrusts the game was every bit the equal of the razzle-dazzle Iowa-Indiana game three weeks ago. The last time Iowa won here was in 1929 and the last Hawk victory over the Badgers was in 1933 by a 26-7 margin at Iowa City.

For sheer fury the game was a headliner. Both teams stood at the Big Ten crossroads. Victory for either meant a favorable position in a race which seemingly is as wide open as a Reno saloon. For the Badgers, another loss would about wreck all hopes for even a fair season. Iowa followers expect little this season but they love these unexpected victories and this was another to rack alongside the Indiana triumph.

Just as the Hoosiers fell before Kinnick's amazing artistry so did the Badgers. Wisconsin scored first, took a short-lived lead in the third quarter, then stumbled and fell in the fire of a team which wouldn't be licked — and was not.

On the ground the Badgers held a marked superiority. The passes looked good at times — they scored twice via the air lanes — but in the proverbial long pull, Iowa had what it took. As the clocks clicked off the final fateful minutes, the Iowa line bounced back from the kicking it had absorbed all afternoon and was stronger than the Maginot and Siegfried lines combined.

Just disregard the statistics in pondering over this notable Hawk effort. The Badgers ripped that Hawk left side of the Iowa line to shreds in one powerhouse drive, which carried almost the length of the field and resulted in a score. The Badgers made seven consecutive first downs in that march and even the most loyal Iowa followers were willing to check in their ticket stubs for a short beer check or less. It was the day's only power drive.

Before opening the symphony of praise for Kinnick, permit a brief back pat for Bergstrom, Iowa's sophomore who tried to fill the famous Jim Walker shoes. Bergie took an awful beating as the Badgers poured power through the right side of its line. But it takes fire to make men and Bergstrom was still on the field when the final gun sounded and he was still demonstrating to Dr. Eddie Anderson that the best way to develop line material is to put it in there and let the chips fall where they may.

Now for Kinnick: 7 of 14 were completed and he threw them all. He was rushed at times like a pop stand on a midsummer day but the Little General cocked his arm and let fly. The Badgers were pinning his arms like a Dionne diaper but he'd shake them off and bing another completion. Iowa's running attack was nothing to write home about. In fact, it might as well have been in Iowa City until the last five minutes of the ballgame. Kinnick tried it 11 times for a total of 12 yards. Murphy with 20 yards in four trials and Green with 47 yards on five journeys were the aces, and even they had plenty of grief.

Before getting into a discussion of how the clubs cashed

Iowa quarterback Al Couppee caught a key pass from Nile Kinnick on the winning drive that put the Hawkeyes on the Wisconsin 29.

the chips, one last bit of whoopee is in order. It deals with the goal-line stand of the Hawks in the final quarter after a 41-yard pass from Cone to Gile gave the Badgers a first down on Iowa's 9.

Get the picture. Iowa led, 19-13. About five minutes remained. Gile leaped high in the air to catch the ball while three Iowans sought to guard him. Just the place for a team to collapse after such a miracle catch. But the Hawks don't fold. Three times the Badgers sought to connect on passes and each time the Old Gold and Black lads batted down the ball.

In came Gradisnik, one of the best ballplayers on the Wisconsin club. He dropped back to pass and Erwin Prasse climbed aboard his shoulders. Gradisnik threw the ball but Bruno Andruska, the Iowa sub center, was there to bat it down and the threat ended. That ended the Badgers. They backed right down the field and when the final whistle blew, Iowa was sitting 20 yards off the goal. Due to playing very, very conservatively.

This fellow Gradisnik, George Paskvan and Billie Schmitz bore the brunt of the Badger load with a sophomore named Cone playing manfully. Lorenz and Moeller were standouts at end, but the best lineman on the field to these prejudiced eyes was big, substantial Mike Enich. What a tackle!

Wisconsin, despite the wind in its face, had control through most of the third quarter but after the teams changed ends, Floyd Dean intercepted one of Schmitz's passes at midfield and carried to Iowa's 48. It was a break for the Hawks but bad generalship on the part of the Badgers made it possible.

Kinnick hit Prasse for a first down on the Wisconsin 40 and then repeated a little later to Al Couppee for another first down on the 29. On the first play, Nile found Bill Green open in the shadow of the goal posts and the catch was as simple as the village halfwit on "Information Please." Kinnick finally found his dropkicking stride and converted.

From then on it was "root hog or die" for the Iowans. Two consecutive holding penalties near the close of the game nullified two nice runs by Green and Dean, but Kinnick booted the old pigskin 60 yards to ease the heat. Then came that long pass which put Wisconsin right in the money, but again these stalwarts from the Tall Corn state were equal to the task, as has been set forth before. Iowa was boss until the finish after that.

Iowa's Ironmen Jar Fighting Irish

By Tait Cummins, The Gazette

Ghosts of Iowa's football immortals stepped respectfully down from the pedestal of champions here Saturday afternoon to make room for the incredible 1939 Hawkeyes, who stunned the gridiron world by outfighting the previously unbeaten, No. 1-ranked Notre Dame team for a spectacular 7-6 victory before a crowd of almost 47,000.

In ending the Irish victory streak at six games, Dr. Eddie Anderson's handful of football opportunists took a leaf from Notre Dame's own book — grab a break and then fight like a bunch of inspired tigers to hold a slender victory margin.

All the hackneyed adjectives — already worn shinier than the seat of an alderman's pants — must be called into play again to adequately describe this heart-stopping, nerve-tingling gridiron battle which was worth 10 times the $2.75 per head the Iowa athletic department received, oh, so gratefully as the Hawkeye athletic renaissance gets under full steam ahead.

As the lengthening shadows of dusk pushed their long fingers across the battle-scarred sod of Iowa field carried new measures of strength for an undermanned but never outgained Iowa team which again proved that it not only is the best fourth-quarter team in the country today but also one of the

Halfback Nile Kinnick scored Iowa's only touchdown against Notre Dame, and also kicked the extra point. The Hawkeyes ended the Irish's six-game winning streak

SCORE BY QUARTERS					
Iowa City, Nov. 11, 1939					
NOTRE DAME	0	0	6	—	6
IOWA	0	7	0	—	7

finest of all time.

Evening brought that final, brutal quarter of a game which saw two inspired teams battle like madmen, yet with such clean sportsmanship that only one penalty was assessed all day and that a mere 5-yard levy against the Irish for offsides.

And with the night a new star rose over the gridiron fir-

mament, the star of Eddie Anderson, a coach who in the space of a few short weeks brought Iowa from the very depths of the Big Ten to a position of national prominence. On every tongue, at every corner store, the subject today is Iowa, those Hawkeyes who couldn't win during the last few years and who won't lose now.

Only 15 men answered the call for Iowa but never a gamer platoon invaded a battlefield anywhere. Two back-field substitutions, two-line replacements, that was all. The ends, the tackles, the center, the quarterback and that inde-scribable little dynamo, Nile Kinnick, went from start to finish against the finest foe Iowa has faced to date — and

"Iron Mike" Enich broke through the Irish line to drop the Notre Dame quarterback for a 24-yard loss to ensure victory.

that doesn't except Michigan.

Line play again turned the trick for Iowa. That and alert backfield work, which snuffed out one Notre Dame threat after another in a game which is startling because it so nearly duplicated that great 1921 victory when Iowa took a lead and then fought with backs to the wall in saving a 10-7 victory.

That game broke a Notre Dame victory streak at 20. This one ended another growing string of triumphs. That one saw Duke Slater come into his own as a legendary figure in Hawk-

eye annals. This game puts at least seven lineman right up alongside Slater, "Spike" Nelson and the rest.

Fingers tremble over a battered typewriter with the fear that some one of the embattled Iowans might be overlooked. The crowd did its part, scooping the entire team off the ground when the final shot was fired and carrying each player off the field.

And well those rabid Iowa followers, reveling in their joy over a truly great team, might swarm onto the field in the greatest display of Iowa spirit in years. The margin was narrow but Iowa had won. That was what counted.

The nation will know of this because as this is written little Nile is still on the field re-enacting a few choice items for the news reels.

But the feats of the backs sparkle through they did, fade into the background for this observer in the light of the final Iowa smash of the day which saw "Iron Mike" Enich break through a desperate Irish line to dump Stevenson for a 24-yard loss in the final minute of play as Stevenson attempted to get off a pass. Notre Dame ran another play in the final four seconds but Enich had turned the trick and everybody in the place knew it.

Just before that play, Kinnick supplied the spark which whipped the flame of Iowa's waning strength into a prairie fire by kicking from his own 21-yard line, over the head of the Irish safety man and out of bounds on the Notre Dame 9-yard line. With less than two minutes to play, Iowa wouldn't be denied. Alert backs knocked down passes and the line did the rest.

About 500 words back in this narrative some reference was made to Iowa snatching a break to score. That's exactly what happened but before it came, Kinnick supplied the impetus for the thrust. Notre Dame had the ball near midfield with the second quarter almost over when Kinnick snagged a forward pass thrown by Stevenson and when he was finally downed the oval rested on the Irish 35-yard line.

Iowa's running attack hadn't been such great shakes and Quarterback Al Couppee knew it, for on the first play he sent Kinnick back to throw a long pass. Bill Green, the sub for Ray Murphy who started at fullback, was the intended receiver over the goal.

He was there but so was Steve Sitko, Notre Dame's sparkplug quarterback. Sitko intercepted the ball, raced back to the playing field and cut sharply to the right when Andruska went for his legs. Bruno nailed Sitko and as the quarterback tried to lateral, the ball rolled free and two hard-charging Iowans, Buzz Dean and Dick Evans, snared it.

Two ground plays were ineffectual over the right side of Iowa's line. Then Kinnick tried the left side where the rookies, Wallie Bergstrom and Ken Pettit, were at the tackle and guard post. These two opened a hole wider than the goal posts and away went Kinnick. One Notre Dame man caught him near the payoff stripe but Kinnick gave one last lunge and fell into the glory dirt. His dropkick was a sweetheart, and well

it was for that kick eventually won the game.

Throughout the game those who occupy the free press seats at these affairs were shouting for Evans and Prasse, bellowing praise for Enich and Bergstrom, cheering for Snider and Pettit and quietly pointing out the superb play of Bruno Andruska. The line that wouldn't give for Purdue had enough left to save Iowa's bacon, even though Notre Dame's march to a touchdown was marked by consistent gains on reverses and drives off tackle.

The big push by the Irish started along toward the close of the third quarter when Iowa should have been progressing due to the advantage of the wind. Instead, the Notre Dame Rough Riders took the play and smashed goalward with a drive which stunned the defenders of a 7-0 lead.

With Stevenson handing the ball to Piepul, Notre Dame plugged away. One drive was stopped by Couppee who broke through to smear Stevenson for a huge deficit on an attempted pass. A little later the teams changed goals for the final period with the ball on Iowa's 10-yard line in Notre Dame's possession. The situation looked desperate and it was.

First Stevenson went over his own left guard for six yards. Then Piepul took the ball from Stevenson on that same old reverse that looked so simple from the press box. He rammed straight forward and rolled off Buzz Dean like water off a duck to score standing up.

A pin dropping in that stadium would have been a cannon shot, so still was the crowd as Zontini warmed up his kicking foot. Back came the ball, Zontini's foot swung through and the attempt went wide. Tense throats broke forth with cheers of relief as the teams went back to work with Iowa receiving the kickoff.

Notre Dame no longer sent in substitutes by the carload. The men who plowed across for the touchdown couldn't be spared in any strategy move. This thing was beyond the strategic stage and bordered on the desperate. As usual in such a plight, the team behind carried the heaviest mental burden and from then until the finish Iowa was the boss like a drunken stevedore at a tea dance.

Iowa never came close to scoring again but neither did Notre Dame. As the final quarter closed the Irish were either passing from behind their own goal, or so close to the last ditch that the back were lucky two or three time's to avoid being thrown for safeties.

Kinnick Leads Iowa Comeback Against Gophers

By Tait Cummins, The Gazette

<table>
<thead>
<tr><th colspan="6">SCORE BY QUARTERS
Iowa City, Nov. 18, 1939</th></tr>
</thead>
<tbody>
<tr><td>MINNESOTA</td><td>0</td><td>3</td><td>6</td><td>0 —</td><td>9</td></tr>
<tr><td>IOWA</td><td>0</td><td>0</td><td>0</td><td>13 —</td><td>13</td></tr>
</tbody>
</table>

The greatest fourth-quarter team in the nation today spotted the hardest-driving team in America nine points in the annual Iowa Homecoming game, and then came from behind with a spectacular display of smart football to win, 13-9.

Translated, that means Iowa's incomparable 11 came back from a seemingly bottomless pit to win over the bruising Gophers of Minnesota and send a crowd of 50,000 persons home with their hearts still in their throats. In breaking the monotonous string of Minnesota victories since 1929, the Hawkeyes hit their peak for the year and made Nile Kin-nick a certain all-American.

It took the combined efforts of the familiar band of Iowa iron men, those embattled heroes who take to the field when the opening whistle blows and never look back for help. Only seven of the starters went the route, but the men who took over in the other four notches went all the way out against parade of smashing, inspired Gophers, who went after this one like a national championship was at stake.

Minnesota has a great ballclub, make no mistake on that score. But Iowa has a miracle team. Nothing else can replace that hackneyed word "miracle" in the light of the happenings in that never-to-be-forgotten final quarter, when a team which couldn't do anything right until the last, fleeting minutes rose to the point where Minnesota was doomed.

Bedlam reigns as this is written. Homecoming at Iowa hasn't been a particularly happy occasion for these many years. And victories over Minnesota have been hard to get since 1891 but this edition of Hawkeye gridmen hasn't learned how to lose.

In getting their sixth victory of the season, the Hawkeyes scaled heights untouched before. As in former games where the opposition seemed certain of victory, Iowa waged a valiant fight to a certain point, saw the big scoreboard list points for the opposition, and then cut loose with football, which not only produces touchdowns with dizzy speed but also bottles up the rival forces until the victory whistle blows.

Every person in the stadium left with the name Kinnick on his or her lips. Great when the Iowa team couldn't find itself, Kinnick became the personification of gridiron glory when the final stack of chips was shoved onto the table was strictly score or else.

But Kinnick is no superhuman being. He needed help to

Nile Kinnick (24) cemented his chances of being named an All-American after leading Iowa's comeback. He passed to fullback Bill Green for the winning score in the fourth quarter.

salvage this one, and when he called the plays which brought home the bacon, there stood Bill Green, Erwin Prasse, Dick Evans, Mike Enich, Wally Bergstrom, Bruno Andruska and Ken Pettit, right at his elbow saying: "Show us what you want done and, brother, we'll do it."

So Kinnick — calling signals after Couppee was benched because of a shoulder injury — told them what he thought would win and they did it. Twice long passes shook receivers in the open, once behind the goal line for the points that won, and Iowa had its Homecoming victory.

And so for another week, Dr. Eddie Anderson can walk through his tiny squad of football artists and wonder just how deep their devotion goes, to just what heights they can scale in the face of odds that would stun an ordinary individual, and just what it takes to defeat an Iowa team which in the space of a year has become a power in America's gridiron firmament.

No team could have won this game without more of an incentive than just personal glory. Love of school is not enough. As these lads dug in for the final drive which brought victory, it was obvious they wanted this one for the little doctor who came out of the east with a football potion which spells trouble for any opponent.

They show their gratitude for the scoring weapons at their command and when they win it is just as much for Dr. Anderson and his coaching associates as for Iowa or themselves.

Seven 60-minute men again adorn the headlines as sports writers go all the way out in describing the great new Iowa team. The ends, Prasse and Evans; the tackles, Enich and Bergstrom; one guard, Ken Pettit; the center, Bruno Andruska (a demon on defense if ever there was one), and Kinnick, toughest of them all, went the route.

Iowa's heaviest loss in the personnel department came early in the game when Couppee was forced to retire. He was hurt on the first play of the game when he put a terrific shoulder tackle on Quarterback Mernik who received the kickoff. Still in the ball game, Couppee showed he was finished and when he left the quarterback spot fell to the subs.

Those subs can stand right up in the front row for their share of applause. Bill Gallagher came into the game for a brief span and sparked the club for its best showing in the third quarter. Ankeny had his fling and backed the line superbly. Finally Henry Vollenweider came into the battle and helped stem the tide in the closing minutes.

Line replacements consisted of Chuck Tollefson at the guard spot of Ham Snider. Tolly worked for a short time in the final half, went out because of injuries and Ham went back to run out the string. A brilliant line, indomitable and charged with a confidence in its own power, the forward wall had a tough afternoon in the face of one of the finest lines the Big Ten boasts.

Iowa attempts to block a field-goal attempt. The Hawkeyes' defense thwarted the Gophers' last-ditch comeback in the fourth quarter.

But to get back to the ball game and that spectacular final quarter. Minnesota had scored in the first half on a field goal and in the third quarter on a short end run before the aerial circus came out of the tent.

Plays no opponent has seen before this year were uncorked as the Hawks generated the steam which was to bring eventual victory.

Two quick passes, each from Kinnick to Dean, started Iowa rolling with 14 minutes left in the ball game, after a Van Every punt from the Minnesota 35 had rolled over the goal. Buzz Dean went 18 yards on the first toss and charged for 12 on the second completion. That put the ball about midfield or thereabouts — who cares for trifling details?

On the second play in the next series of downs, Dean took the pass from center and handed the ball to Kinnick. Nile was rushed by the Gopher linemen but when he saw Prasse loping far downfield, he cut loose. Right into Prasse's arms the ball came down and he smashed the other 10 yards with a would-be tackler trying to halt the march.

The stands went wild as Prasse scored. Kinnick's drop kick split the uprights and the Gophers elected to receive. A fumble by Sweigert after one first down put the Hawks in scoring position again as Mike Enich added another spectacular play to his string by snaring the loose ball.

That threat faded, however, when Sweigert intercepted a pass and brought the ball to Minnesota's 25-yard line. Sweigert, Smith and Van Every combined to fashion a first down but the Hawks dug in and Van Every's long punt was brought back by Kinnick to the Iowa 21. That put the issue squarely up to the slinging brigade.

One pass failed before Kinnick hit Dean and Buzz smashed his way to the Iowa 38-yard line. Another pass was intercepted by Van Every but a Gopher was caught holding Dean, and Iowa took the ball at midfield.

Bill Green twisted forward to the 35-yard line and Kinnick made it first and 10 on Minnesota's 28-yard line. Just three minutes and 25 seconds remained.

On the first play, Bill Green went far to the left of the line of scrimmage. Kinnick took the snap from center, raised his foot high in the air and let fly. Green was racing like mad toward the end zone. The fastest man on the Iowa squad, he passed the Gopher secondary and was there waiting when the pigskin finally came down.

Such a scene as followed never has been duplicated on Iowa field. Emotional fans raced into the end zone and hoisted Green off the ground. So wild were the Iowa followers that the officials were forced to appeal for help in clearing the field. When Kinnick finally tried to dropkick for the point after, it was blocked but nobody cared.

Minnesota received and its ace, Sonny Franck, took the kickoff. Up the field he raced until Green met him on the 26-yard line. Two passes failed and Van Every then carried the ball almost to a first down. Christiansen hit the line for a first down and again the Gophers tried to pass for the winning points. On the first pass, Dean almost intercepted but couldn't hold the ball. On the next thrust, Kinnick was

there and he hugged that lemon like a long lost brother.

Less than two minutes remained and Iowa ran out the string with Kinnick blasting his head into the center of the line.

Last week's mad house on the field after the game was just a dress rehearsal for the scene which followed the final gun in this Minnesota battle. If any player reached the Iowa dressing room with uniform intact, it wasn't the fault of these fans who go daffy at the sight of an Iowa team which fights, and fights and fights.

The more unimportant and uninteresting details of this sheer drama of the gridiron deal with the first half and third quarter. Minnesota had command like a European dictator and seemingly could advance as they pleased — up to a certain point which was the Iowa goal or vicinity.

Twice the Gophers knocked at the scoring door but each time the Hawkeye line found an extra ounce of strength and refused to give. Mernik's first attempt at a field goal went wide but his second attempt, in the second quarter, was between the posts.

The third quarter saw Van Every, Franck, Christiansen & Co. blasting their way to the final line. The Gophers used one pass to help in a long march, finally getting a first down on Iowa's 6-yard line. Sweigert had his turn first and couldn't gain. Then Franck hit center for a yard. Van Every, as fine a plunger as football boasts today, knocked heads with the Iowa line but had to be content with a single yard. That was the payoff shot.

Iowa set itself for another power play, seven men in the line and two linebackers ready to leap into the breach, if one showed. But Minnesota sent Franck wide toward the east of the field and it was nip and tuck whether he would be able to slant in and score. It was a dead heat as he dove for the end zone, his body knocking the goal sign loose. But the officials who were right on top of the play saw Franck's lithe body wipe out the double stripe before he rolled out of bounds and it was a touchdown. The conversion failed.

The statistics testify to the power developed by the northland giants. Sixteen first downs should win most any game, particularly when the other side gets only eight — four of those on passes — but the old adage about touchdowns, etc., still stands and it was Iowa that scored the touchdowns.

NILE KINNICK

He Had Energy, Ambition, Intelligence and Courage

By Ron Fimrite, Sports Illustrated

Every few years or so, as often as they can, the Ironmen get together in Iowa City to tell all the old stories. "You remember how bowlegged old Ham Snider was," Erwin Prasse, the team captain, is saying. "Well, my mom and dad saw me play just once, in our last game against Northwestern. My folks were bakers, and neither of them knew a football from a loaf of bread. Anyway, that Northwestern game was tough. Everybody seemed to get hurt. We were all pretty beat up. So on one play they're helping old Ham off the field, and my mother looks down at him, and she's horrified. 'Oh my God,' she says. 'Look what they've done to his legs.' "

Prasse, Al Couppee, Chuck Tollefson, Wally Bergstrom and George (Red) Frye are having dinner at a restaurant called The Lark. When they were all Ironmen on the University of Iowa's legendary 1939 team, the same spot was known as Ken and Fern's, and it was a pretty tough roadhouse where they would get into real trouble from time to time. "Hey, Tolly," says Couppee, "remember the night the town marshal chased us out of here after we broke that slot machine and we hid in the parking lot of that funeral home?"

They are men in their late 60's or early 70's now, still robust and fun-loving, and they are as close as any old teammates can be. "Some call it love," Couppee says. Al was the quar-

Nile Kinnick dreamed of more than a pro football career, but he died at age 24 during a routine Navy training flight.

terback and he still pretty much calls the signals at these casual reunions. Couppee, a semi-retired newspaper columnist and broadcaster, articulates perhaps better than the others their experience together so many years ago.

"It's a shame," he says in his big voice, "but my perception of things as a kid back then was so shallow. I couldn't see beyond the surface of things. There was so much happening at once, such a combination ... the Great Depression, people in bread lines ... I can remember the desperation in my mom's face when it came time to buy coal. The whole state was in a bad way. Farms were closing down, people were hungry. Then, out of a clear blue sky came this one little group of people with just the right chemistry — our team. There was an almost hysterical relief at having something at last to grab hold of, to believe in. And ... we had Nile. ..."

The others nod, their ruddy faces beaming in the soft blue light of the restaurant. "Yes, Nile," says Prasse. "You know, I think about him all the time. I think of him whenever I get in a conversation about players from our time and the ones now. Everyone says how much better they are today. Sure, but I say Nile could've played anytime. He was so smart, He'd have found a way to play. I was never envious of Nile — he wouldn't let you feel that way — until I saw this big scrapbook his father had kept for him. I was jealous of that scrapbook, because I never had one."

"All the cliches fit Nile," says Couppee. "He was Jack Armstrong and Frank Merriwell rolled into one. He was the smallest — only about 5'8", 170 to 175 pounds — and the slowest of all our backs. Our coach, Eddie Anderson, used to say that if that man could've run a 10-flat 100, the Big Ten would've banned him. Roger Pettit was a better punter, and Bill Green was a better runner. But never in a game. In a game, you just knew he'd do something in the last minute, find a way to pull us out. In my 66 years, I've never met anyone who had the self-discipline that 21-year-old had. There was just an aura about him. He didn't try to create it, it was just there. You really had the feeling you were in the presence of someone very special."

And would Nile show up at a reunion such as this?

Laughter all around, "Oh, no. ..."

"No, I tell you where Nile Kinnick would be right now," says Couppee. "He'd be in the White House. And with him there, we wouldn't have any of the junk that's going on now. Nile would've been so far ahead of these people. ..."

NILE CLARKE KINNICK JR. WOULD HAVE TURNED 69 this past July 9 (1987). He was that rarest of beings — rarer now, lamentably, than ever before — a scholar-athlete, a Heisman Trophy winner and a Phi Beta Kappa. He was a truly humble and compassionate man. "One of the few athletes who could rise to the top without making enemies," teammate Bill Green once said. And he had the soul of a poet. "I flew up in the clouds today — tall, voluminous cumulus clouds," he wrote in his World War II diary. "They were like snow-covered mountains, range after range of them. I felt like an alpine adventurer, climbing up their canyons, winding my way between their peaks — a billowy fastness, a celestial citadel."

Kinnick's Heisman acceptance speech after the 1939 season was so eloquent and touching that the audience at the Downtown Athletic Club in New York was too stunned at first to respond. But then, as Whitney Martin of the Associated Press described the scene, "seven hundred men and women rose and cheered and whistled ... You realized the ovation wasn't alone for Nile Kinnick, the outstanding college football player of the year. It was also for Nile Kinnick, typifying everything admirable in American youth." Wrote Bill Cunningham of The Boston Post, "This country's O.K. as long as it produces Nile Kinnicks. The football part is incidental."

Today, of course, the football part is never incidental with Heisman winners; it's pretty much all there is. And Nile Kinnicks are getting awfully few and far between.

Iowa football in the 1930's kept pace with the national economy. It, too, was in a Great Depression. Under Howard Jones in the early 1920's the school fielded some of its finest teams, including the back-to-back undefeated Big Ten champions in 1921 and '22 that featured such stars as Duke Slater, Gordon Locke and Aubrey Devine. But following a bitter quarrel with members of the Athletic Control Board, Jones left Iowa after the 1923 season and moved first to Trinity College (now Duke University) and then to the University of Southern California, where his famous "Thundering Herds" won five Rose Bowl games. With Jones's departure, Iowa football declined. When the school built a new 53,000-seat stadium for the 1929 season, it soon became a monument to bad timing.

"No, I tell you where Nile Kinnick would be right now. He'd be in the White House. And with him there, we wouldn't have any of the junk that's going on now. Nile would've been so far ahead of these people. ..."

Al Couppee

Nile Kinnick, right, was an all-around athlete.
He was Iowa's quarterback, but also punted,
kicked and returned punts and kickoffs.

In January 1930, just before the members of the Big Ten were to meet to arrange the schedule for the following season, Iowa was suspended from the conference for alleged recruiting violations. It was reinstated only a month later, but by then 11 members of the team had been declared ineligible and only one Big Ten school, Purdue, agreed to change its schedule to accommodate the Hawkeyes.

High school athletes were shunning the university, and its teams quickly became an embarrassment to a conference that considered itself the best in the country. Between 1930 and 1938, Iowa won only 22 games, and in five of those seasons the Hawkeyes did not beat a single Big Ten opponent. The teams coached by the unfortunate Irl Tubbs in '37 and '38 were 2-13-1. The 1938 team was outscored 135-46 and did not score a touchdown in its last five games.

Nile Kinnick, then a junior, had played the '38 season with what was quite probably a broken ankle. No one knew for certain, because, as a practicing Christian Scientist, he would not allow the injury to be examined or treated. "I used to watch him wince in pain when he punted," says Couppee, a freshman that year. "It was amazing what he put himself through."

Kinnick had been All-Big Ten as a sophomore in '37 and, broken ankle notwithstanding, the following year he completed 43 percent of his passes (a respectable ratio in an era of unsophisticated passing attacks) and averaged 41.1 yards on 41 punts, fourth-best in the nation. He was healthy again for his senior year, and in a letter to his family just before the start of spring practice he wrote with uncharacteristic bravado, "For three years, nay for fifteen years, I have been preparing for this last year of football. I anticipate becoming the roughest, toughest all-round back yet to hit this conference."

A new coach and a new system would give him the chance to fulfill the boast. Tubbs had resigned after his 1-6-1 '38 season. His team had gone scoreless against Colgate, Purdue, Minnesota and Nebraska and had just a field goal against Indiana. Football gate receipts had been only $65,000, and the athletic department was in the hole by more than $10,000 — big figures in the Depression. Still, the school was prepared to spend whatever was necessary to hire someone able to reverse the sorry descent of Iowa football.

The choice — for a three-year contract at $10,000 per — was the 38-year-old Dr. Edward N. (Eddie) Anderson, a native

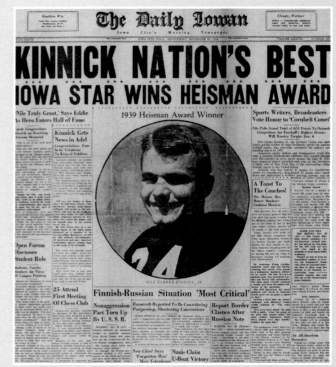

Nile Kinnick displays the Heisman Trophy he won in 1939, a year he was voted the nation's top male athlete.

Iowan who had coached Holy Cross to a 47-7-4 record the six previous seasons. Anderson had been a star end at Notre Dame, captain of the 1921 team, a Rockne pupil and a George Gipp teammate. He had played professionally with the Chicago Cardinals while at the same time earning his M.D. from Rush Medical College. He was a urologist, but as Ironman Frye has said, "He's the only physician I've ever known who thought the cure for everything from a hangnail to appendicitis was 'running it off.' "

Anderson was indeed a fanatic for physical conditioning, and his spring practices were so arduous that from an original turnout of 80 or more candidates, only 35 survived into the season. Of these only about 20 would play regularly, and 12 would play the full 60 minutes in at least one of the eight games.

Anderson brought with him to Iowa City two fellow Notre Dame alums, backfield coach Frank Carideo, an All-America quarterback for Rockne in 1929 and '30, and line coach Jim Harris. Both shared the good doctor's obsession with conditioning. Carideo had the additional distinction of being an expert at punting and drop-kicking, and Kinnick, who had learned both skills from his father, became his star pupil. Before and after every practice — Kinnick was always the first on the field and the last to leave it — the coach and player would kick to each other from various points on the gridiron. "They were so accurate," Couppee recalls, "it was like watching two guys playing catch."

From Carideo, Kinnick mastered the technique of "coffin corner" punting, and he refined his skills as perhaps the last serious practitioner of the then outdated, now lost art of drop-kicking field goals and points after.

Anderson's offensive system was the Notre Dame Box, with variations. The T-formation revolution, led by Clark Shaughnessy's Stanford Wow Boys, was a year away, and in 1939 the dominant formation was the single wing. In the Notre Dame system, the team first lined up with the backfield in a tight T, from which the quarterback called the play and the snap count. Only in an emergency would the Iowa team huddle before a play. On the quarterback's signal, the backs shifted into the box formation, which differed from the single wing only in that the line remained balanced.

No more than 20 times during the '39 season, and then merely for shock value, did Iowa run a play from the T. The tailback (usually the left halfback) and the fullback were the deep backs in the box. The quarterback played close to the line and was the principal blocking back. The right halfback, or wingback, was flanked outside or directly behind the end on his side. The tailback was the workhorse. He was the triple-threat man — a runner, passer and kicker. Kinnick was Anderson's tailback.

The '39 Iowa team was relatively small in stature even at a time when 200-pound linemen were considered "behemoths." Anderson did start the season with three "big" men—260-pound guard Henry Luebcke, 212-pound tackle Mike Enich and 202-pound tackle Jim Walker. But Luebcke suffered an abdominal hernia in the second game and Walker went out with a bad knee in the third. With those big men gone, Iowa averaged 191 pounds on the line and 181 in the backfield. If the team had any advantage, it was in age. Three players—guard Tollefson, tackle Bergstrom and guard Max Hawkins—were approaching their middle 20's. Tollefson had dropped out of school for three years to "go on the bum," Bergstrom had shipped out on a South American banana boat and Hawkins had done a tour of duty in the Navy before starting school as a 22-year-old freshman.

Preseason polls picked Iowa to finish at the bottom of the Big Ten. Bill Osmanski, the Chicago Bears fullback who had played for Anderson at Holy Cross, had no illusions about the team's potential after helping coach at spring practice. "Among 5,000 male students at the University of Iowa," Osmanski said, "there are only five real football players." But Anderson's confidence was unshaken. In Kinnick, he said, he had potentially the best back in the country. "All of which sounds quite rosy," Kinnick wrote home, "but I shan't be put off my base or guard the least bit. However, I can't deny that I was happy to hear him say this for the simple reason that I have practiced all my life to learn to run, throw and kick and haven't, as yet in college, had the opportunity to show myself a good single wing back."

KINNICK WAS BORN IN ADEL, IOWA, ON JULY 9, 1918, the oldest child in a farming family of three sons. Although they were far from wealthy, the Kinnicks did have a certain station in the community because Nile's maternal grandfather, George W. Clarke, had been governor of the state from 1913 to 1917. Nile Sr. had been a scholar-athlete at high

Nile Kinnick's Heisman Trophy acceptance speech was so moving that the audience at the Downtown Athletic Club was too stunned to respond.

school in Adel and at Iowa State, where he was celebrated for drop-kicking two field goals once against Missouri. "The trouble is," the elder Kinnick recalls, "while I was kicking field goals, they were scoring touchdowns."

He and Frances Clarke were married on Dec. 14, 1916, and Nile was born 19 months later. Ben came 13 months after that, and George eight years after Nile. Between farm chores, Nile and Ben learned to play every sport, but it was Nile who excelled. In the eighth grade he caught a hard-throwing pitcher of his age from the neighboring town of Van Meter named Bob Feller. Nile was a superb basketball player, naturally ambidextrous, and he could do everything on a football field. He was also, it became apparent to his family and friends, an unusually sensitive boy. When one of his friends was punished by a teacher for failing to give a correct answer in class, Nile came home in tears. "He couldn't tell her the answer," he complained to his father, "because he didn't know it." "He had this natural sympathy for the less fortunate," his father says.

The Depression finally forced the Kinnick family off the farm and into Omaha, where Nile Sr. found work with the Federal Land Bank in 1934. At Benson High, Nile Jr. was all-state in football and basketball and graduated as an A student. At Iowa, to concentrate on football and his studies, he quit the baseball team after his freshman year and the basketball team after two seasons. "The athlete," he confided to his diary before his junior season, "learns to evaluate — to evaluate

"This country's O.K. as long as it produces Nile Kinnicks. The football part is incidental."

Bill Cunningham

between athletics and studies, between playing for fun and playing as a business, between playing clean and playing dirty, between being conventional and being true to one's convictions. He is facing the identical conditions which will confront him after college — the same dimensions and circumstances. But how many football players realize this?"

IN A DECADE OF DESPAIR 1939 HAD BEEN A comparatively upbeat year. The worst of the Depression was over. Hollywood was flourishing — Gone With the Wind, The Wizard of Oz and Mr. Smith Goes to Washington would all be released that year — and the big bands had an entire country dancing to the swing beat. But it was dancing in the dark, for in September, Hitler marched into Poland and Europe was at war. Kinnick told his college friends he feared America would soon become involved. "We didn't want to believe him," Prasse recalls.

Kinnick's father had not seen Iowa win in his son's first two years on the team. He reasoned that his best and possibly only chance to witness a victory would be the 1939 opener on Sept. 30 against South Dakota, the weakest opponent on a schedule that included Notre Dame and six Big Ten teams. The elder Kinnick was right — the Hawkeyes won, 41-0. Nile Jr. carried eight times for 110 yards and three touchdowns, one on a 65-yard run, passed for two more scores and drop-kicked five extra points. His 23 points scored were the most by an Iowa player since Oran (Nanny) Pape had scored 24 in 1928. Nile Sr. decided he would make the drive from Omaha to Iowa City for every home game.

The following Saturday the opponent was Indiana, whom the Hawkeyes had not beaten since 1921. The game was played in punishing 94 degree heat at Iowa Stadium. Indiana had a 10-0 lead in the first half, but Iowa came back to win 32-29. Kinnick rushed for 103 yards on 19 carries; he ran for a touchdown and threw scoring passes of 25, 50 and 15 yards to Prasse. He set a school record that still stands by returning nine punts for 201 yards, an average return of 22.3 yards. Kinnick also had 171 yards on kickoff returns and he quick-kicked for 73 yards. He played the entire 60 minutes.

Sportswriters of the time were rarely restrained, but Tait Cummins of The Cedar Rapids Gazette was driven to apparent distraction by Kinnick's heroics: "A new gridiron star blazed across the Big Ten horizon here Saturday, a spectacu-

lar comet with brilliant touchdown tails which cleared away the shadows of despair which have hovered over Iowa's big stadium for the last six years, and which completely eclipsed Indiana's lesser constellation in a 32-29 game never equalled in Hawkeye history."

In Ann Arbor the next week, Kinnick completed a 71-yard touchdown pass to right halfback Floyd (Buzz) Dean in the first quarter, but that was about it for the "Cornbelt Comet." Michigan won, 27-7, with Tom Harmon, who would win the Heisman the following year, scoring all the points. One of his touchdowns came on a 90-yard interception return of a Kinnick pass in the flats. "I wish we could play it over," Nile wrote his father. "That is the ruthless part of this game sometimes ... once it is over nothing can be done about it ... It breaks my heart to have sort of let him [Coach Anderson] down."

But in their next game, at Madison, Kinnick and his teammates came from behind once again to beat Wisconsin, 19-13, Iowa's first win there in 10 years. Kinnick threw touchdown passes to Couppee, to Dick (Whitey) Evans and the game-winner to Bill Green. He, Bergstrom, Hawkins, Tollefson and Enich all played 60 minutes. Anderson told the press he was coaching "Ironmen." The expression made headlines. The team was on its way to becoming a legend.

The following week against Purdue the Hawkeyes scored two safeties after blocking punts, and that was all the scoring, as Iowa beat them by the bizarre score of 4-0. Eight Hawkeyes played the entire game, Anderson using only 14 players from his traveling squad of 26. The coach was clearly reveling in the Ironman image. His team had an identity, and he, as a Notre Dame man, knew from the Four Horsemen the value of a catchy nickname.

During the halftime of the Purdue game, Anderson reviled Couppee for not using Kinnick as the ballcarrier when the team was close to the Boilermaker goal line. He embarrassed both the quarterback and the star by "introducing" them to each other before the entire squad, but the point was well-taken. On the following Saturday, when Iowa reached the Notre Dame 4-yard line on a recovered fumble with only 40 seconds left in the first half, Couppee called for a rare huddle, one of perhaps three he convened all year. The Irish had been plugging the right side of the Iowa line all day, so Couppee called a run to the left. He also wanted Kinnick to carry the ball,

Nile Kinnick rushed for 103 yards and a touchdown, and passed for three scores in a victory over Indiana in 1939.

and in the huddle he ordered the halfbacks to switch positions. Buzz Dean was furious, and Prasse told his quarterback not "to screw things up like this." But Kinnick got the ball and lowered his shoulder through two tacklers to score. His extra point gave the team its ultimate 7-6 win, one of the great upsets of the season.

In addition to his touchdown and extra point, Kinnick's punting was crucial to the Iowa victory. In all, he had 16 punts for 731 yards, a 45.6-yard average. The number of punts and yardage total remain school records. But it was his last punt that finally broke the spirit of the previously unbeaten Irish. With two minutes to play, Kinnick punted from his own 34, the ball going out of bounds on the Notre Dame five.

"When I saw that ball sail over the safety's head, I knew we had beaten Notre Dame," Couppee says. "I have played in 147 football games, college, service and pro, but that was the single most exhilarating moment I've ever experienced in sports." Kinnick's teammates carried him from the field.

The Ironmen and their indomitable little star had overnight become national heroes. They could scarcely walk between classes on the Iowa campus without being mobbed. Classrooms were empty on Monday, and impromptu rallies were held all week long. Mighty Notre Dame had fallen. But Bernie Bierman's Golden Gophers of Minnesota were next. They led the Ironmen, 9-0, in the fourth quarter; Kinnick hit Prasse with a 45-yard touchdown pass and, with three minutes left in the game, connected with Green for a 28-yard game-winner.

"There's a golden helmet riding on a human sea across Iowa's football field in the twilight here," rhapsodized James S. Kearns of The Chicago Daily News. "Now the helmet rises as wave upon wave of humanity pours onto the field. There's a boy under the helmet, which is shining like a crown on his head. A golden number 24 gleams on his slumping, tired shoulders. The boy is Nile Clarke Kinnick Jr., who has just now risen above all the defenses that could be raised against him."

Kinnick had played every minute of six straight games, but not even he was indestructible. In the last game of the season, against Northwestern, he was forced to leave in the third quarter with a separated shoulder. Iowa was held to a 7-7 tie. Couppee was frantically calling pass plays near the end of the game in an effort to break the tie, but Anderson believing incorrectly that a tie would give Iowa the Big Ten title, pulled him to the sideline and sent in substitute quarterback Gerald Ankeny with instructions to "sit on the ball." The tie gave Ohio State the Big Ten championship, and Anderson, in an unprecedented act of atonement, apologized to Couppee.

The Ironmen hadn't won the championship, but they had revived Iowa football and given a state beaten down by poverty and despair something to cheer about. This was a far larger triumph. "It was the damnedest thing you've ever seen," says Couppee. "We couldn't go anywhere without people cheering us. They even stopped movies to turn on the lights and cheer us. We were forever the Ironmen."

Their star, the most durable of them all, was heaped with honors. Kinnick was named to every major All-America team. He won the Heisman Trophy, the Maxwell Award and the Walter Camp Trophy. He also won The Chicago Tribune Silver Football Award, given to the Big Ten's Most Valuable Player, by the largest margin to that date. An Associated Press poll picked him as the nation's top male athlete for 1939. He finished ahead of Joe DiMaggio, who merely hit .381 that year, and Joe Louis, who had KO'd all four challengers for his heavyweight championship.

In accepting the Heisman, Kinnick sounded more like a world statesman than a 21-year-old football player. After thanking his coaches, teammates and the sportswriters, he paused dramatically and then said, "I would like, if I may, to make a comment which I think is appropriate at this time. I thank God that I was born to the gridirons of the Middle West and not to the battlefields of Europe. I can say confidently and positively that the football players of this country would much rather fight for the Heisman award than for the Croix de Guerre."

Kinnick completed his undergraduate years with a 3.4 grade point average in the school of commerce and was one of 30 Iowa seniors elected to Phi Beta Kappa. He was also elected to the school of commerce's Order of Artus honor society. He won the Iowa Athletic Board Cup for excellence in scholarship and athletics, and he was elected senior class president for the College of Liberal Arts and president of the senior class presidents of the 10 colleges and schools at Iowa. His fellow students voted him athlete of the year, and his teammates elected him their Most Valuable Player. "There was not a man on that team who didn't like Nile," Couppee says. On

After winning the Maxwell Award, the NFL's Brooklyn Dodgers wooed Nile Kinnick. But he said law school was his priority.

June 3, 1940, he was awarded the John P. Laffey law scholarship.

Kinnick was first in the balloting for college players in the 1940 College All-Star Game against the Green Bay Packers, and he was on the cover of the game program. In the game itself, on Aug. 29, 1940, he passed for two touchdowns and drop-kicked four extra points in the All-Stars' 45-28 loss to the NFL champions. And, with that, Kinnick's football career came to a sudden end. He never played again, even though the NFL Brooklyn Dodgers drafted him and offered him $10,000, a princely sum then, to play in 1940. Dodger owners John (Shipwreck) Kelly and Dan Topping paid separate visits to Iowa, urging him to turn pro. Topping even brought along his wife of the moment, film and figure skating star Sonja Henie, for one meeting with Kinnick at the Jefferson Hotel in Iowa City. Kinnick asked Couppee, Prasse and Enich to come along and meet the glamorous couple. "My football career is over," Couppee remembers Kinnick as saying. "Law is my first priority."

In fact, Kinnick was already contemplating a future in politics. Less than a month after the All-Star Game, he appeared at a political rally in Iowa Falls and introduced presidential candidate Wendell Willkie to the crowd of 10,000. Kinnick, the grandson of a governor, later addressed a gathering of Young Republicans himself: "When the members of any nation have come to regard their country as nothing more than the plot of ground on which they reside, and their government as a mere organization for providing police or contracting treaties; when they have ceased to entertain any warmer feelings for one another than those which interest or personal friendship, or a mere general philanthropy may produce, the moral dissolution of that nation is at hand."

"We Want Willkie" was the Republican rallying cry that year, but at that particular convention, there was heard another cry: "We Want Kinnick." He was becoming the spokesman for a generation, another duty he would not shirk. Writing a year later to another politically ambitious friend, Loren Hickerson, Kinnick said, "Yes, Loren, some day I would like to meet you as a fellow senator or representative in Washington, D.C. Whether this can ever be my lot none can say now." Getting the jump on other newspapers, The Marion (Iowa) Sentinel announced after the Iowa football season that it was endorsing Kinnick for President in 1956, the first election in which he would be eligible to run for the office.

Kinnick finished his first year of law school third in a class of 103, then enlisted in the Naval Air Corps Reserve. He was called to active duty three days before the attack on Pearl Harbor. "May God give me the courage and ability to so conduct myself in every situation that my country, my family and my friends will be proud of me," he wrote in one of the black notebooks he kept as a record of his war service.

The words, thousands of them, that he wrote on those lined pages serve as a vivid testimony of what might have been. They reveal a much more complicated and vulnerable man than the all-American boy he seemed to be. On these pages, he is sometimes a man in pain. Conditions in the South, which he witnessed while undergoing flight training in Florida, appalled him. "The inequities in human relationships are many," he wrote, "but the lot of the Negro is one of the worst ... kicked from pillar to post, condemned, cussed, ridiculed, accorded no respect, permitted no sense of human

dignity. What can be done I don't know ... When this war is over the problem is apt to be more difficult than ever. May wisdom, justice, brotherly love guide our steps to the right solution."

Despite the rigors of flight school, he read and wrote with the prodigious energy of a man racing to fulfill himself. "Finished Sandburg's *Prairie Years* on Lincoln. Want to get started on *War Years* soon ..." "Picked up a biography of Mr. Churchill just recently written by Philip Guedalla. Read it straight through ..." "Finished St. Exupery's book *Wind, Sand and Stars*. ..." "Did some Science reading for an hour and a half. Read more in Pringle's biography of Theodore Roosevelt ..." "Finished Steinbeck's *Grapes of Wrath* ..." "Started reading Tolstoy's *War and Peace*, the greatest novel ever written. It is 1,350 pages long. ..." These entries were all made between May 21 and July 22, 1942. *War and Peace* took him a few weeks.

He somehow found time to go to the movies — *Mrs. Miniver* was a favorite, *The Maltese Falcon* was not — and to the theater. He was enraptured by a Marian Anderson performance at the Metropolitan Opera House in New York. "Miss Anderson was dressed in a beautiful, full-length velvet gown of quiet green with a splash of silver extending diagonally across the front from waist to hem ... Her powerful heartfelt rendition of *Sometimes I Feel Like a Motherless Child* was marvelous. I could hear the moan and wail of the Negro soul echoing through the centuries ... The perfection of her tone and interpretation swelled out over her listeners and we all closed our eyes and felt as if we were in church."

He listed his favorite swing records: *Elmer's Tune, Moonlight Cocktail, Blues in the Night, Chattanooga Choo-Choo*. And he, who had scarcely a free night in college for dating, in his diary sounded very much like the young man he was. "I must admit that there is nothing I enjoy more than the companionship of a beautiful woman who also possesses breeding, grace, charm and wit. There have been a few such women in my life but not enough ... I shall not consider my mortal existence complete until I have loved and won a woman who commands my admiration and respect in every way. It looks as if it will be some time before that comes about."

Kinnick, a self-assured boy wonder, was, his diaries disclose, afflicted on occasion with a nagging self-doubt. "More than once in the past few months, speeches that I have made have come to mind. It is strange that what I considered then

"There's a golden helmet riding on a human sea across Iowa's football field in the twilight here. Now the helmet rises as wave upon wave of humanity pours onto the field. There's a boy under the helmet, which is shining like a crown on his head. A golden number 24 gleams on his slumping, tired shoulders. The boy is Nile Clarke Kinnick Jr., who has just now risen above all the defenses that could be raised against him."

James S. Kearns of The Chicago Daily News

as a pretty good talk now seems naive, unimpressive, possessing little merit. Sometimes I momentarily feel embarrassed — I wonder what others thought. Would it all have been better unsaid?" "Feel kind of low today. Used to worry about getting into a field of life endeavor that would be sure to press my capabilities. Now I am wondering whether I didn't have a rather exalted idea of the extent of those capabilities."

The final entries, in the spring of 1943, are pithy, hurried, epigrammatic, the words, prophetically, of a man who seemed to be running out of time. "Yesterday's gardenias. ..." "It is a real mistake to try to be head man in everything you attempt ..." "Freedom another name for hunger? ..." "sans culotte. ..." "Tolstoy claims there is no such thing as chance or genius ..." "How I wish I could sing and play the piano ..." And, on June 1, 1943, the last entry: "People must come before profits." The rest of the pages are blank.

On June 2, at 8:30 a.m., Nile Kinnick took off in a Grumman F4F Wildcat Navy fighter plane on a routine training flight from the deck of the carrier U.S.S. Lexington, which was then sailing in the Gulf of Paria in the Caribbean Sea off the coast of Venezuela. Shortly before 10 a.m., another pilot, Ensign Bill Reiter, noticed that Kinnick's plane had an oil leak. He warned him of the trouble by radio and started to follow him back to the ship. About four miles from the carrier, the leak became much more serious. Kinnick could not land on the Lexington without endangering other planes on the deck, so he elected to ditch in the water.

"He was calm and efficient throughout and made a perfect wheels-up landing in the water," Reiter wrote the Kinnick family. Reiter saw Kinnick in the water free of the plane, so he flew back to the carrier to direct the rescue craft. When the vessels reached the crash site, there was no trace of either plane or pilot. Nile Kinnick was five weeks short of his 25th birthday. His brother Ben, born 13 months after him, died 15 months later as a Marine pilot shot down over the Pacific. Their father, Nile Sr., now a vigorous 94, has outlived his two elder sons by 43 years.

THE FACE ON THE COIN TOSSED BY OFFICIALS AT the start of every Big Ten game is Nile Kinnick's. The Iowa football team, a true Big Ten power now, plays in Nile Kinnick Stadium. In the lobby of the Ironmen Inn on the outskirts of Iowa City, there is a giant oil reproduction of the photograph of Kinnick scoring the winning touchdown against Notre Dame. Portraits of all the Ironmen are there. Kinnick, photographed in a frazzled practice jersey, looks, with his cropped sandy hair, wide eyes and dimpled chin, to be no more than 15 years old. There is sort of shrine to Kinnick in the players' lounge downstairs from the football offices on campus. Another picture of the winning touchdown run against Notre Dame is there also, and so, in a glass case, are the Heisman Trophy and the Maxwell Award. By pressing a button below this trophy case, a visitor can hear Kinnick's recorded voice accepting the Heisman. It is a firm, confident voice, a voice older than the man. His number 24 has been retired. Two books have been written about Kinnick and the Ironmen — *Kinnick, The Man and the Legend* by D.W. Stump and *The Ironmen* by Scott M. Fisher.

In 1989 the surviving Ironmen will return to the campus in Iowa City for the 50th anniversary of their team. They will be honored in the stadium named for the man whose memory they keep alive. He is like a friendly ghost to them. "I could not believe it when they said this indestructible man was dead," says Couppee. "I can't recall ever being more emotionally upset. I still find it hard to believe."

Those who knew him have long wondered what this exemplary human being might have accomplished. He had energy, ambition, intelligence, courage, sensitivity. "Offhand, it is hard to think of any good quality which Nile Kinnick did not possess in abundance," Eric C. Wilson wrote in The Daily Iowan after Kinnick's death. "And now he is gone, and his dreams with him," Whitney Martin of the AP wrote. "Why does war have to take such really human humans. It doesn't seem fair."

And yet, almost 50 years after his success, Nile Kinnick remains a presence on the green hills and riverbanks of the Iowa campus. He is not forgotten there, and that is only just, because he would never have forgotten it. "It is almost like home to me," he wrote a friend visiting there. "I love the campus, the people, the trees, everything about it. And it is beautiful in the spring. I hope you strolled across the golf course just at twilight and felt the peace and quiet of an Iowa evening, just as I used to do."

Reichardt Spurs Iowa Comeback vs. Oregon

By Pat Harmon, The Gazette

SCORE BY QUARTERS						
Iowa City, Oct. 29, 1949						
IOWA	6	0	7	21	—	34
OREGON	0	10	14	7	—	31

T

hey're off and running at Memorial stadium.

The track season opened here Saturday and Iowa, by its mastery in the 94-and 99-yard heats, tipped a terrific but fumbling Oregon 11.

Or so it seemed to 37,976 spectators, who were sent home starry-eyed by a record exhibition of running with a football. Iowa defeated Oregon, 34-31, with the last tilt on a teeter-totter that swayed back and forth all day.

Iowa shook one of its runners loose for 99, another for 94, and had scoring plays worth 26 and 21 yards on forward passes.

Oregon contributing mightily to the afternoon of unrestrained thrills, scored with zooming runs of 74, 54 and 37 yards. The Ducks also gave their all for the $3.50 customers with a nifty field goal from 24 yards.

Then there was a 2-yard plunge for the Oregon fullback and a 1-yard jab by the

Iowa fullback. But who will remember those on a day like this?

The prosaic plunge by Iowa's fullback, Bill Reichardt, was the most important 1 yard of the game. It scored the finishing touchdown and pulled Iowa up to its 34-31 victory in the last quarter.

Iowa started the scoring with a 6-0 lead, was knocked back to a 24-6 deficit by the hustling Webfoots, and then came banging back for victory. When the Hawkeyes got up to 24-20, they saw Oregon make another grasp at clinching the game, 31-20. Two Iowa touchdowns followed, and the Hawks had won.

Oregon outdowned the Hawkeyes, 16-14, and had an edge of 395-262 in yards rushing plus passing. But the Ducks couldn't keep up with the flying Hawkeyes on kick returns. Iowa ran six of them back for 265

Fullback Bill Reichardt
scored Iowa's final two
touchdowns, including one on
a 99-yard kickoff return.

yards. This statistic included a 99-yard kickoff sprint by Reichardt and a 94-yard punt rebound by Bob Longley.

Oregon contributed to the Iowa rally with three fumbles. Two of them set up the shorter Iowa touchdowns. The third choked an Oregon drive that had reached the 4-yard line.

Even on the last play, with every spectator standing, the Webfoots threatened to regain the decision. With one second of playing time left when the ball was snapped at center, Jim Calderwood tried a pass to Darrell Robinson that skipped over the latter's fingertips in front of the goal line.

Along with their nonconference victory — the first scored by Iowa against a Pacific Coast opponent — the Hawkeyes went into a tie for first place in the Big Ten race Saturday. Illinois' defeat accomplished this and also allowed Ohio State to step into a share of the lead.

On its last 10 plays, Iowa scored four touchdowns. This included a kickoff return, a punt return and eight tries from scrimmage.

Both Reichardt's 99-yard kickoff return and Longley's 94-yard punt run were new stadium records for distance.

Iowa pulled its halfback pass again, with Jerry Faskie throwing once and completing a touchdown as he had done last week against Northwestern. Jack Ditmer was the receiver, giving him a record of six touchdowns in as many games.

The long gainers for Oregon were Woodley Lewis, who got away for 74 yards from scrimmage and for 33 after scooping up a teammate's fumble; and Johnnie McKay, a deceptive runner who picked off 37 yards in one scoring dash.

Mixed with the speedy rushing of halfbacks Lewis and McKay was some excellent line backing by fullback Bob Sanders.

The nine touchdowns and one field goal showered down on Memorial stadium in this order:

1. Iowa marched 98 yards for a touchdown. Halfback Mearl Naber, punting for 11, 14, and 6 yards, was the spearhead. The scoring play was a 26-yard forward-pass gainer, Glenn Drahn to Don Commack. Reichardt missed the extra point. This was the only failure all day by either placekicker. Iowa 6, Oregon 0.

2. In the second period Sanders plunged over from the 2, closing a 56-yard drive. "Cool Papa" Daniels made the point by placement. Oregon 7, Iowa 6.

Donald Commack (22) gave Iowa a 6-0 lead on a 26-yard touchdown reception from Glen Drahn. Oregon then scored 24 unanswered points.

3. Oregon drove from its own 36 to the Iowa 8. On fourth down, Daniels dropped back to the 14 and placekicked a field goal. Oregon 10, Iowa 6 — at the half.

Lewis went through the middle of the line, was hit in the secondary by one tackler but not stopped, and sprinted 74 yards to a touchdown. Oregon 17, Iowa 6.

5. Oregon scored on a 54-yard play. McKay had made a good gain when he fumbled the ball. Lewis snatched it 21 yards beyond the line of scrimmage, and ran 33 yards for a score. Oregon 24, Iowa 6.

6. Longley caught a Calderwood punt on the Iowa 6 and apparently was pinned in to the east sideline. An Oregon man missed a flying tackle just as Longley set out. Two others had a shot at him as he swung out to the middle of the

field, but they veered in the wrong direction as he swung back toward his original course. He then ran straight ahead, 94 yards, for a touchdown. The third quarter ended during his run. Oregon 24, Iowa 13.

7. Reichardt's short kickoff was fumbled by Oregon tackle Sam Neville and recovered by Iowa tackle Don Winslow on the visitors' 44. Commack ran for 12, Faske for 12, and Reichardt for 8. Two penalties set the Hawkeyes back 10 yards. Faske passed 21 yards to Dittmer for a score. Oregon 24, Iowa 20.

8. McKay ran wide around the Iowa left end, and shot straight down the west sideline. Duane Brandt, defensive halfback on the other side of the line, and Bob Hoff, defensive end on the other side, cut across the field and took aim at him on the 10-yard line. At that instant McKay cleverly cut into the middle of the field and completed a 37-yard bolt to the goal line. Oregon 31, Iowa 20.

9. Lewis kicked off, and the entire Oregon lineup

swarmed down to contact Reichardt, who took the ball on the 1, he started to the sideline, swayed into the middle of the field, and burst through the pack to run 99 yards. Oregon 31, Iowa 27.

10. Sanders' fumble was recovered by Hoff on the Oregon 10. Reichardt smashed across in three plays. Iowa 34, Oregon 31.

Reichardt kicked four extra points after missing the first one. Daniels went 4 for 4 in the Oregon extra point department.

After the last Iowa touchdown, six minutes remained, and Oregon had the ball all this time. The Ducks surged 51 yards down to the Iowa 4, on the gains of McKay, 9 yards, Lewis 11, and Bill Fell, 11 and 17, plus the punching of Sanders.

At first down on the 4, Sanders missed a pitchout pass from Calderwood, who regained the ball after a 15-yard loss. As the game ended, Earl Stelle's pass to Darrell Robinson went incomplete.

EDDIE ANDERSON

Coach Engineered Renaissance at Iowa

By Gus Schrader

Many of those who followed Iowa football from 1939 through 1949 insist Dr. Eddie Anderson could have amassed one of the school's greatest records if two things had been different.

First, of course, was World War II. Anderson, a physician, volunteered to enter the U.S. Army's medical corps, and he was in uniform from 1943 through 1945. This kept him away from coaching football for the 1943, '44 and '45 seasons.

Second was the fact he didn't devote full time to coaching and recruiting in the seasons he did coach. His medical specialty was urology, and he spent many of his hours seeing patients at the University of Iowa Hospitals, located a block away from his office in Iowa Field House and from Kinnick Stadium.

There are football experts who will tell you Anderson would be the man you wanted if you needed a coach to devise strategy for winning any one big game. His skills at motivating players and planning offenses and defenses were outstanding.

Anderson came to Iowa in the depths of one of the university's dismal football periods. The Hawkeyes hadn't won or tied for a championship since Coach Howard Jones' teams completed back-to-back unbeaten campaigns in 1921 and '22. (Actually, they didn't win another until Forest Evashevski coached them to the 1956 title). Iowa was suspend-

ed from the Big Ten in 1930 for alleged recruiting violations, and this affected recruiting for years.

Jones left for Southern California after a 5-3 record in 1923. In the next 15 years before Anderson's famous Ironmen lit up the football landscape in 1939, Hawkeyes teams had a collective record of 50 victories, 61 losses and nine ties. In only six of those 15 seasons did they finish with a winning record.

Iowa didn't win a Big Ten championship in Anderson's nine seasons (35-33-2), but his teams provided a great tonic for a state that was long overdue for some football to get excited about.

It all began soon after Anderson was hired away from Holy Cross in 1939 at an attractive salary of $10,000. The former Notre Dame star immediately fired the imagination of Iowans by making optimistic speeches about the Hawkeyes' potential for that fall. Iowa was a little numb after suffering through 1-7 and 1-6-1 records under Coach Irl Tubbs the previous two years.

What's more, Anderson's arrival came at a time when Iowans, like Americans everywhere, were desperately eager to escape from the lingering pall of the 1930's Great Depression. Many people were still out of work. Iowans were still losing their farms after several years of crop-killing droughts. Interest on the bonds for Iowa Stadium hadn't been paid for five years because of poor football attendance.

Deep down, Anderson couldn't have had a very a rosy outlook after watching his Hawkeye squad in spring practice. Sure, there was Nile Kinnick, a relatively small halfback with immense all-around talent, and several other promising players, but Anderson knew his ranks were very thin.

Assisted by backfield coach Frank Carideo and line coach Jim Harris (each was hired for an annual salary of $4,000), he began to see some light at the end of the tunnel, provided injuries didn't further weaken his squad.

But who would dream that before the 1939 season was over the school could come up with a star who would win the Heisman, Maxwell and Walter Camp trophies, knock off such powerhouses as Notre Dame and Minnesota, compile a 6-1-1 record and miss tying Ohio State for the Big Ten title only because of a 7-7 tie with Northwestern in the final game, when Kinnick was knocked out with injuries?

Indeed, even with the Northwestern tie and a loss to Michigan, Iowa's total season record (6-1-1) was the best of any conference team in 1939.

Eddie Anderson played at Notre Dame under Knute Rockne, and beat the Irish in his first two years as Iowa's coach.

Accustomed to seeing huge squads of players today, people ask what was meant by calling the 1939 teams "the Ironmen." Because their talent was so thin and their games so close, many of Anderson's players had to perform 60-minute games almost every week. The coaching staff was ingenuous in putting patches on top of patches to shore up positions where injury took tolls.

The change in starters began in the second game when Hank Luebcke, giant senior guard, was lost for the season with a hernia that required surgery. A week later tackle Jim Walker suffered a knee injury. He probably could have returned to action after a couple of weeks with today's arthroscopic surgery, but in 1939 he was limited to brief spots of limping action in the last five games. Just a week later, against Wisconsin, center Bill Diehl was knocked out, also with a knee injury.

Anderson had to dig deep after that. Max Hawkins and Ham Snider inherited Luebcke's guard spot. Wally Bergstrom became an Ironman at Walker's tackle. Bruno Andruska took over at center, but Anderson finally had to start sophomore George (Red) Frye there for the final game against Northwestern after Andruska was injured against Minnesota.

Obviously there was some drop-off in experience and talent, so Anderson decided his best players simply would have to play the whole way in close games.

You must understand the rules of football in 1939. There was no platooning, so each man played both offense and defense. A player removed from action could not return until the start of the following quarter. Teams with deeper material and those getting ahead by big margins could afford to rest their regulars the last few minutes of each quarter, but Anderson had neither of those luxuries. By midseason, Iowa newspapers were hailing the "Ironmen" who had to play complete games, or close to it.

Speaking of platooning, here's an example of how well Kinnick played as a two-way performer: He competed in 24 games at Iowa, playing both offense and defense, and he intercepted 18 passes for a school career record. From 1982-85, Devon Mitchell had the chance to play in 49 games. Performing only on defense, he was able to tie Kinnick's record. What's more, think of how many more passes were thrown in the 1980's, what with wide-open attacks and longer games because the rules were changed to stop the clock frequently.

Anderson loved to coach football, but like many coaches he didn't enjoy recruiting. Much of the time he could have devoted to scouring the Midwest for more and better players were spent at the urology lab. If it hadn't been for his assistants and several dedicated Iowa friends and alumni, his records in later years would have been far worse

One of those who helped Anderson most in landing key players was George Foerstner, who later founded Amana Refrigeration. Among the stars he helped recruit were Emlen (The Gremlin) Tunnell, later to become an all-pro defensive star with the New York Giants; "Tulsa Bob" Smith, who starred for the Detroit Lions; and Lou King, a left-handed quarterback chosen for the 1947 Blue-Gray game.

Anderson's debut in 1939 was a 41-0 rout of South Dakota. That didn't start the Hawkeye faithful dancing in the streets, but a week later Kinnick threw a long touchdown pass to Captain Erwin Prasse in the closing minutes for a 32-29 upset of Indiana in Kinnick Stadium. The arena was known only as Iowa Stadium then, but in 1972 the Iowa Board in Control of Athletics finally listened to the pleading of alumni and fans, changing the name to honor the school's only Heisman Trophy winner who died in a Navy airplane accident in 1943.

The Iowa fans really did dance in the streets after the win over Indiana. Happy fans collected downtown and halted traffic, held pep rallies at intersections and tried to rush the movie theaters before being held at bay by police.

Michigan, led by Tom Harmon and Forest Evashevski, cooled this ardor in the next game with a 27-7 triumph, but then the Hawkeyes broke loose for consecutive wins over Wisconsin (19-13), Purdue (4-0), Notre Dame (7-6) and Minnesota (13-9) before the 7-7 tie at Northwestern.

That 4-0 final score at Purdue may have caught your eye. It was achieved on safeties after Iowa tackle Mike Enich blocked two punts. When newsmen questioned Enich about how he managed to accomplish this feat twice in one game, he replied, "After the first one, I just wanted to make it decisive." Enich made two All-America teams the following season.

While Kinnick's passing usually was a great asset, his results at Purdue were miserable. He completed only one and had four passes intercepted, three of them by Purdue's Tom Brown. You can guess from the close scores of Iowa's victories how

the fans reacted for four straight weekends. There were only four home games, but excitement reached climaxes after consecutive upsets over Notre Dame and Minnesota in the final two in Iowa City.

Anderson, a native Iowan, had a special motive against the Fighting Irish. He was born in Oskaloosa and reared in Mason City, where he was a contemporary of the famous "Music Man," Meredith Willson. He played four seasons for Notre Dame (because freshmen were eligible in 1918). His coach was the immortal Knute Rockne, and George Gipp ("The Gipper") was a teammate. The Irish were unbeaten and untied in 1919 and '20. Anderson was captain in 1921 when Notre Dame was shocked by a 10-7 upset at Iowa, which claimed a perfect season of its own.

He won All-America honors as an end in 1921. Then he coached three years at Columbia College of Dubuque (now Loras) before taking the head football job at DePaul in Chicago. Imagine this: In addition to coaching DePaul, he was a player-coach of the Chicago Cardinals, played with a Chicago pro basketball team and attended the Rush Medical College. Oh, yes, he also found time to marry an Irish lass named Mary Broderick and start a family of three sons.

With that as a springboard, Anderson was hired as head coach at Holy Cross, which then had an enrollment of about 1,200 students. He also practiced medicine part time. His football record there was 47-7-1. That's an 87 percent winning record. It might be noted Rockne also had an 87 percent record in 13 years at Notre Dame.

Anderson, 39 when he took the Iowa job, obviously looked forward to facing his alma mater in the sixth contest of 1939. The Hawkeyes' only touchdown was scored on a 4-yard slash by Kinnick after the backfield alignment had been adjusted to fool the Irish defense.

Then Kinnick dropkicked the decisive extra point, 7-6. Although Kinnick dropkicked 11 of Iowa's points that season, observers felt his boot against the Irish may have succeeded because their rushers were accustomed to charging in to block placekicks. Some of their men did penetrate, but they overshot their target as Kinnick took two steps forward to launch his dropkick.

Anderson took no chances in preserving the upset of his alma mater, which had won its first six games and was ranked No. 1 nationally. He had Kinnick punt 16 times in this contest for an average of 45.7 yards and that was in the years when a punter was docked 20 yards for kicking the ball over the goal line. Talk about your triple threats!

Despite their astonishing upsets, the Hawkeyes were given little chance against Bernie Bierman's Minnesota Golden Gophers in the home finale. "The Thundering Horde from the Northland" had routed Iowa by such scores as 34-0, 48-12, 52-0, 35-10 and 28-0 in recent years. However, an estimated 10,000 showed up for a Friday-night rally that fired everyone's hopes. Kinnick again was the standout. In the final minutes he hurled a long touchdown pass to sophomore halfback Bill Green for the 13-9 shocker.

The 7-7 tie with Northwestern in the last game did dampen the enthusiasm of the Iowa fans, but they listened to their radios to hear the details of the contest in Evanston, Ill. Most of them agreed the outcome might have been different had Kinnick been able to play at full strength the whole game. Kinnick belonged to the Christian Science Church, and he was one of those who refused to accept the fact they were ill or injured. Although he obviously could not function because of a shoulder separation, he wanted to stay in the game until ordered by Anderson to return to the bench. He was out of action for the first time in seven games, 402 consecutive minutes against Big Ten opponents and Notre Dame.

Honors poured in after the season. Anderson was named Coach of the Year by several organizations. Iowa fans presented him with a new Cadillac and gave Carideo and Harris new Fords.

Kinnick reaped the most honors. He was a consensus All-America pick. He won the Big Ten's Most Valuable Player award, and captured the Heisman, Maxwell and Walter Camp trophies as the nation's best college player. Get this: He was voted U.S. Athlete of the Year, topping even baseball's Joe DiMaggio and boxing's Joe Louis.

As a student, Kinnick was senior class president. He was a member of Phi Beta Kappa for maintaining a 3.4 grade-point average while participating in two sports. He graduated from the College of Commerce in 1940 and was enrolled in Iowa's Law College when he was killed in the 1943 Navy plane crash.

The attendance at Hawkeye games certainly improved. Indeed, the net profit from football in 1939 was $85,700, compared with a net loss of more than $10,000 in 1938. It wasn't long before the stadium indebtedness was paid off.

After the excitement of the 1939 season subsided, Anderson found winning tougher in the next three years before departing for the armed service. His 1940 team had a 4-4 record, defeated South Dakota and Wisconsin to start the season and finishing with victories over Notre Dame and Illinois. However, the middle four contests were losses to Indiana, Minnesota, Purdue and Nebraska.

At that time, it seemed the Hawkeyes really had the number of Notre Dame in football. Iowa had started this with a victory in its unbeaten 1921 season, and Anderson's 1939 and '40 victories made the school one of the very few with such a record against the Irish. Alas, it couldn't last forever, as Notre Dame defeated Iowa, 56-0, in 1945 and added other victories in 1946, '47, '48 and '49 after Anderson returned from service.

Along that line, here's a strange fact about the Iowa-Notre Dame rivalry. Anderson's successor at Iowa in 1950 was Leonard Raffensperger, a native of Victor, Iowa. Notre Dame's coach then was Frank Leahy, who was born in Winner, S.D. But in the two years their teams met in football 1950 and 1951 the contests ended in ties.

After the 1939 season, this comment by Jim Gallagher in Chicago's Herald-American was typical of the way Anderson was regarded: "It's doubtful if any coach in football history ever accomplished such an amazing renaissance as Eddie Anderson has worked at Iowa."

What kind of offensive system did Anderson use? It was a rather complicated offense in which the Hawkeyes lined up in a T-formation while the quarterback, usually sophomore Al Couppee, barked the signals in open formation.

That's right, Iowa rarely used a huddle. Then the team shifted into one of a variety of formations single wing, double wing, Notre Dame box or long or short punt. Couppee recalled what an achievement it was for him and his mates to master Anderson's system.

Later, Couppee was asked what it was like to perform under Anderson.

"Man, he was a SOB when I played for him," he replied, "but I know now he is a great coach and gentleman."

Couppee was the man who nominated Anderson for admission to the College Football Hall of Fame in 1971, and nobody was more proud than Couppee when his old coach was the one chosen to give the acceptance speech for the incoming group.

CAL JONES

Evashevski Says Lineman Was Best He Ever Coached

By Gus Schrader
....

I owa has retired only two uniform numbers to honor stars in its 109-year football history.

One is No. 24, worn by 1939 Heisman Award winner Nile Kinnick. The other is No. 62, worn by Calvin Jones, the All-America guard, from 1953-55.

Small wonder that Forest Evashevski, his Hawkeye mentor, called him "the greatest lineman I ever coached." Jones might have gone on to become a great in pro football as well, but he was killed in an airplane crash atop an icy Rocky Mountain peak near Vancouver, British Columbia, on Dec. 9, 1956, following his first pro season.

After Evashevski came to Iowa in 1952, he started vigorous recruiting to supplement his supply of players. One of his biggest triumphs was landing three stars from Steubenville, Ohio: Jones, end Frank Gilliam and halfback Eddie Vincent.

It wasn't easy getting Jones. He was sought by many major schools, especially Ohio State, where Coach Woody Hayes already was becoming accustomed to collecting most of the top talent from his area.

A Hawkeye player drove to Steubenville in late August 1952 and picked up Gilliam and Vincent. Then he went to Jones' home, where his mother told them to go away, that her son had already committed to Ohio State. But Calvin did not agree. He was upstairs, and, while his two buddies waited in the auto out front, he tossed his suitcase from the window. Then he managed to get past his angry mother and join the

Calvin Jones was a three-time All-American at Iowa and won the Outland Trophy in 1955. He died in a plane crash on Dec. 9, 1956.

group heading for Iowa City.

Hayes protested the loss of Jones to the Big Ten office, but Commissioner Tug Wilson decided Iowa had not violated the rules. Jones was the instant star on the freshman team and went on to three years as a varsity starter.

College football still did not have free-substitution rules in those years, so Jones was a standout on both offense and defense. Statisticians did not start keeping track of tackles until 1966, but surely he would have been one of the leaders. He also was known as a very fast, devastating blocker.

He was a three-time All-Big Ten choice, and he made All-America first teams 22 times in his career, including an Iowa record of 15 in 1954.

Despite his play, the Hawkeyes had so-so records of 5-3-1, 5-4 and 3-5-1 in his three seasons, and included were narrow losses to Ohio State in 1954 and '55.

The year after Jones finished, the Hawkeyes soared to a 9-1 record and their first Big Ten championship since 1922, but the state's celebration of it was marred by the news of Jones' death.

After his first season with the Winnipeg Blue Bombers, he had been chosen to play in the Canadian League's all-star game in Vancouver. Next morning, he and Coach Bud Grant were scheduled to fly back to Winnipeg together. However, Grant said Jones reported he was unable to get ready in time and would catch another flight that evening. What a tragic coincidence that was.

The four-engine North Star airliner that Jones boarded took off at 5:45 p.m., and a short time later the pilot radioed he had a fire in the No. 2 engine and requested permission to return to Vancouver, as there was no landing field large enough between there and Calgary. The plane descended from 19,000 feet and struck a 6,000-foot mountain top just east of Hope, B.C.

There were 59 passengers and a crew of three aboard. There were no survivors, making it the worst air accident in Canada's history up until then. The Royal Canadian Air Force was not able to spot the wreckage for many days because of bad weather. When it was located, the Royal Canadian Mounted Police announced it would not allow anyone to try reaching the site because of the dangerous altitude and climbing conditions.

There was one report that inflamed the imagination of treasurer seekers. A Chinese official was on the plane who had visited North America. He supposedly had more than a million dollars in gold on his person or in his luggage.

Search parties eventually did get there, of course, but it wasn't reported if they found the treasure.

Two days after the crash, seniors on Iowa's Rose Bowl-bound squad were honored at an annual banquet in Cedar Rapids. The large assembly was asked to say a silent prayer for Jones and others on the plane.

"I can't help but feel if anyone could come through such a desperate situation it would be Cal," Evashevski said, "and I offer a silent prayer for his safe return."

Among his former teammates was Bob Commings, the rugged little guard from Youngstown, Ohio, who served as Iowa's head coach from 1974 through 1978. Commings matriculated with the Steubenville trio in 1952 and lettered in 1953. Then he went into the military for two years before returning to become a regular in 1955 and '56.

"Cal was the greatest football player I ever knew, and there's no two ways about it," Commings said. "There are so many wonderful things I could say about the big guy. It's awfully tough on Frank Gilliam. He and Eddie Vincent were as close as brothers to Cal."

Jones, who was single, had been proud of a 3.0 grade-point average in his four years at Iowa, and he had planned to return to school in February 1957 to finish work on his degree.

He was captain of the 1955 team, and that season he was awarded the Outland Trophy by the Football Writers Association of America as the nation's top lineman. A consensus All-America choice in both '54 and '55, he was elected to the Halls of Fame by both the National Football Foundations and Helms Athletic Foundation.

Jones was named to Iowa's all-time team in 1989, and was in the first group inducted into Iowa's Lettermen Hall of Fame. He finished 10th in the Heisman Trophy voting in 1955.

It is ironic to note that despite his many honors, Jones was not voted Most Valuable Player on the Iowa squad in any of his three seasons. End Bill Fenton was chosen in 1953, center Warren Lawson in '54 and quarterback Jerry Reichow in '55.

Jones was drafted in the ninth round by the Detroit Lions in 1956, as the NFL clubs apparently had word he was interested in going to Canada. Later, he signed with Winnipeg in the Canadian League. He and Reichow were selected to play in the East-West Shrine game after their senior season.

Iowa Escapes After Purdue Misses Late Extra-Point Attempt

By Gus Schrader, The Gazette

SCORE BY QUARTERS
Lafayette, Ind., Oct. 27, 1956

PURDUE	7	7	0	6	— 20
IOWA	7	14	0	0	— 21

Iowa's hair-breadth Hawkeyes, the only unbeaten, untied team in the Big Ten, staved off Purdue's frenzied challenge, 21-20, Saturday as Fullback Fred Harris came through with two tremendous clutch plays in the final three minutes.

Hawkeye heroes were numerous, but it was Harris' vicious tackle that jarred Purdue halfback Erich Barnes loose from the football to give Iowa precious possession just 1:13 before the end.

Frank Bloomquist, believed to be out of action in this contest because of a lame ankle tendon, made the vital recovery to thwart Purdue's last, desperate surge.

That drive might have been successful if Harris had not forced the favored Boilermakers to start from their own 4-yard line. That was where his perfect punt rolled out of bounds with three minutes left.

Punting was one of Iowa's weakest links in the first four games, but Saturday Harris and John Nocera averaged 44 yards on four kicks. This was a large contribution to putting the Hawks on top of the Big Ten standings with a 3-0 record.

Iowa did all of its scoring in the first half, showing by far the best offensive work of the season.

First, end Jim Gibbons made a superb catch of Kenny Ploen's 14-yard pass in the end zone. Then Iowa struck twice in the second quarter on Billy Happel's slashing darts of 6 and 30 yards to take a 21-14 lead.

Purdue's Lennie Dawson, as great a passing quarterback as the Big Ten has seen in many, many seasons, matched Iowa touchdown for touchdown the first two times.

The senior from Alliance, Ohio, hurled three strikes of 17, 20 and 6 yards to set up the first score. With the ball on the 6, fullback Mel Dillard lunged over for the first score on his third carry.

Dawson paved the way for the second one with his own running. Although reputed to be a timid runner, Lennie traveled 7 and 24 yards. Then he dropped back and hurled a strike to Tom Fletcher, who took the ball on the 10 and completed the 18-yard play for a touchdown.

Iowa was able to rest its regulars more than Purdue, but

the Boilermakers turned into fierce fanatics in the fourth quarter, egged on by a Dad's day crowd of 41,415.

They penetrated Iowa territory three times without scoring, then rambled 51 yards in nine plays, Dawson hitting three passes in seven tries for gains of 16, 14, and 20 yards.

The final one was a 20-yard dandy. Lamar Lundy, Purdue end and basketball center who stands 6-6, caught Dawson's pass on the 10 and waded through two Iowa defenders to the goal.

Then came the really crucial moment of the game, although it wasn't to become fully apparent until nine minutes of playing time later.

Dawson, whose missed extra point last year caused a 20-20 tie with Iowa, made Purdue's first two points, as he usually does.

But after the third touchdown, he stepped into the ball a little too eagerly, perhaps kicking before Bob Khoenle had the ball in perfect position. The ball veered off a little to the left, missing the post by a couple of yards.

Purdue players, including Dawson, were seen to demonstrate briefly with the referee, but his decision was given unhesitatingly, and it stood. It will stand forever among the many close calls in this thrill-packed contest.

Iowa was outgained for the first time this year. Purdue rolled up 242 yards on passing. All but 20 yards of it came on Dawson's tosses. Kenny Mikes surprised Iowa by throwing his first pass, and it was good for 20 yards in the first touchdown drive.

That was the first time any Purdue player aside from Dawson has thrown a pass in competition all season.

Purdue ended up with an amazing 405 yards total to Iowa's 349. Purdue also won the battle of first downs, 21-17.

Individually, Purdue had only one runner to match the brilliance of Iowa's Bill Happel and Don Dobrino. Dillard gained 94 yards, but he had to carry 19 times to do it.

Happel led everyone with 99 yards, and he needed only 12 carries. Dobrino had 94 yards in 15 tries. Mike Hagler totaled 11 carries for 45 yards, and Ploen hit six passes for 43 yards.

Iowa halfback Don Dobrino shows off his passing arm, but he was more effective running the football. Dobrino gained 94 yards on 15 carries against the Boilermakers.

Rose Bowl Berth Beckons After Win vs. Mighty OSU

By Gus Schrader, The Gazette

SCORE BY QUARTERS						
Iowa City, Nov. 17, 1956						
IOWA	0	0	6	0	—	6
OHIO STATE	0	0	0	0	—	0

I owa's unranked team of destiny came out of Saturday's game smelling roses — Rose Bowl roses.

Thirty-four years of Big Ten football frustration boiled over as delirious Iowa fans wrenched the steel goal posts from their cement moorings amid the bedlam that was Iowa Stadium.

The 57,732 unbelieving customers had just seen the magnificent Hawks pulverize mighty Ohio State's 17-game Big Ten winning streak, 6-0, and clinch no worse than a share of the conference title.

So Iowa marches to the Rose Bowl against Oregon State Jan. 1 with the proudest Hawkeye record since the unbeaten 1922 team tied for the conference title.

Iowa's final 5-1 conference record is greater even than the 4-1-1 mark posted by the famous Ironmen of 1939. The Hawks can even win the championship all alone, if Ohio State loses or ties in its finale with Michigan next Saturday.

The Rose Bowl contest will be the first "rematch" contest since the Big Ten and Pacific Coast conference initiated their contract in 1946.

Iowa edged Oregon State, 14-13, at Iowa City on Oct. 6 with two touchdown passes and Bob Prescott's two perfect conversions in the last 11:17.

It will be the first trip to the colorful Pasadena classic for both teams, although Oregon State played in a "transplanted" Rose Bowl game at Durham, N.C., in 1942, when wartime regulations banned the game at Pasadena. Oregon State beat Duke, 20-16.

Oregon State clinched its right to represent the Pacific Coast conference Saturday with a surprisingly narrow 14-10 win over underdog Idaho.

Neither team will be selected officially until next Sunday, Nov. 25, when the athletic directors cast their votes in both conferences. But it would take a special session of congress to keep either one out.

The Hawkeyes of Iowa, defeated only by Michigan this season in a 17-14 heartbreaker with a minute to go, seldom have played as ferocious a contest as the upset of Ohio State.

No one would have dreamed a six-point score would be enough to defeat an Ohio State team that had rolled up a

End Jim Gibbons gets ready to catch the winning score from quarterback Ken Ploen in the fourth quarter despite the efforts of Ohio State halfback Don Clark. Iowa's victory ended Ohio State's 17-game Big Ten winning streak.

record 17 straight Big Ten victories and only last week gained 465 yards rushing against Indiana, another Big Ten mark.

But defense did it! Only four times did the Hawks let Ohio State cross the 50-yard line, and none of these drives penetrated deeper than the Iowa 32-yard line.

That was the Buckeye sortie that ended in a futile field-goal try, a kick that was a grounder instead of a line drive.

Ohio State's other noteworthy attempts ended on the Iowa 35 (fumble recovered by Sleepy Klein), on the Iowa 38 (downs) and on the Iowa 42 (downs). The last mentioned

drive was Ohio State's only penetration of Iowa territory in the second half.

In fact, Ohio State gained only 47 yards rushing and 6 yards by passing in the second half.

The statistics were amazingly close to being even in the first half, but the Hawks played a second half like they never have before.

Indeed, it was the first time in the last four games that Iowa had scored in the second half.

But when the dam broke, it gave away with a flourish

that turned Iowa Stadium into a madhouse.

The Hawks had made the only important scoring threat of the game up to that time, a push to the 19-yard line in the first quarter that ended for want of more downs.

But the Hawks took the second-half kickoff and never gave it up until end Jim Gibbons had possession of Kenny Ploen's precious pass in the end zone.

This march covered 63 yards. It required nine plays and was helped by an Ohio State pass-interference penalty that gave Iowa a first down on the Buckeye 20.

The Hawks were worrying Ohio State with their double reverse then, but suddenly on second down Ploen drifted to his left from the 17 and flipped a high toss into the front part of the end zone.

It cleared one Buckeye defender, quarterback Frank Ellwood, and Gibbons captured it cleanly in front of halfback Don Clark.

Iowa joy was short-lived. On the extra-point try, Bob (Automatic) Prescott missed his first kick of the season after 13 straight successful ones.

It could have been that the pass from center was a bit high, causing Ploen to hurry the ball into position. At any rate, the kick was off to the right, and the stands groaned with fear that Ohio State might come storming from behind like Michigan did two weeks previously.

But Ohio State never got beyond the Iowa 42-yard line after that; so aroused was the Hawkeye line.

The Hawks gave it an iron-man performance Saturday that one wouldn't believe possible in these days of frequent substitutions.

Gibbons, fullback Fred Harris and halfback Don Dobrino went all the way, 60 minutes of skin-tight action. Coach Forest Evashevski used only brief relief at the other eight positions.

Chuck Pierce and giant Mac Lewis spelled co-captain Don Suchy during the times when the brave Iowa center was sent to the bench because of injuries.

The other co-captain, Dick Deasy, relieved tackle Sleepy Klein briefly in each of the last three quarters. John Burroughs spelled tackle Alex Karras for a minute or two in the fourth quarter

Gary Grouwinkel and Hugh Drake gave short relief to the starting guards, Frank Bloomquist and Bob Commings.

Mike Hagler got into the game a couple of times for Bill Happel, the game's rushing leader, with 58 yards on 13 carries.

Randy Duncan spelled Ploen for only two plays just before the half, and one of them almost went for a touchdown.

The Hawks had the ball on their 37, second down with 2:32 to go in the second quarter. Duncan threw down the middle and the ball barely eluded the fingertips of Dobrino as he sped all alone into the open. Six inches shorter and the pass would have been good for an Iowa lead in the first half.

A foot or so was all that kept Iowa from clinching the contest with 2½ minutes to go, something that would have saved wear and tear on the hearts of the 57,732 fans.

Iowa stopped an Ohio State drive on the Iowa 42. Using Harris on quick openers over left guard, the Hawks soon

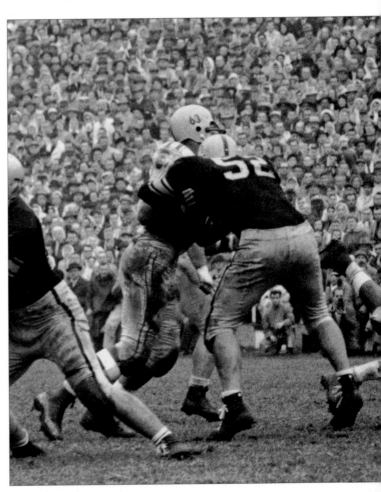

had a first down on the 15. Two plays lost 3 yards to the 18.

Then the Hawks played it carefully. Ploen sent the scraping Happel over left tackle to the 15 in a move designed to get the ball in the middle for a field-goal try.

Then the Hawks called for Prescott and his kicking tee. The pass from center again seemed a bit high, causing Ploen to reach up and maybe forcing Prescott to kick before the ball was ready.

At any rate, everyone held his breath as the ball sailed straight toward the posts, finally falling short of the crossbar by a foot.

Ohio State never got out of the hole, although the Buckeyes would have made it mighty interesting had it not been for a crucial clipping penalty that nullified a 15-yard gain and set the Bucks back to their 25. The officials ruled Jim Roseboro clipped Iowa's Harris on the 40-yard line.

Ohio State's passing went from bad to worse. Roseboro tried one to end Leo Brown that was dropped. Then Iowa's Frank Gilliam and Karras rose to new stature.

Ellwood went wide to his right on a passing attempt, but the agile Gilliam climbed all over him and dropped him for a 13-yard loss on the 12.

Roseboro threw a pass that was much, much too low for Brown to handle. Twenty-five seconds remained, and this time Karras smashed through to drop Roseboro on the 3.

Iowa took over there, and the Hawks tried one play as confusion reigned. It ended with red handkerchiefs all over the field, and spectators starting a demonstration that didn't end until the 6-inch steel goal posts were uprooted.

Iowa's Randy Duncan flips a pass to end Bob Prescott. The Hawkeyes' victory clinched a share of the Big Ten championship and virtually clinched a spot in the Rose Bowl.

Iowa Enjoys Sweet Su

By Gus Schrader, The Gazette

California is famous for its Iowa picnics, and the Rose Bowl game turned into one Tuesday as Kenny Ploen led his Hawkeye mates to a 35-19 triumph that further lengthened faces in the misfortune-pocked Pacific Coast conference.

Oregon State's Eager Beavers were the victims this time, marking the 10th setback in 11 games against the Big Ten in the colorful postseason classic.

A crowd of 97,126, witnessing Iowa's first Rose Bowl trail, watched Ploen spark the Hawks to a 14-0 lead before the first quarter was half over. Then, before the Hawks got pos-

SCORE BY QUARTERS					
Pasadena, Calif., Jan. 1, 1957					
IOWA	14	7	7	7 —	35
OREGON STATE	0	6	6	7 —	19

session of the ball again, Ploen was carried to the bench with a wrenched right knee.

Still, the Hawks were able to swap touchdowns with the Pacific Coast champions the rest of the way to win going away with the fourth-highest score in the 11-year Rose Bowl series.

Ploen was patched up enough to lend considerable help in the second half, pitching a 16-yard touchdown pass to end Jim Gibbons on fourth down.

The game hardly followed the form chart, although the

Iowa's Bill Happel (40) and Don Dobrino (20) help bring down Oregon State fullback Nub Beamer during the Hawkeyes' first appearance in the Rose Bowl.

ccess In 1st Rose Bowl

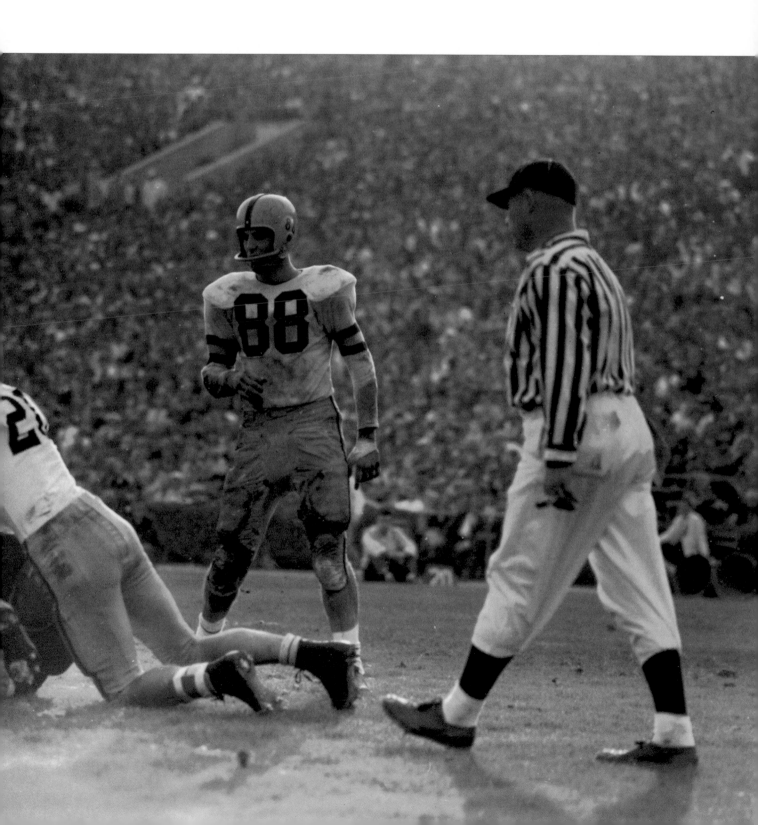

Iowa ran away from Oregon State from the start of the Rose Bowl and never looked back. The Hawkeyes scored 14 points in the first quarter, led 21-6 at halftime and 28-12 after three quarters.

Hawks were a nine-point favorite going in. It had been billed as a defensive duel, with both teams well aware of each other's offensive tendencies, because they had played earlier this season and traded scouting movies.

When Iowa won the first meeting, 14-13, at Iowa City, Oct. 6, plenty of folks thought the Hawks were lucky to win. No one left Pasadena's vast Arroyo Seco saucer Tuesday with that impression. The Rose Bowl crowd probably has seen greater individual accomplishments, but none seemed more vital than the contribution made by Ploen.

Many of the spectators were still struggling down from the gorgeous Tournament of Roses parade and were seeking their seats when Ploen hurled the first bombshell into Oregon State's hopes for an upset.

Dependable Frank Gilliam pounced on an Oregon State fumble to check the Beavers' first frenzied rush. Four plays gained 11 yards to the Beaver 49, and Ploen suddenly rolled out to his right on the familiar pass-run option play.

The Hawkeyes chopped black-shirted Beavers in key spots, and the shifty quarterback quickly sported his way down the right sideline. The Beavers had him for sure on the 25-yard line, and he was knocked almost flat, saving his knees from touching the turf by balancing with one hand.

Back upright before you could deliver a one count, Kenny cooly counted noses and found two friends left standing to only one enemy. The buddies, Dick Klein and Gibbons, flattened Oregon State's Tom Berry and Ploen raced on for an electrifying 49-yard touchdown run that was the turning point of the whole game.

The Beavers couldn't help but be shaken. Vicious Iowa tackles soon forced another fumble, and the Hawks rattled 66 yards in four plays to make it 14-0 with 7:40 gone.

The big play this time was a 37-yard romp by big Don Dobrino to the 9-yard line. From there, Mike Hagler, the only man to score more than one touchdown, socked into the end zone on the first play.

It might have been a picnic for the estimated 15,000 Iowans and the many former Iowans and their friends, but the Hawks found the Beavers to be a fast, dangerous team that could scare the daylights out of you on every play. Oregon State took considerable satisfaction in being the second team to score three touchdowns against the Big Ten champions this season, but the Beavers had no defense capable of holding an Iowa attack that had come of age since the conference season ended.

The Hawks used to rely on a hard-nosed defense that held four opponents scoreless. But just as they proved in the Notre

Dame game, the Hawks have learned how to manufacture touchdowns. And they came from all sorts of ranges Tuesday. In addition to Ploen's 49-yard streak, Hagler hit the end zone on a 66-yard double reverse that started Iowa off anew in the second half.

Hagler disproved the great emphasis placed on Oregon State's speed advantage, for he outraced the fastest Beaver backs, once he got the step on them at midfield.

Iowa stuck to the offense it has used all season, except for some variations late in the fourth quarter. But the Beavers proved they have been taking full advantage of secret sessions staged on the UCLA practice lot.

The Iowans were hardly prepared to see both of the Beavers' feared tailbacks, Joe Francis and Paul Lowe, in the backfield at the same time. But that was the spectacle that greeted them early in the game, giving the Black Bandits from

Victory wasn't the only thing the Hawkeyes got to taste during their first trip to the Rose Bowl. Actress Jayne Mansfield plants a kiss on Iowa's future All-America quarterback Randy Duncan.

Benton County even more speed than was expected.

Oregon State also used a fullback flanker for the first time, and for the first time this season the Beavers threw passes to their fullbacks.

The results were effective enough to keep Iowa's best combinations in the lineup most of the time. It wasn't until late in the fourth quarter that Coach Forest Evashevski was able to relax enough to send in the rest of his Rose Bowl squad.

Six Hawks figured in the scoring. In addition to the touchdown plays already mentioned, Billy Happel of Cedar Rapids scored on a 5-yard shot around left end to make it 21-6 at halftime. This was a key touchdown, too, because it helped the Hawks prove they could score even without Ploen. All five extra points were booted perfectly by Bob Prescott. This gave him 24 of 26 for the season.

Iowa left a convincing stamp on the Beavers in another way, too. Frank Gilliam and Fred Harris each blocked one of Oregon State's first two extra-point tries.

This was especially shattering to John Clarke, reserve end for the Beavers. He had been successful on 16 straight extra point tries up until then. He started kicking 'em right after the Beavers dropped their 14-13 nod at Iowa City.

With Clarke unable to return to the game because of the sub rule in the fourth quarter, the Beavers decided to run across with their final point. Or maybe it was just that they were fed up with seeing white-shirted Iowans blocking the kicks. At any rate, they sent fullback Nub Beamer spinning across for the point, marking the first time in many years that a team in the Rose Bowl has purposely converted by another means than kicking.

The first two Oregon State touchdowns were scored from short range. Fullback Tom Berry hit from 3-yards out in the second quarter after the score was set up by Sterling Hammack's 25-yard punt return to the Iowa 15.

The Beavers marched 70 yards in 15 plays for the second one, with Beamer diving over from a foot out.

The final touchdown came suddenly. In fact, the Beavers went 62 yards in only two plays, assisted by a pass-interference penalty.

Francis threw to Hammack on the 2-yard line to complete a 35-yard touchdown play.

The Hawks never trailed by fewer than 14 points after scoring the first two touchdowns.

ALEX KARRAS

All-America Tackle Turned From Ugly Duckling to Swan

By Gus Schrader

Alex Karras would not be flattered if someone compared his football career at Iowa to Hans Christian Anderson's "The Ugly Duckling," but the big tackle from Gary, Ind., did morph from a stubborn tackle who didn't win a letter as a sophomore into a player who performed as beautifully as a swan.

Karras was a four-time Indiana all-stater at Gary Emerson, and almost every major college sought to enroll him in 1955. Iowa finally won the recruiting derby, after a bitter, last-ditch fight with Indiana, but it wasn't until two years later that the big tackle fulfilled what had been expected of him.

He was an All-America choice in 1956, when Iowa went to Pasadena in its first-ever bowl appearance, and he made it again in 1957, winning the Outland Trophy given by the Football Writers of America to the nation's outstanding lineman.

More than that, he was runner-up to Texas A&M's John David Crow in the Heisman Trophy voting. No "down lineman" has ever finished higher than that since the Heisman was started in 1935. He made Iowa's all-time all-star team and was the No. 1 choice in the 1958 draft. Then, of course, came his 13-year career as an all-pro with the Detroit Lions.

He morphed again, becoming first a TV football commentator and then a featured star in Hollywood motion pictures. Who will forget his acting in *Blazing Saddles* and *Babe*, the story about Babe Didrickson Zaharias? For several years he was a star on the *Webster* television sit-com.

He also wrote a book (co-authored by Herb Gluck) called

Alex Karras didn't win a letter during his sophomore season. He was the Heisman Trophy runner-up in 1957.

72

Even Big Guys Cry in which he candidly admitted some of the mistakes he had made before and after finding fame and fortune. Get this: Karras got crosswise with Iowa head coach Forest Evashevski and one of his assistants, Bob Flora, and didn't even play enough to win a letter as a sophomore. How many All-America players improve that much in one year?

It all began on July 15, 1935, when Alex was born in Gary. His father, Dr. George Karras, was a Greek immigrant who graduated from the U. of Chicago and got his medical degree in Halifax, Nova Scotia. There he met Alex's mother, a Canadian of Scotch-Irish descent. They were married in 1926 and two years later moved to Gary, where he opened a medical practice.

His father died a relatively poor man in 1948, when Alex was 13 years old. Alex already had started playing football at the Sears-Roebuck parking lot near his home. His older brother, Teddy, played at Purdue, then transferred to Indiana.

Because of this, Alex said "Indiana had the inside track" on recruiting him. Teddy encouraged him to go there. An Indiana alumnus who owned a string of doughnut shops in Gary, gave Alex a job, let him stay at his house, had the Karras house painted free and bought Alex a suit of clothes.

However, late in the summer of 1954, after he graduated from Emerson High, four coaches from the U. of Iowa came to Gary and flew him to Spencer, in the northwest corner of Iowa. Alex discovered he was being hidden out there while Indiana alumni scoured the Gary area in search of "their" recruit. Even his brother Teddy didn't know where he was, and he took heavy pressure from Indiana coach Bernie Crimmins and Hoosier alumni.

Alex moved to Iowa City when freshman practice began. He said he had a fine relationship with Wally Schwank, the freshman coach, but developed a strong dislike for Bob Flora, whom he claims called him "greaseball" and "pool-room Johnny."

Alex admitted his appearance wasn't much when he showed up for registration in Levis and a stained Indiana University T-shirt, carrying two pairs of pants and Teddy's black double-breasted suit over his arm. He said his hair hung down to his collar, at least a month overdue for the barber.

"Maybe I looked like a gangster," he confessed, "or what a gangster was supposed to look like."

Alex probably would have gone back to Gary if he hadn't met Ernie Pannos, an Iowa City theater owner, also of Greek descent. He gave Alex a job ushering in one of his movie hous-

es. He also developed a fine relationship with Calvin Jones, Iowa guard, who won the Outland Trophy in 1955 when Alex was a soph.

That season started badly when Alex reported for practice 20 pounds overweight. He also was set back by a cracked ankle bone, but still managed to play briefly. After being disappointed at not getting to play in the finale against Notre Dame, he recalled he threw his shoe at Evashevski and went home to Gary. Evashevski lifted his scholarship.

Pannos finally talked him into returning to school, but he went back to Gary again after the 1956 opener against Indiana. He said Evashevski had promised to start him against his brother Teddy, but held him out for the first two minutes. This time it took a call from Evashevski to induce him to come back. He did it only after making Evashevski and Flora promise they wouldn't talk to him. After the final regular-season game he got into a physical battle with the two coaches.

Karras made five All-America teams that year and 10 in 1957 when he finished his college career. He also met Joanie Jurgensen, an Iowa coed from Clinton who later became his wife. This marriage ended in divorce, and Alex later married Susan Clark, who played Babe Zaharias in the movie *Babe*.

He was chosen for the College All-Star game in 1958, but he didn't get along with Coach Otto Graham, who called him a loafer and a trouble-maker and predicted, "You'll never make it in the NFL."

When he arrived in the Detroit Lions' camp later, he was faced by Coach George Wilson.

"I have a report from Otto Graham about you," said Wilson. "It's awful. He thinks you're not going to make it here. What do you have to say for yourself?"

When Alex stammered an answer, Wilson added, "If Otto Graham says that about you, you must be one great SOB. I'm glad to have you here."

Alex's brilliant career as a Detroit defensive tackle for 13 years had many highlights and a few lowlights. Like being elected team captain. Like the time he and Paul Horning were suspended from play for the 1963 season after they admitted to betting on games. Like being named all-pro tackle for most of his 13 seasons.

Like being told by Coach Joe Schmidt on the phone that the Lions were releasing him. Small wonder that "Even Big Guys Cry."

Hawkeyes Run Roughshod Over U-M to End Jinx

By Gus Schrader, The Gazette

....

SCORE BY QUARTERS					
Ann Arbor, Mich., Nov. 1, 1958					
MICHIGAN	0	6	8	0	— 14
IOWA	7	7	7	16	— 37

Iowa released the greatest storm of long-distance scoring lightning in its history Saturday to blast a 34-year old football jinx into smithereens.

Michigan, scrapping to regain respectability, hampered the celebrated passing of Randy Duncan, but the Wolverines had nothing to match the speed of halfbacks Willie Fleming, Ray Jauch and Bob Jeter.

It's likely the 31-year old Michigan Stadium never saw such running before.

These Hawks contributed touchdown runs of 61, 74, 61, 24 and 3 yards to bury Michigan, 37-14, in the first Iowa victory over the Wolverines since 1924.

When it was over the hilarious Hawkeyes swept their coach, Forest Evashevski, up on their shoulders and paraded him to the middle of the same field where he attained stardom for Michigan. There, they let him down to accept the congratulations of Benny Oosterbaan, his old friend who directs Michigan.

The win marked Evy's first over Michigan in six tries, although his team battled back to obtain a 21-21 tie last year after four straight bitter defeats.

Many of the 68,566 customers in this vast 101,001-seat sta-dium thought another Michigan comeback would break Iowa's old heart again Saturday, but they reckoned not with another Iowa team of destiny that has a mighty closing kick of it's own.

Tied at 14-14 by a furious Michigan counterattack at the start of the second half, Iowa thundered to its last three touchdowns inside a glorious 16-minute stretch of the third and fourth quarters.

The gate was opened by another sparkling defensive play by an Iowa team that didn't figure to be tough defensively this year.

Michigan was backed up to its own 19, where Hugh Drake and Don Horn nailed Reid Bushong for a 5-yard loss. Then Drake, one of Iowa's senior Rose Bowl veterans, broke through and knocked quarterback Stanton Noskin head over heels.

The ball squirted free for Michigan's only fumble of the game and guess who was Johnny-on-the-spot to retrieve it. Jeff Langston, who picked off a Wisconsin fumble of the

touchdown that beat the Badgers, grabbed the ball on the 3.

Jeter, a smiling junior from Wierton, W. Va., sped far around right end on the next play to give Iowa the lead it never relinquished.

Both Michigan and Iowa hearts were thumping during the next 10 minutes, as the teams took turns giving the ball away, Michigan on a pass interception and again when faced by a fierce Iowa goal line stand, and Iowa on a pair of fumbles by Jauch and Jeter.

But the Hawks shook off their errors like a duck shedding water. After halting the Wolverines on their own 6-yard line, the Hawks stabbed 94 yards in eight stunning plays to put the game beyond reach.

Fleming, a 5-9, 170-pound soph from Detroit who gave his home folks a great show, grabbed one of Duncan's passes for the biggest gain, a 37-yarder to the Michigan 41.

Duncan regained his passing form after a cold first half and hit Curt Merz with another first-down pass to the 27. Then Randy Duncan handed the ball to Jeter and sent him slashing around the right end. Jeter seemed stopped twice, but he sifted through the sagging Wolverines like a Halloween ghost for the final 24 yards.

It still wasn't over, even when captain John Nocera hoisted a perfect pass to Merz for the 2-pointer that made it 29-14.

Michigan punted with 6½ minutes to go, and Jeter circled right end again for 6 yards to the Iowa 39. There, Fleming tucked the ball under his arm, found running room outside left tackle and suddenly was all alone again. The little bombshell outran his futile pursuers for a 61-yard touchdown run. Iowa was penalized for delaying the game for the second straight time, but against the Hawks merely shrugged and went for the 2-pointer. This one came on Duncan's little pitch to the reliable Merz.

Just to show their scorn for Michigan's long domination in this series, the Hawks threw Michigan back for losses of 2, 6, 9, and 11 yards before the wolverine finally took the hint and punted.

But the overeager Iowa subs lost the ball on an interception of Mitch Ogiego's pass, and Michigan was knocking on the

Senior Randy Duncan shook off a cold first half to quarterback Iowa to its first victory over Michigan since 1924.

door against Iowa tailenders when the game ended. Michigan was primed for an upset, and who can say they wouldn't have got it without Iowa's long-distance operating technique?

Indeed, Michigan played most of the first quarter in Iowa territory, twice kicking over the goal line when Iowa snubbed drives spearheaded by Darrell Harper, Fred Julian and Bob Ptacek.

Michigan had the better of it with the final play of the opening quarter. Then Harper got off a 40-yard punt that Fleming bobbled momentarily on the Iowa 28. Iowa fans who have been waiting six weeks to see Willie run, finally got their chance.

He fled through the Michigan tacklers like a thief, almost knocked off his feet at the Iowa 40, and again on Michigan's 40. This last encounter required Willie to pull free of a Michigan defender with a beautiful pivot, and when he stopped spinning he was in the open.

It was a touchdown run of 72 yards, Iowa's first punt return for a score since Earl Smith used to run 'em back in 1954. But the folks hadn't seen anything yet.

Two minutes later, Iowa got the ball again on a Michigan punt. This time the Wolves were more respectful, kicking the ball out of bounds on the Iowa 26.

But on the very first play, Jauch sprang through an opening at left tackle, cut back to his right and saw daylight

Game Ball Goes to Evy

By Lou Breuer, The Gazette

Calvin Coolidge was president. Rudolph Valentino was the big box office attraction and Bobby Jones had just won his first U.S. Open golf title.

The year was 1924 and until Saturday that was the last time Iowa whipped Michigan on a football field.

But the floodgates opened here Saturday and the Hawks surged to a 37-14 victory.

How does it feel:

"There have been so many frustrations in this series for me, I just don't know what to say," explained Coach Forest Evashevski as he sat in the dressing room clutching the game football.

"This was a big one for me.

"I'm proud of our Iowa boys and I'm proud of the way those Michigan players fought back and I'm mighty proud of the Michigan kids who played for Iowa today."

Evy got the game ball, seconds after the final gun. Quarterback Mitch Ogiego grabbed it from the ref-

eree and ran over to Evy, who was coming out on the field.

"This is for you, Coach," Mitch said proudly as he handed Evy the ball, "You deserve it."

There was no question among the players that the ball would be Evy's if he succeeded in coming through with a win.

"Heck," explained jubilant John Nocera, "we've been dedicating the ball to him every year for 3 years, but this is the first chance we've had to give it to him."

Getting back to the events of the day, Evy revealed that Michigan's surprise balanced line had caused plenty of trouble during the first half.

"Michigan hasn't run with a balanced line at all," Evy explained. "We just weren't expecting it and we had a tough time adjusting.

"It took away our 'keys' but in the end we had too much depth and too much speed for them."

Evy called the game "a pretty even one outside of a few long runs."

The game plan, he revealed, was to run the ends and pass, and Michigan's ends proved vulnerable, ahead. He zipped 74 yards, escorted the last half of the way by Don Prescott, who kept a careful eye on tackle Don Deskins until the goal line was assured.

Michigan didn't give in easily. The Wolverines bounced by for a 67-yard touchdown drive to cheat the half gun by 26 seconds. That push required 16 plays, and the Hawks twice threw Michigan passers for losses.

But it should go as a credit to the Wolverine determination that they were able to claw back and keep the drive going. Ptacek completed five passes in the stretch, and they needed one to put the ball across.

Michigan had a first down on the Iowa 5, and two plays gained only 1 yard. Then Ptacek flipped a little flat pass to Harper for the touchdown.

Michigan failed on a pass attempt for extra points after its first touchdown, but tied the game at 14-14 right after the half when a 2-point run followed its second touchdown.

Michigan used 14 plays to cover the 74 yards following the second half kickoff. Harper did most of the lugging, and Ptacek the passing. Ptacek finally sneaked for the final foot, then sent Brad Myers driving outside right tackle for the extra points.

That was Michigan's high-water mark, because the Wolverines never threatened again until Iowa was out in front.

especially in the second half.

Evy also said the Michigan passing attack, which he termed "a good one," had proved troublesome to the Hawkeyes.

Quarterback Randy Duncan said the Iowa attack didn't really get going in the first half because, "I wasn't running the ends enough."

"They were stunting in the middle and giving us a lot of trouble, but once we got started around the ends in the second half, we moved a lot better."

In all, Michigan threw the ball 25 times and on several other occasions Michigan passers were tossed to the ground on what had started out to be pass plays.

"I've never rushed a passer so much in my life," said an exhausted Don Norton, "but it was worth it. This is a wonderful day."

Jeter Turns On Jets as Iowa Rolls

By Gus Schrader, The Gazette

L ike many a desperate gambler, California put its chips on the wrong "horse" when Iowa's star-studded entry went to the post in the 45th running of the annual Rose Bowl handicap Thursday.

Underdogs by 18½ points, the Golden Bears figured their best bet for an upset was to stop the golden armed passing of Randy Duncan and the will-o-the-wisp running of Willie Fleming.

But they reckoned not with another galloper in the Hawkeye stable, Bob Jeter, a shy, pleasant young West Virginian, belted them from their blind side and almost ran the Pacific Coast champs right through the hazy San Gabriel mountains that towered over the 98,297 fans in the New Year's classic.

Iowa routed California, 38-12, for the most lop-sided Big Ten victory since Illinois clawed Stanford, 40-7, seven years ago. And, although California had won only 2 of 7 previous bowl games, its most lopsided loss up to Thursday was 14-6 to Michigan in 1951.

Rose Bowl experts who named Kenny Ploen the player of the 1957 game when Iowa clouted Oregon State, 35-19, went into even greater superlatives in trying to describe Jeter.

The jet-propelled Jeter caused the biggest stir locally since the San Andreas fault began kicking up earthquakes.

Jeter broke two long-time Rose Bowl records with his flying feet, and the Hawks shattered two team marks and

Iowa's victory over California was the most lopsided in the Rose Bowl since Illinois defeated Stanford, 40-7, in 1952.

SCORE BY QUARTERS Pasadena, Calif., Jan. 1, 1959						
IOWA	7	13	12	6	—	38
CALIFORNIA	0	0	6	6	—	12

The game was so one-sided after the opening exchange of the ball's possession that you'd have to say the "turning point" came when Duncan dived over from 1½-yards out for the first touchdown, and Bob Prescott kicked the extra point.

The Hawks added two more in the second quarter, the first on Duncan's 7-yard pitch to Jeff Langton and the other on fullback Don Horn's 4-yard belt into the end zone.

tied still another.

Duncan, who outshone California's brilliant Joe Kapp in their personal duel of All-American quarterbacks, had a direct hand in the scoring of Iowa's first two touchdowns, then turned the duties over to his halfbacks and fullbacks.

California, which gained only 137 yards to Iowa's 227 in the first half, finally shook out the kinks from its famous option-play offense as the second half began and scored a touchdown.

Halfback Raymond Jauch and the Iowa offense generated Rose Bowl records of 429 yards rushing and 516 total yards.

Iowa fans flocked to Pasadena, Calif., for their second Rose Bowl trip in three years.

It came against Iowa's first unit, too, and many of the thousands of Iowans began fearing the Bears and found a mortal chink in Iowa's defensive armor.

But the Hawks sealed that off completely, and the Bears couldn't score again until they passed for one against the Iowans in the final 37 seconds.

Meanwhile, Fleming climbed into the act by cutting back 37 yards through sieve-like California defense for the touchdown that broke the host team's hearts.

Just when the Bears had begun to convince themselves that was all a dreadful mistake, Jeter roared through the opposite side for the 81-yard touchdown run that was the longest in Rose Bowl history. Never since the classic began in 1907 had another run that far from scrimmage.

That did it. Fleming's second touchdown run in the fourth quarter only added insult to injury, because the bettors who had taken the 18½ points had long since abandoned hope. Willie simply waltzed through the Bear secondary on that last one, doing a buck-and-wing as he crossed the goal.

Jeter's 194 yards in nine carries comprised a Rose Bowl record, the old individual rushing high being 151 yards by Bobby Grayson of Stanford 25 years ago.

The Hawks' great Winged-T offense, which set a Big Ten record and led the nation this season, had its greatest day of the whole campaign. Both the rushing total of 429 yard and the total offense of 516 yards stand as Rose Bowl records.

The old marks were: 320 yards rushing by Illinois in 1947 and 491 yards total (passing and running) by Michigan in 1948.

The record tied was 24 first downs, the game total compiled by Georgia in 1943. And California didn't do too badly in that department, getting 20 of its own.

Because of the mismatch of personnel, Kapp had to make a back set as a runner, but his passing was better than expected. He hit 8 of 17 passes for 126 yards, and his final toss covered 17 yards and Jack Hart gathered it in for the final touchdown.

Kapp had great help from his receivers. Hart gathered in 4 for 61 yards, and Ted Bates nabbed two for 37.

Cal Couldn't Contain Jeter

By Jack Ogden, The Gazette

"I didn't have much chance to study him" confessed California Coach Pete Elliott as newsmen queried him here Thursday on the merits of Iowa's jet-like Bob Jeter. "Every time I saw him he was running."

That feeling was echoed by California players as they looked back on their 38-12 loss to Iowa in a game in which Jeter raced for 194 yards in nine carries, setting two Rose Bowl records.

Elliott should have asked the advice of Iowa fans, because they found a way to halt the junior speedster from Weirton, W. Va.

After the Rose Bowl game was over, Iowans stopped Jeter as he headed for the dressing room. He was almost 10 minutes late getting inside.

"Somebody got my helmet," grinned Jeter. "I guess I'm lucky that I kept my jersey."

Before the game had ended, the 182-pounder who also threw some key blocks, had set a Rose Bowl record when he went 81 yards for his only touchdown, and another when he clipped off 194 yards in just nine carries, an average of 21.6 yards.

The old records were 71 yards by Frank Aschenbrenner of Northwestern against another California team in 1949 and total running yardage of 151 by Bobby Grayson of Stanford way back in 1934.

Bob Jeter gained 194 yards on nine carries, setting a new Rose Bowl record.

Jeter also lost a race to officials, who kept him on the field to present him with the Helms Foundation trophy, given annually to the player they rate as the best performer of the Rose Bowl game.

The smiling Hawkeye clutched the trophy as he stood up on bus ride back to the Huntington Sheraton hotel.

"Yes," he grinned. "I guess this is my biggest day."

Jeter and speed were the big topics in the California dressing room after Iowa's second straight smash success in the California classic.

"It's the best team we've played all year," admitted Elliott, a carbon-copy in speech and mannerisms for his brother, Bump, former backfield coach for the Hawkeyes.

"They just had too much speed," said Pete as he talked things over with newsmen.

"We expected them to run a lot. They didn't do anything that we hadn't expected. At least they basically ran the same things, but they just had too much speed."

Elliott figured that the two key points in the game came in the first and third quarters.

"When we couldn't move the ball after getting that fumble in the first quarter, and when we let them score on that 37-yard touchdown by Willie Fleming after we had cut the score to 20-6, it really hurt us.

"I thought our offense did a good job. We moved the ball well, but we just didn't score.

"Fumbles and mistakes hurt us."

No. 2 Iowa Halts Purdue Rally in Thriller

By Gus Schrader, The Gazette

SCORE BY QUARTERS						
Iowa City, Oct. 22, 1960						
IOWA	0	14	7	0	—	21
PURDUE	0	0	7	7	—	14

Before anyone even mentions the name of a backfield man, let's salute those gallant Hawk-eye linemen who kept Iowa atop the national rankings and Big Ten football race Saturday in a spine-tingling 21-14 homecoming win over Purdue.

Guard Bill DiCindio and tackle Chester Williams, who filled so magnificently for injured Sherwyn Thorson and Charles Lee. Both played about 55 minutes, as did Al Hinton, the other tackle who also outshone Purdue's All-American candidates.

Guard Mark Manders, who celebrated his 22nd birthday with another fine performance. Center Bill Van Buren and his understudy, Lloyd Humphreys. Bill performed many key tackles, and Humphreys had the distinction of making the final one on Purdue's last-gasp effort.

Iowa's ends, led by Felton Rogers, the man who shook Purdue's Bernie Allen loose from the ball on the game's big play.

Who else did you say? Oh, a sophomore named Dayton Perry? And what did Dayton do?

Well, he was the latest Hawk to be kissed by Lady Luck as Iowa scared the life out of its fans with a third straight cliff-hanger. Dayton was the happiest guy among the 59,200 people who attended Saturday's thriller.

"It seemed as though it took me at least five minutes to run for that touchdown," the 6-1, 215-pound Perry panted. "It was my first touchdown in my whole life!"

"How far did I go? Eighty-four yards wow! That was the first time I ever carried the ball. How's that for an average 84 yards a shot!"

"All I thought about when that ball popped into my arms was run just run. I thought I'd never get there. I'll bet I looked over my left shoulder 12 times on almost every step.

"I kept seeing that big No. 86 (Purdue's Menzie Winters) and I thought sure he was gaining on me. Another 10 yards and I'm afraid I'd have pooped out. It was like a dream."

It WAS a dream, a lineman's dream come true. And Perry's touchdown, coming 50 seconds before the half ended, gave Iowa a 14-0 lead at a time when it should have been only 7-0 or maybe even 7-7 if Purdue could have pushed a touchdown across in the final minute instead of fumbling.

The Hawks shot ahead by 21-0 in the third period when

ah, here comes the mention of those backs, Wilburn Hollis, barreled over for his second touchdown. Hollis, the piker, had to go only 6 yards, but he showed Purdue one of the prettiest stiff arms the old Big Ten has seen in many a moon.

It was all wrapped up at that point less than 24 minutes to play and a 21-0 lead. Tom Moore kicked his 3rd straight extra point. But the people who had seen Iowa squander 14 points at Michigan State and against Wisconsin didn't settle all the way back in their seats.

Sure enough, Purdue marched right back and got a touchdown — also with a smile from Lady Luck. Allen passed from Iowa's 16-yard line, and the ball glanced sharply off the fingers of end John Elwell. The ball caromed perfectly into the end zone and into Jimmy Tiller's eager arms, 21-7.

The Boilermakers went 92 yards for their second score. It took 16 plays. Play No. 15 was a pass by Allen that went over the end zone. But an official charged Iowa's Bernie Wyatt with interference on Dave Miller, and Purdue had a first down on Iowa's 1.

Iowa quarterback Wilburn Hollis rushed for two touchdowns against Purdue.

Allen slipped over center for a touchdown, then kicked his 2nd straight extra point, 21-14.

Iowa hearts were in Iowa throats now. But the Hawks, the nation's No. 1 team, with backs up against the wall, were equal to the occasion. They took the kickoff and marched to Purdue's 26.

The big play here was a real clutcher. Using the risky double-handoff reverse play that had gained ground consistently, Sammie Harris careened 29 yards on third-and-14.

But on the third-and-11 on the Purdue 26, Hollis rolled out on the option and spotted end Bill Perkins all alone on the goal line. He let fire for the old clincher, but Tiller made a tremendous leaping interception on the 3 and legged it back to the 22.

Know what Allen did then?

Sure, he passed, but how he passed!

He called seven straight pass plays. Twice the Hawks managed to haul him down before he could throw. But on each of the other five times he hit his man.

When Purdue finally ran out of time-outs and other ways to stop the clock, the Boilermakers had reached Iowa's 42-yard line, and no crowd was ever happier to hear the final horn sound.

Iowa had the better of the fist-half statistics, but Larry Ferguson's fumble on Iowa's 43 gave the Riveters a golden chance in the opening minutes. But Fergie promptly dropped Miller for a 5-yard loss on the next play and Purdue punted.

Purdue's deepest penetration in the first period carried only to Iowa's 26. Then came Iowa's touchdown marker of 39 yards in six plays following a personal foul on Purdue's Forest Farmer.

Penalties, a pass interception and Iowa's poor passing connections blunted other Hawkeye sorties in the first half. Purdue pushed down to Iowa's 16-yard line and first down there when the big break came.

Allen went back to pass, changed his mind, started to run, then seemed to think about passing again. But as he raised his arm, Rogers and Hinton smashed into him. The ball squirted up in the air and into Perry's hands.

He went the distance. Some called it 76 yards, others 84 yards. The official statistics said 84. When the movies are inspected they probably will show Perry caught the ball on the 20-yard line.

FOREST EVASHEVSKI

Iowa Head Coach Had Fierce Compulsion to Excel

By Tim Cohane, Look, Sports Editor

Forest Evashevski would need only a dueling scar, a bristling mustache and a monocle to pass for the dean of men, or the equivalent, at Old Heidelberg. As he is, Iowa's football coach — big darkly handsome, almost gloweringly direct — makes a formidable picture. He is as dynamic as a punch in the teeth.

When he came to Iowa in 1952, Evy was asked by a writer. "Do you think Iowa could ever really have a consistently winning team?" Evy's eyebrows poised like thunderheads. "Why in the hell," he snapped, "do you think I took the job?" Afterward, a photographer said dreamily, "I think that man truly believes he's the savior of Iowa football."

There is no doubt he did believe it, and because his spirit is as free as it is tough, he said what he believed. "Evy is an honest guy," says his close friend, Coach Dave Nelson of Delaware, who was a class behind him at Michigan. "He's just naked. It's part of the directness of thought that makes him a great football mind. He recognizes the thing to do and does it. He's impulsive too. Don't ever dare him to do anything."

The Iowa job was a dare. The Hawkeyes had been "have-nots" for most of three decades. In Evy's eight seasons, their records (conference, 28-20-2; overall 44-26-4) rank fourth in the Big Ten, despite schedules like mine fields. His 1956 and '58 teams won Big Ten titles and ran away from Oregon State and California in the Rose Bowl. The Grantland Rice Award, won by the 1958 team, represented Iowa's first formal national championship in any sport. To accomplish all this required more than coaching skill. Evy needed his "heavy qualities: quick aggressiveness, a drive to dominate, a disregard of controversy." No coach ever nursed a fiercer compulsion to excel. Under his cold facade, a tethered emotionalism strains. Even as an assistant, kick-off minus five minutes often left him unable to keep down his lunch.

It is fortunate as well as diverting, perhaps, that his "heaviness" is relieved by an imaginative humor the gift of self-appraisal. Otherwise, he might drive himself into the psychic dislocations observable of late in some celebrated coaches.

He has, for example, the flair, rare among ostensibly self-confident men, for so telling a story that it will be interpreted not as self-praise, but as subtle self-kidding. As Michigan's quarterback, in 1938-40, he was one of those nearly extinct paragons: single-wing field general, linebacker and obliterating blocker all in one. Yet his talent was overshadowed by the ball carrying of Tommy Harmon, the Heisman Trophy halfback candidate for whom he ran crushing interference.

Evy is often asked what made Harmon so

great. "I'll tell you," he is likely to reply. "When I was out in front blocking, Harmon was the only man in the country who could stand the sight of all the blood."

The Wolverines won 20 of 24 games in this three-year period. His coach, Fritz Crisler, called him, "the greatest quarterback I ever had."

The more serious, basic side comes into focus when he is asked why Michigan's 1938 team was almost upset in the Yale Bowl. Had a 7-6 loss to Minnesota the week before left the Wolverines down? Or were they overconfident? "Neither," says Evy. "Yale's line stunting was new, and I was a sophomore quarterback, too inexperienced to adjust."

His dynamism is not something Evy would use to court popularity for its own sake. He puts himself out only for his family, his football teams his other objectives and a few well-tested friends. That these friends include important business people doesn't suggest, however, that he would strive to cultivate them. Position, rank and wealth do not set him to tugging at an invisible forelock.

At a Delaware dinner, he was kidded by Bob Carpenter, the millionaire owner of the Phillies, for borrowing Nelson's brain child, the tricky winged-T. "Nobody would ever have heard of you if you hadn't run it," said Carpenter. "Yeah," Evy countered, "and nobody would ever have heard of you if it wasn't for your old man's money."

It is not meaningful that when Evy assisted Clarence (Biggie) Munn, first at Syracuse, later at Michigan State, they sometimes saw things chin-to-chin, for Biggie also is a man of opinion and no introvert. A truer measure of Evy is his readiness to speak forcefully even to the presidents of colleges he works for. He is not even averse to bearding them in their dens.

Well publicized was Evashevski's feud with Paul Brechler. As Iowa athletic director, he had hired Evy from Washington State. They presently developed differences. Brechler was as good at his job as Evy was at his. During the feud, Brechler turned down offers from Pittsburgh, Indiana and Arizona. He finally stepped out last winter to become Sky-

line Conference Commissioner, and Evy succeeded him. No public explanation of the feud ever made much sense, and couldn't have, since their trouble traced less to administrative disputes than to divergent philosophies.

Evy's other celebrated conflict involved a magazine, which in 1957 ascribed to him quotes criticizing the failure of Indiana's president to back up Coach Phil Dickens when he was suspended a year for recruiting irregularities. Evashevski vehemently repudiated the quotes.

Later that fall, after Iowa was tied by Michigan, a sister publication accused the Hawkeyes of quitting. Evy called this a reprisal for his denying the earlier quotes. He then announced he was canceling his subscription to the entire stable. "I did the only thing I could," he said, with the air of a man forced to move his family out of a neighborhood that had seen better days.

A footnote to the magazine affair reveals the whole man. Evy regularly attends the Methodist church in Iowa City. The Rev. Dr. L.L. Dunnington considers him a pillar, with good reason. Even Evy's enemies will acknowledge that he is a devoted family man with high standards of personal morality. After church the Sunday following the incendiary quote, Evy phoned Nelson, who asked him if he was really that mad.

"Yes, I am," said Evy. "Among other things, it has caused me two broken legs." Now Nelson is used to Evashevski's quips. (Letters from 6-feet-1 Evy to 5-feet-7 Dave are addressed: "Head Dwarf, Athletic Department.") But he went along and asked, "Broken legs?" "Yes," said Evy. "The minister today devoted his sermon to eulogizing me. He said it was a terrible thing that magazine did. Afterward, I just couldn't wait to try my new wings. So I climbed on top of the field house and tried them. That's how I broke both legs."

Although Evy rejected the angelic life, his record in recruiting ethics probably would be acceptable to St. Peter or Avery Brundage. When football "have-nots" climb to riches, they sometimes get caught breaking laws. Except for some airplane maneuvers by E. K. Jones, the "I" Club sec-

> "The greatest quarterback I ever had."
>
> *Fritz Crisler*

Reporter: "Do you think Iowa could ever really have a consistently winning team?"
Evashevski: "Why in the hell do you think I took the job?"
Photographer: "I think that man truly believes he's the savior of Iowa football."

retary, for which he was permanently grounded, the Hawkeyes under Evy have been unharassed. An official from Big Ten Commissioner Kenneth L. (Tug) Wilson's office says he wishes all Big Ten schools would give him as few problems as Iowa does.

Evy recruited some of his finest players out of state, including the late Cal Jones, a great Negro guard, from Steubenville, Ohio. Jones was supposed to attend Ohio State, and when news reached Broad and High in Columbus that he wouldn't, the frightful groans caused Commissioner Wilson to visit Iowa City. Iowa's position proved unassailable, because Jones really wanted to go to school there. Evy implies that Jones arrived unsolicited with two other players from Steubenville, and adds that Cal become so enamored of the campus that he could not be made to tear himself away. Evy never claimed however, that he took Cal by the ear, faced him toward Ohio and thundered, "Now, get back there where you belong!"

The football Evy teaches is striking like himself: fundamental and forceful, with exciting, unexpected overtones. He believes it is easy to overcoach. "You can teach a simple ball exchange," he says, "in a whole day — or a half hour. You can get so involved in details you miss the purpose of what you are doing."

Like any superior coach, he never would underestimate defense. But his background as a quarterback under Crisler at Michigan, one of the offense classicist, and his own nature condition him to think in terms of attack. This may also influence his recruiting. He is too realistic to consider systems of attack important beyond suitability to personnel and the problems of the year — or that week.

The week of the Ohio State game, his first season at Iowa, he replaced the multiple offense pro tem, with a haphazard, unbalanced-line version of the split-T, and with it upset the Buckeyes for a keynote victory.

After seeing an Evashevski team for the first time, in Iowa's 35-19 Rose Bowl win over Oregon State, Arthur Simpson, The Boston Herald football expert, commented: "Iowa's attack is as advanced as I have seen. Every play is a possible run or pass and smoothly executed."

This was the Nelson winged-T, which Evy adapted in 1956. The winged-T, later picked up effectively by Louisiana State and others, masks single-wing blocking behind the T formation and combines power, deception and all-area threat. While publicly crediting Nelson, Evashevski also needled him.

"Nelson," he explained, "you were absolutely nothing — like a punk song writer trying to sell a song everybody was ignoring. Finally, you brought it to old Uncle Frosty up at the big publishing house. He put it on television, got it into the Rose Bowl and made it famous from coast to coast. Now, I think it's time you did something for yourself."

Evy was only 16 when he was graduated from Northwestern High in his native Detroit. His weight shot up from 140 to 180 from his junior to senior year. That's why he didn't go out for football until he was a senior.

Forest Evashevski, right, quarterbacked the University of Michigan from 1938–40. But his talent was overshadowed by Tom Harmon.

"I made center," he says, "but in the second game, I suffered a cerebral hemorrhage. They did three spinal taps on me before they decided to operate. I was supposed to be through with football. But when something is taken away from you like that, I believe you want it even more than you did before."

His recovery was remarkable. So was the fact that he started at quarterback the first varsity game of his sophomore year, just a week after Crisler switched him from center. Only a person of Evy's mental affinity for the position could have made transition that rapidly.

"As a quarterback," says Tom Harmon, who has remained his close friend, "Evy seemed to think right with Crisler.

Fritz seldom faulted his strategy. As a linebacker, he had a fantastic instinct for smelling out the play. He could run the 100 in a shade over 10 seconds and was an excellent pass receiver. As a blocker, I never saw a better one."

At Harvard one day, Evy kept trap-blocking a guard, picking him up and slapping on the butt with a "Nice going, fellow!" "Anyhow," the guard finally retorted, "we're better students than you guys!" Actually, Evy won the Big Ten Medal, awarded to the best senior student-athlete. He was football captain, baseball catcher, senior president and honor-society member. He is remembered for his piggy bank with the mechanical organ and monkey. Curious students accepted Evy's invitation to put a quarter in the monkey's mouth. The monkey danced briefly, while the quarter dropped into the bank. None of this, apparently, was "out of compliance with" the Big Ten aid code.

Stray quarters were not unimportant to Evy, whose father, a machine-tool salesman, could not afford to send him to college. Evy worked for a year and a half at the Ford Motor Co. before matriculating. Summer vacations, he labored as an Upper Peninsula dock hand. On campus, he hashed and did other jobs. He had to work for his schooling. This conditioned his belief that no aid code is harmed by a decent job program.

"Chris Fisler," as Evy sometimes calls Crisler, was sedate, articulate and in command. He was also too astute even to try modifying any of his quarterback's attitudes. After being taken out of the 1939 Ohio State game, safely won with 30 seconds to play, Evy astonished his coach and teammates by lighting a cigar on the bench. Before the Minnesota game, when Crisler impassionedly called for eleven lions on offense and eleven tigers on defense, Evy spoke right up and said he wouldn't play unless he could be a leopard.

The 1940 Michigan team, defeated only by Minnesota (7-6 again) and called by Crisler "the craziest gang I ever coached," was cued in all things by Captain Evashevski. One day, Crisler, who demanded punctuality, arrived for practice a little late. "Fritz," Evy barked, "we begin at 3:30. It's now 3:35. Take a lap around the field." Crisler obeyed.

En route, to the Ohio State game, the squad was so larkish that Crisler took them off the train during the Toledo stop for a lecture. "These guys," he confided to Evy and Harmon, "are going to get killed." Evy told him not to worry. Just before the kick-off, he reminded his mates this would be their last game together. They beat Ohio State, 40 to 0.

Evy studied prelaw and would have been something to see in a courtroom. But law was gradually nudged aside by 42 months in the Navy and by the Lorelei song of coaching. Now, he has said he will coach no more after this year. He has always held that it is a job for young men and that he never would become a "Mr. Chips." He is only 42, but coaching tension bothers his stomach.

He is under no financial pressure to coach. His income as athletic director alone would be substantial, and he enjoys wise investments and good contacts. Big-money offers to

coach elsewhere would not in themselves attract him.

He would like to spend more time with his wife, Ruth, the daughter of Prentis Brown, the former senator from Michigan, and their family: Forest, Jr., or Frosty, 18; Jim, 16; Marion, 14; John, 10; Tom Harmon (for his old buddy), 7, and Bill, 3. Frosty, a good passing quarterback at Iowa City High, entered Michigan this fall. Jim, a junior at Iowa City High, plays halfback and wrestles. Both boys have finished runner-up in the state junior golf championship.

"I'd like more time to play golf with Frosty, Jim and John," says Evy. "John is the only one I can beat now, so I may have to play Ruth. Frosty, Jim and I have taken fishing trips to Canada, even one to the Arctic Circle. At our summer home in Upper Michigan, we fish and water-ski. To keep up with them for a 12-hour day is getting tough on me, yet I'd like more time to try it."

Close friends are not at all sure he will quit. They feel he is not sure himself. There could be two reasons he might want to coach Iowa a little longer: 1) if this season is mediocre; 2) the promise of the current sophomore backs, especially Joe Williams from New Jersey. Jerry Burns, Evy's assistant and choice as successor, would still be available.

It is also possible that if another Big Ten school made him an offer, he would study it attentively. He has always regarded the Iowa job as especially tough. He might decide to try a last few years at some other Big Ten school he thinks would be easier.

He might even be attracted by the challenge that confronts today's athletic directors in the Big Ten. This conference, next to the late Pacific Coast, has been most vexed in working out a sensible aid program. If Evy could help the other athletic directors (four of whom, like himself, have coached Big Ten football) to sell faculty senates on the validity of the cost-of-living code, it would be more than a great contribution. It would be a minor miracle.

To help bring it about might even qualify Evy to don wings again. This time, he might break only one leg.

Forest Evashevski posted a record of 52 wins, 27 losses and 4 ties in nine seasons and led the Hawkeyes to two Rose Bowl wins, in 1957 and 1959, and a national championship in 1958.

Lawrence's Four Scores Help Iowa Ground Gophers

By Gus Schrader, The Gazette

L arry Lawrence, who became the first Iowa Hawkeye in modern times to score four touchdowns in one game, took pains to explain Saturday that it wasn't his idea to be a scoring hog even though this was indeed the day of the pig.

Larry crossed the goal line on runs of 1, 4, 9 and 8 yards as the Hawkeyes brought Floyd of Rosedale home after the famous pig statue had lived in Minnesota the last four years.

Iowa's victory was the third of the 1968 season and marks the first time the Hawks have won that many games in one season since 1964.

The score was 35-28, but only after an electrifying finish that saw first Iowa and then Minnesota score in the final 78 seconds before a crowd of 57,703.

Even then, the Gophers, unwilling to let Iowa escape with its first victory here since 1958, mounted another threat that was thwarted only by Charles Bolden's pass interception on the Hawkeye 10-yard line.

The delirious joy of Iowa's first road victory in 16 games, dating to the Oregon State game at Portland early in the 1965

SCORE BY QUARTERS						
Minneapolis, Nov. 2, 1968						
IOWA	7	7	7	14	—	35
MINNESOTA	7	13	0	8	—	28

Ed Podolak, left, with Coach Ray Nagel and Steve Wilson, right, and Iowa won at Minnesota for the first time since 1958.

season, overflowed at that point, and the Hawkeyes rushed over to rescue Floyd from the Gopher bench.

"Those first three touchdowns of mine all were scored on the option play in which I fake to Eddie Podolak and keep the ball," said Lawrence. "On that last one (with Iowa leading, 28-20), I wanted to give Tim Sullivan the ball so he could score a touchdown after all his hard work today.

"But Coach Nagel sent in Podolak with instructions for the next play, and I scored on it.

Yes, it was a great thrill to score four times today, but I'm much happier that we just won."

Lawrence, who scored three touchdowns total in the first six games of his sophomore season, showed he certainly began to get the feel of the end zone by the time the fourth quarter arrived.

As soon as he crossed the golden strip with the 8-yard run that hiked Iowa's lead to 28-20, he paused and hurled the ball 40 rows up into the end zone bleachers where many Hawkeye fans sat, incidentally.

On his final touchdown jaunt, he was rolled over by a tardy tackle, but he leaped up and again passed one of Minnesota's $26 game footballs into the spectators.

The features of Iowa's tingling victory lay in several things. Foremost among them, certainly, was a big defensive improvement over last week, when Purdue mauled Iowa's rushing defense for 483 yards and a 44-14 victory without completing a pass.

Iowa still gave up big chunks of yardage, but the defenders came through with key plays time and again to turn back Minnesota's comeback.

Another highlight was Iowa's offensive change. The Hawks installed a slot double wing in which Podolak, as well as Barry Crees, plays up a yard behind the line of scrimmage. This gave the Hawkeyes the threat of a power sweep in both directions, and Podolak charged through Minnesota's confused defenders for a whopping 129 yards in 29 carries.

This also loosened things up for Crees, the flyweight who has been specializing in catching passes. He darted 10 times for 76 yards, and fullback Sullivan rammed for an even 100 yards on 20 carries.

The drama, however, came in several places. Like when the Hawkeyes, trailing by 20-7 and seemingly headed for their 16th straight loss on the road, suddenly came back to life in time to score a touchdown 76 seconds before the first half ended.

It took the Hawkeyes only 4:32 to take the lead from the gophers for good. They went 54 yards in 8 plays, with Sullivan stampeding 11, 5, 20 and 1 yards to put the ball on the 4-yard line.

From there, Lawrence skipped across to tie the score, 20-20. Then Marcus Melendez, one of nine children of a career army man, calmly soft-shoed one of his five perfect placements across the bar to give Iowa a 21-20 lead.

Not only did Melendez make all five kicks to run his record to 25 of 26, but he also did an excellent job of kicking off, twice putting the ball into the end zone.

Once the fourth quarter arrived, Iowa was ready to sew up its victory. Some more rugged running by Podolak and Sullivan mixed with some of Lawrence's passes to Ray Manning put the ball in position and Lawrence shot across from 9 yards away.

This was the third play of the final period and the thousands of Iowans here throught that ought to sack it up for sure. But the Hawks felt they needed another one, and they were right.

They got it with 1:18 to play on Lawrence's 9-yard run after Mike Phillips intercepted Phil Hagen's pass.

This time reserves Bill Powell and Tom Wallace helped Melendez swing his foot for the final time, and people started leaving with the score 35-20 and only 78 seconds to play.

It took the furious Gophers only 22 seconds to score.

They went 70 yards after the next kickoff in just three plays.

The longest pass of the day was Ray Stephens' 53-yard heave to Chip Litten, who was run out on the 17-yard line. Another 14-yard pass and Stephens' 3-yard sneak put the ball across.

Barry Mayer carried 26 times for 179 yard, tying a Minnesota school record set in 1951 when all-American Paul Giel had the same yardage against Iowa.

Larry Lawrence's four-TD parade broke a modern (since 1939) Iowa record and historians say you'd have to go back to the 1920's to find out when someone scored that many TDs for the Hawks. It is believed Gordon Locke tallied six TDs in 1921 or 1922.

Cilek's Spartan Effort Lifts Iowa Against MSU

By Gus Schrader, the Gazette

SCORE BY QUARTERS					
Iowa City, Oct. 25, 1969					
IOWA	0	9	0	10	— 19
MICHIGAN STATE	3	0	7	8	— 18

Jinx, schminx. Pinch-hitter Mike Cilek delivered a home run pass to Kerry Reardon Saturday to let Iowa end a nagging streak of five homecoming defeats.

Stepping into the breach left when Larry Lawrence was injured halfway through a thrilling race against a perfidious clock, Cilek's 6-yard aerial actually only tied the score at 18-18 with 1:25 to go. Well, maybe there was only 0:25 to go, but we'll get into that detail later.

Michigan State used a precious time-out to set up a special maneuver, hoping to block Iowa's extra-point kick, just as Ron Curl had come through to block a Hawkeye punt earlier.

But the Hawks were used to pressure by this time. They had been tested by fire in the late innings of their bitter defeats at Wisconsin and Purdue. With all this added pressure, Alan Schuette booted the decisive point perfectly, 19-18.

And then there were skyrockets set off in an adjoining practice lot, someone set fire to the homecoming monument on the east-side campus; the Iowa band paraded out of Iowa stadium with their hats on backward, and there literally was dancing in the streets of Iowa City.

It was fortunate Iowa scored before the final minute showed on the clock. A few fans in the crowd of 57,471 had noticed the official clock had stuttered with 12 minutes left. The teams actually played 61 minutes instead of 60. Neither coach knew of the mechanical hiccup until after the game, and neither did the official timer.

Michigan State went ahead, 18-12, with 12:18 remaining in this see-saw game that practically erased any remaining hope the Spartans had of slipping home with the Rose Bowl bid.

Perhaps Iowa's hope vanished with the losses at Wisconsin and Purdue, but you wouldn't have known it to see the joyful celebration the Hawkeyes and their fans touched off at the game's end. Iowa might still be jinxed at Wisconsin and Purdue, but at least the Hawks proved they don't always lose their own homecoming.

It was a fascinating game, end-around plays, the old Statue of Liberty was dusted off, a trans-continental pass, and

Iowa's offense — third best in the nation before Saturday — was held to 321 total yards by a bristling Michigan State defensive line.

But Iowa, the team that has been hamstringing itself with individual mistakes, suddenly came up with a near-perfect game in the error department. Not one turnover on a pass interception or fumble.

Michigan State, the team that also has been wounding itself with errors, kept on doing so. The Spartans suffered from three interceptions and two lost fumbles.

Rich Solomon was the lad who drove the last nail in Michigan State's coffin. He intercepted Bill Triplett's pass with a diving, shoe-string grab on the Iowa's 46, and soon the Iowa students were hilariously counting off the dying seconds.

The Spartans entered the game boasting of a peculiar distinction owned by Ron Curl, defensive tackle. He had blocked three punts in the first five games, and let it be

Larry Lawrence, left, Jim Miller and Iowa helped make it a happy homecoming for Hawkeye fans. Lawrence left the game with 1:57 remaining in the first half because of an injury.

known he would try to do it again.

The first time Iowa punted, Curl shot through and blocked Reardon's punt. It was recovered back on the Iowa 8. The Hawkeye defensive platoon was equal to its first test, but Michigan State got on the scoreboard first with Hans

Sudar's 20-yard field goal.

Reardon got lots more punting practice in the first half. He kicked five more, but Curl never came close to blocking another. But the Hawkeye offense sputtered in the face of a merciless rush by Rich Saul and his Spartan mates, so it became a 3-3 standoff on Schuette's 35-yard field goal early in the second quarter. It came after Layne McDowell recovered Don Highsmith's fumble on the MSU 29.

Michigan State lost at least two touchdowns on mistakes. Frank Foreman dropped Triplett's perfect pass at the goal line in the first quarter, and a 38-yard Spartan touchdown pass in the second quarter was called back because an ineligible receiver (tackle Dave VanElst) was downfield.

The Spartans got away with another mistake. Tom Kutschinski foolishly tried to field Reardon's punt on his own 14 and fumbled it away to Iowa's Al Cassady.

Triplett suffered two interceptions in the first half both wide-open grabs by Chris Hamilton. Michigan State survived the first one, but Hamilton ran the second one back to the Spartan 35 just before the first half ended.

Four plays later, Iowa got its first touchdown. Lawrence tossed a little flair pass to Don Osby, the soph from Steubenbille, Ohio, and the latter legged it into the end zone. Schuette's kick was delayed by a low snap, and Michigan State blocked the low attempt.

Michigan State's defensive line kept Iowa in the hole most of the third quarter.

Meanwhile, the Spartans got into scoring position on Kutschinski's 32-yard runback of a punt to the Iowa 8. A face-mask penalty put the ball on the 4, and an Iowa off-side moved it 2 yards closer. So fullback Kermit Smith scored on a 2-yard shot off right tackle. Sudar's kick made it 10-9 with 3:37 to go in the third period.

Iowa launched a long drive after the ensuing kickoff. Lawrence's running and passing accounted for the big gains, but Denny Green, Tom Smith, Steve Penney and Reardon also had gains. Lawrence was thrown for a 6-yard loss back on the 10, and Schuette's 28-yard field goal returned Iowa to the fore, 12-10.

A 63-yard pass play, Triplett to Steve Kough, got Michigan State back on top, 18-12, with 12:18 to go, and it brought a sudden chill to the Iowa homecomers. Triplett passed to Highsmith for a two-point conversion.

Iowa's Fate Lies with Fick in Upset Over UCLA

By Gus Schrader, The Gazette

SCORE BY QUARTERS					
Iowa City, Sept. 21, 1974					
IOWA	0	14	0	7 —	21
UCLA	3	0	0	7 —	10

Wuxtra! Cow kills butcher! Read all about it! Wuxtra!

Couple of retreads lead Iowa, a 24-point underdog, to a 21-10 upset of No. 12 ranked UCLA!

There were a jillion other angles: A high school coach who had to stage a political type campaign even to get a one-year contract at his alma mater is rewarded with first collegiate victory! An Iowa defense that leaked for 401 points in 11 losses last year puts brakes on vaunted John Sciarra.

No, the Hawks weren't scared of Sciarra, and a defense headed by Lynn Heil and Dan LaFleur got a share of Sciarra on almost every play. The same man who personally rolled up 390 yards total offense against Tennessee was limited to 113 by the team rated No. 10 in the Big Ten.

And when it was over, some of the most exuberant Iowa fans in the crowd of 47,500 swarmed over the Astroturf and actually succeeded in ripping down the huge iron goal post in the north end of Kinnick Stadium.

The long drought was over. Happiness reigned. But two of the happiest Hawkeyes were strangely restrained and quiet

Bob Commings won his first home game as Iowa's new coach.

amid the dressing-room bedlam below.

Rob Fick and Dave Jackson, two players who Coach Bob Commings rescued from the discard pile fulfilled the promise they gave as freshman when Ray Nagel coached his last season here in 1970.

It was Fick's 38-yard touchdown pass to Jackson that opened the gates for Iowa's fist victory in 13 straight starts and its first over UCLA after five previous failures.

Fick, who outgained and outplayed UCLA's Sciarra, was cast aside by the Frank Lauterbur staff. Jackson, also playing in his fifth year at Iowa, was booted off the Iowa squad as a sophomore but scrapped his way back to play some the last two seasons.

Some of the 47,500 here Saturday could recall when these two hooked up in a deadly passing combo that led the

Fullback Mark Fetter scored two of Iowa's three touchdowns — which were all by passes from Rob Fick.

Hawkeye yearlings to exciting victories over Minnesota and Iowa State in 1970. Saturday, they were back, and how!

They had plenty of help. Chelsea's Mark Fetter scored Iowa's other two touchdowns. One was on a picture-book 30-yard screen pass from Fick to stretch Iowa's first-half lead to 14-3. The other was a marvelous 4-yard spin with 1:28 to go that sealed UCLA's fate.

Fetter was the game's leading rusher with 84 yards in 14 trips. Davenport's Jim Jensen wasn't far behind with 78 yards in 18 shots. Fick had 44 in nine carries and his protection was so good he wasn't sacked once as he completed 5 of 10 passes for 110 yards.

Rod Wellington, the god-son of former Iowa great Ozzie Simmons, picked up 33 yards in 14 hard-won attempts.

It wasn't a cut-and-dried decision. Not with the way the Hawkeyes opened the game. Earl Douthitt, who led the nation in kickoff returns last year, bobbled the opening boot at the goal line and returned it only 4 yards.

The Hawks were lucky — or their defense was good.

Their first thee scrimmage plays went like this: Minus 1, minus 2 and no gain.

But UCLA took the ball from the Iowa 34 and then was snubbed on the Iowa 4. Brett White kicked a 21-yard field goal for a 3-0 first-quarter lead.

The second quarter was all Iowa, with Fick throwing the two TD strikes to Jackson and Fetter. The second was set up when Andre Jackson, playing a standup nose guard in the middle of Iowa's 4-3 defense, recovered Bobby Ferrell's fumble on the UCLA 30.

"I thought that was a great call that Coach Commings sent in," Fick said later. "UCLA was looking for us to throw a bomb on the unexpected turnover, so they were not set up for the screen pass. Mark (Fetter) did a super job of running with it."

The third quarter was scoreless. UCLA penetrated to the Iowa 6 but Sciarra's fumble was gobbled up by Shanty Burks. But the next drive was consummated on the first play of the final period when Sciarra sneaked the final yard. White kicked the extra point and the Uclans trailed only 14-10.

The Iowa fans, many of whom have been accustomed to leaving before the last quarter begins, were too nervous to depart in this one. They cheered themselves hoarse as Iowa's defense stopped UCLA twice, forcing punts.

Then it happened. In the old days, the Hawkeyes wore out and the visitors rambled for the winning scores. This time, the Hawks gathered themselves together and marched 90 yards for the clincher as Sciarra and his offensive playmates sat helpless on the sideline.

The winning drive took 14 plays and six minutes off the clock. Fancy this: So sound was Iowa's blocking and running that Fick never even so much as faked a pass. All 14 were rushing plays that Woody Hayes or Bo Schembechler would have envied.

The last one was something. Fetter careened off left tackle and got hit at the scrimmage line. But the former South Tama All-Stater wheeled with a great second effort, shook his tackler off like rain and pranced into the end zone.

Then Fetter, caught up with the exuberance of the moment, threw the ball high in the air. The officials, quite properly, paced off a 15-yard punishment on the ensuing kickoff for Marks' display, but nobody cared.

Nick Quartaro, the refugee from Xavier's football foldup, kicked his third straight point, 21-10.

Hawkeyes' Road Warriors Topple No. 11 Penn State

By Gus Schrader, The Gazette

SCORE BY QUARTERS					
University Park, Pa., Sept. 25, 1976					
IOWA	7	0	0	—	7
PENN STATE	0	0	0	6	—	6

Bob Commings' bald head gleamed with sweat as linebacker Dean Moore squeezed past a ring of newsmen surrounding the Iowa football coach after Saturday's 7-6 shocker of No. 11-rated Penn State.

"There goes the best football player on the field today, Dean Moore!" exclaimed Commings, like a professor using visual aids, as he had just been talking about that very person.

Again, as if on cue, an aide yelled at Commings that he was supposed to take a call on the dressing-room telephone.

"It's probably the President!" deadpanned the Hawkeye coach. (It wasn't: it was ABC-TV calling to tape a quick interview, but later Commings claimed he couldn't even remember what questions were asked.)

The newsmen turned to Moore, who had made 11 unassisted tackles as Iowa's newly named "Wild Bunch" swarmed over the Nittany Lions like an angry hive of bees. Penn State gained 159 yards on the ground, but the longest was 13 yards.

What turned on Moore to play with such intensity?

"I got torn knee ligaments in last year's loss to Penn State," said the junior from Akron, Ohio, "so I was determined to do my best today.

"We didn't do much stunting on defense. Just took it to them. I got most of my tackles chasing 'em down."

Moore said he got his fingertips on the ball when Penn State missed a 25-yard field goal attempt with 47 seconds left. But he added that he didn't think he deflected it much. The kicker, freshman Herb Menhardt, seemed to "duck hook" the ball from the right hash mark with his soccer-style attempt.

Iowa called time-out with 51 seconds left just as Penn State lined up for Menhardt's try.

"I was watching their kicker," said quarterback Butch Caldwell, who led Iowa's rushers with 57 yards, "and I know it had to worry him extra to stand around and think about it."

"We called the time-out for two reasons," added Commings. "First, we wanted to make the kicker have the chance to get tense out there. Second, with only 51 seconds left, we didn't want to let Penn State run the clock down to a few seconds in case they made the kick and we had to come back."

When the referee signaled Menhardt's kick was wide to the left, the rest of Iowa's 54-man traveling squad gushed onto the field to congratulate with the Wild Bunch. That cost Iowa 5 yards for delay of game, but the Hawks shook it off, just as they had 55 other yards in penalties on this beautiful afternoon in Beaver stadium.

Penn State's time-outs were exhausted, so Caldwell fell on the ball twice to preserve Iowa's first nonconference victory on the road since the second game of the 1965 season 27-7 over Oregon State.

Each side got a touchdown and each missed two field-goal tries.

The Hawks got their TD early, not long after the fourth-largest crowd in Beaver Stadium history — 61,268 — had finished their tailgate lunches. They won the coin toss for the third straight week and scored on their third possession.

The TD drive was only 33 yards, and Iowa used sev-

Quarterback Butch Caldwell was Iowa's leading rusher against Penn State. Caldwell helped Iowa earn its first victory on the road against a nonconference opponent since 1965.

en plays. Dennis Mosley, who had the best average on the field 17.5 yards on four carries dashed 13 yards on the first carry, and Jon Lazar, Ernie Sheeler and Caldwell took turns to pick up a first down on the 7.

Sheeler, who had 53 yards in 17 tries, wormed to the 5. Then the little freshman back, Tommy Renn of Lowell, Ind., took the ball into the end zone on two slams, the second one from 2-yards out.

Nick Quartaro kicked the extra point with 2:26 left in the first quarter.

Iowa got another chance almost immediately. Towering Nate Washington leaped high to bat John Andress' pass out of the sky, and linebacker Tom Rusk was there waiting for it to come down. The former fullback legged it back 11 yards to the Penn State 7.

Renn drilled to the 7, but then Penn State proved why it is the NFL's biggest supplier of linebackers. Sheeler was nailed for no gain, Iowa was penalized for Tom Grine's offside, Caldwell was chased all over the field and out of bounds on the 13, a clipping penalty moved it back to the 37 and Caldwell was sacked on the 38.

So Quartaro tried a 56-yard field goal (it would have been a school record) that was far short. In the third quarter, Quartaro's 47-yarder was blocked after a slightly high snap from center.

Penn State's Matt Bahr was short on a 48-yard, three-point attempt, also in the third quarter. Actually, the Lions never got inside Iowa's 31-yard line until they recovered the first of three Hawkeye fumbles that came one-two-three in the final quarter.

Lazar, who gained 39 yards in 13 caries, had a big gain when he was whirled around and the ball knocked loose. Neil Hutton recovered it on the Iowa 30.

Rich Milot, third-string soph tailback who led the Lions with 76 yards rushing, did most of the carrying and Matt Sukey dived across from a half-yard out. That made it Iowa 7, Penn State 6, with 9:01 to go.

Coach Joe Paterno was ready to gamble for a victory. He sent in orders for his sub quarterback, Chuck Fusina, who had replaced Andress just before the TD drive, to run or pass for two points. The Hawks ran Fusina down, so he threw a desperation pass that was incomplete one of the biggest plays of the day.

Sears Comes To Iowa's Defense Against Badgers

By Gus Schrader, The Gazette

SCORE BY QUARTERS						
Madison, Wis., Nov. 12, 1977						
IOWA	7	7	10	0	—	24
WISCONSIN	0	0	0	8	—	8

The traditional Sears catalogs don't offer much more than Iowa's Rod Sears did Saturday as the Hawkeyes ruined Wisconsin's final home game under retiring Coach John Jardine, 24-8.

Here's what the 5-10, 192-pound senior walk-on did Saturday: Blocked a Wisconsin punt and recovered it on the 16-yard line to set up Iowa's second touchdown.

Recovered two of the five fumbles Wisconsin lost to Iowa, one on the Badger 5 and one on the 37.

Intercepted a Wisconsin pass and ran it back 15 yards.

Made three solo tackles and three assists, and knocked down another Badger pass. Returned a punt 10 yards. Held the ball for Dave Holsclaw's 39-yard field goal, as well as his three extra points.

There was no confirmation to the rumor that Sears also took tickets, played in the band and popped corn in the concession stand.

"Yes, I guess it was my best game ever," grinned Sears, a 3.7 student in business administration.

"On the blocked punt, Tom Hayes (assistant coach) spot-

ted a weakness in Wisconsin's punt blocking and set up a special plan. I lined up inside, but looped outside of the right end and came in without being blocked. I hit the ball right off his toe. It hit me right in the gut, but it didn't hurt.

"On the interception, we were in a man-for-man defense, and our front people put on a good rush. Their passer (Tony Dudley) wasn't able to make a very good throw and I picked it off.

"On the two Wisconsin fumbles, I just happened to be in the right place."

Iowa Coach Bob Commings mentioned Sears first when lauding his team's defensive play, saying that Sears "was always around the ball."

When told by newsmen that it was Sears who had blocked the punt, Commings laughed and added:

"Why didn't he get up and run with it?"

Sears did get up and the official statistician credited him with recovering the ball on the 16. Three plays later, Jim Arkeilpane rammed up the middle for Iowa's second touch-

Dave Holsclaw kicked a 39-yard field goal and three extra points for Iowa. Rod Sears, the holder, recovered two fumbles, blocked a punt and made an interception.

down and a 14-0 lead.

The Hawks scorned a chance to add a field goal to that lead just before the half, but in the third quarter they added Holsclaw's three-pointer plus Jimmy Frazier's 13-yard end run to take a 24-0 lead. That equals the most points they've scored in any game this season (Iowa beat Northwestern 24-0 in the opener).

Iowa's first TD came after Holsclaw's 46-yard field goal try hit the crossbar and bounced back. On the Hawks' next sortie, they overcame a 15-yard holding penalty, thanks to Tom McLaughlin's 32-yard pass to Jim Swift. McLaughlin sneaked the final yard.

Wisconsin partisans in the crowd of 71,723 probably are saying their team's demise was more of a suicide than a homicide — just as Hawkeye boosters claimed in last week's 24-21 loss to Indiana.

Indeed, the Badgers did lose five of their nine fumbles and had two passes intercepted.

Once Wisconsin reached Iowa's 6-yard line before Shanty Burks stole one of Dudley's passes.

Another time they were on the Iowa 9 when Tom Rusk recovered Kevin Cohee's fumble (Steve Wagner and Burks recovered the other two Wisconsin fumbles).

But Commings and his aides proudly pointed out most of the fumbles came after lusty Iowa tackles. As usual, Rusk was the tackle leader. He had six solos and five assists. Safety Dave Becker was next with eight solos and one assist.

Indeed, Wisconsin's two quarterbacks were sacked six times for 59 yards in losses. Mark Mahmens had two of them for 13 yards, Wagner one for 18, Cedric Shaw one for 12, Tim Gutshall one for 10 and Dean Moore one for 6.

The victory brought Iowa's record to 4-6 (3-4 in the Big Ten) but the Hawks will be able to match last year's 5-6 only by upsetting Michigan State in next Saturday's finale at Kinnick Stadium.

Probably more important, it was Iowa's first victory at Madison since 1958. The Hawkeyes finished with a 4-4 count against Jardine, who announced his retirement last Monday night after getting his fill of the abuse from "low-class Wisconsin fans" after the team's fourth straight loss (22-0 to Purdue).

Most fans expected the Badgers to play with renewed motivation, and the statistics showed how well they did do: They had only 71 net yards in 37 rushes, but they gained a whopping 222 yards passing.

Their touchdown wasn't much consolation to the faint-hearted boosters, but it was a relief to a coaching staff and team that had been outscored 129-7 in the previous four games. Indeed, Wisconsin had only seven points in 20 straight quarters when the big play came with 1:15 to go.

Quarterback Charles Green hurled a sideline pass to Tom Stauss, who ducked around Iowa's secondary, somehow stayed inbounds and legged it to the end zone to complete the 58-yard play. Green pulled a naked reverse for the two-point conversion.

Commings explained Iowa also intended to pass more, but credited Wisconsin with putting too much heat on QB McLaughlin. He particularly singled out left linebacker Dave Crossen for praise saying, "That No. 35 was in there on top of Tommy Mack all afternoon."

Crossen was credited with 10 solo tackles and 14 assists, one of the Big Ten's top performances of the season.

Phillips & Iowa shock No. 7 Nebraska, 10-7

By Mark Dukes, The Gazette

....

SCORE BY QUARTERS
Iowa City, Sept. 12, 1981

NEBRASKA	0	0	0	7	—	7
IOWA	7	3	0	0	—	10

So you were wondering how Iowa would react after last year's 57-0 drubbing at Nebraska?

Forget it.

You were apprehensive about the inexperience in Iowa's offensive unit?

Forget it.

You were wondering how long Iowa's defense could contain a Cornhusker running game that ranked No. 1 nationally last year?

Forget it.

The Incredible Cornhusker Conquest answered all those questions — and many more — Saturday as Iowa rocked the nation by knocking off seventh-ranked Nebraska, 10-7.

The Hawkeyes, efficient in their offensive game plan and absolutely unbreakable on defense, opened their season by giving 60,160 sun-soaked fans a record crowd for Kinnick Stadium a treat they'll not soon forget.

And you were wondering how a hungry Hawkeye fan reacts when his appetite is satisfied?

Forget it.

For example, it took a group of fans less than 30 seconds to tear down the North goal post when the final seconds had expired. Then they went to escort Coach Hayden Fry and his Conquerors to the tunnel leading to the dressing room.

As could be expected, Fry and some of his players could hardly contain their excitement when they met the media. For example:

Fry: "At this minute, this is the greatest victory of my life. I'm getting to be an old man and I don't want to hurt any of my other teams that pulled off some upsets. But while I've been at Iowa, this is far and away the greatest victory.

"If you stay with this game long enough, the worm is bound to turn. Don't think we didn't earn this one either. We did it fair and square, plus we showed a lot of character."

Running back Eddie Phillips: "I don't think they (Nebraska) wanted it as much as we did."

Defensive tackle Mark Bortz: "It's a dream come true. A lot of people had doubts about our winning, but the coaching staff got us going. Everybody was relaxed and we just put it all together. I think the difference over last year was more mental than physical."

Iowa quarterback Pete Gales (12) completed 6 of 10 passes for 34 yards against seventh-ranked Nebraska on the day of his sister's wedding. "This is definitely the biggest thrill of my athletic life," Gales said.

Quarterback Pete Gales: "This is definitely the biggest thrill of my athletic life. It's even more thrilling since my sister (Deborah) got married today in New Jersey, so this will be a good present for her."

Iowa fans probably haven't had cause to celebrate the defeat of a major power since a 7-6 triumph at Penn State in 1975, or maybe the 21-10 home-field shipping of UCLA in 1974.

Even so, Fry said he already "is scared to death" from thinking about next week's game at Ames against Iowa State, which opened with a 17-13 victory over West Texas State.

"I'm happy as hell, but keep in mind this is just one game," said Fry, who will be seeking his 100th career victory Saturday.

"We've got to make sure and keep our heads screwed on tight. We can't be high school Harrys and start rejoicing. We can't be too high, but we're damn sure not going to be low."

Nebraska Coach Tom Osborne was gracious in his praise for Iowa, which held the Cornhuskers to their lowest-scoring total since a 20-3 opening-game loss to Alabama in 1978.

Nebraska has been shut out just once in Osborne's eight-year reign — 27-0 to Oklahoma in 1973.

"This is one of the hardest losses for us since I've been here," said Osborne, who has a 75-21-2 record at Nebraska. "They outplayed us and outcoached us. Anytime we lose a game it is my fault. If our players aren't good enough, then I should have done a better job recruiting.

"If our players don't perform well, then we should have done a better job of preparing them. I think we have better players overall than Iowa does, I think."

This was a Nebraska team that averaged 378 yards rushing and 506 yards in total offense last year. Yet the swarming Iowa defenders allowed the Cornhuskers just 150 yards on the

Iowa scored on its first possession when Eddie Phillips ran in from 2 yards out with 9:16 remaining in the first quarter. In 1980, Nebraska outscored its opponents 111-6 in the first quarter, but in this game, Iowa took the early lead.

ground and 231 total, in addition to keeping them out of the end zone for the first 48 minutes. And when was the last time a Nebraska team was outgained on the ground?

The Cornhuskers, who gave away just 88 rushing yards a game last year, yielded 174 to Iowa this time, including 94 by Phillips, a sophomore running back from Chicago who also scored the Hawks' only touchdown.

But the Hawkeye defenders had to leave their helmets strapped right up until the final minute. Indeed, Nebraska was well into Iowa territory on three of its last four possessions, but couldn't cash in.

With 6:30 remaining, Kevin Seibel missed a 37-yard field-goal attempt wide to the right.

The Huskers advanced to the Iowa 34 with 2:51 left, but

Mark Mauer fumbled the snap from center Dave Rimington and Bortz recovered.

Nebraska got another opportunity when Iowa running back Phil Blatcher fumbled on third down at the Iowa 41 and Husker cornerback Allen Lyday recovered. Iowa stopped the threat at the 39 with 1:25 left, though, on an incomplete pass.

Reggie Roby, who set a one-game punting record for Iowa with five boots for a 55.8 average, pinned Nebraska on a 53-yard kick with 55 seconds left. After Bortz sacked QB Nate Mason on first down, Lou King iced the outcome with an interception with :39 showing.

Iowa, under the direction of senior quarterback Gales, scored on its first possession when Phillips plunged over the left side from 2-yards out with 9:16 showing. Lon Olejniczak, who remained perfect in extra points and field goals for his career, kicked the extra point to make it 7-0.

Phillips gained 34 yards in the seven-play, 44-yard series. The Hawks had gained possession at the Cornhusker 44 when King stormed in and partially blocked Grant Campbell's punt.

Nebraska had to be stunned, or at least wondering, at this point. After all, Big Red outscored opponents 111-6 in the first quarter last year.

Iowa challenged moments later when Mel Cole's tackle forced Roger Craig to fumble and Bortz recovered at the Nebraska 24. However, Roby's 42-yard field goal sailed wide to the right.

But Iowa got three more points on the scoreboard the next possession when Olejniczak booted a 35-yard field goal

on the first play of the second quarter. Brad Webb's interception put Iowa in position to score at the Nebraska 43.

Meanwhile, Nebraska and its much-publicized back, Davenport Central's Craig, experienced all kinds of problems with Iowa's inspired defense. It was a team effort in the truest sense, as 10 Hawkeye defenders had five tackles or more.

The Cornhuskers managed to penetrate Iowa territory only twice in the first half. The first drive failed when Seibel missed a 47-yard field goal with 1:38 left in the half.

Craig, who rushed for 769 yards and 15 touchdowns as a third-string I-back last year, was thwarted constantly in his bid to break free. He finished with 74 yards on 19 carries, but his longest run was only 13 yards.

Fullback Phil Bates had Nebraska's longest gainer with a 22-yard run to the Iowa 24 in the fourth quarter.

Phillips, who inherited a starting assignment when first-string back J.C. Love-Jordan suffered an ankle injury, used 19 carries to gain 94 yards. His long run of 13 yards also was Iowa's longest play.

Gales, who played most of the game, completed 6 of 10 passes for 34 yards. Olejniczak caught four for 34.

Nebraska's chance of getting on the winning track doesn't get any easier Saturday. The Cornhuskers entertain Florida State (2-0), which won at Lincoln last year, 18-14.

Eddie Phillips (18) finished with 19 carries for 94 yards against Nebraska. Phillips was Iowa's starting running back because J.C. Love Jordan suffered an ankle injury.

Iowa Defense Brutalizes Bruins in 20-7 Upset

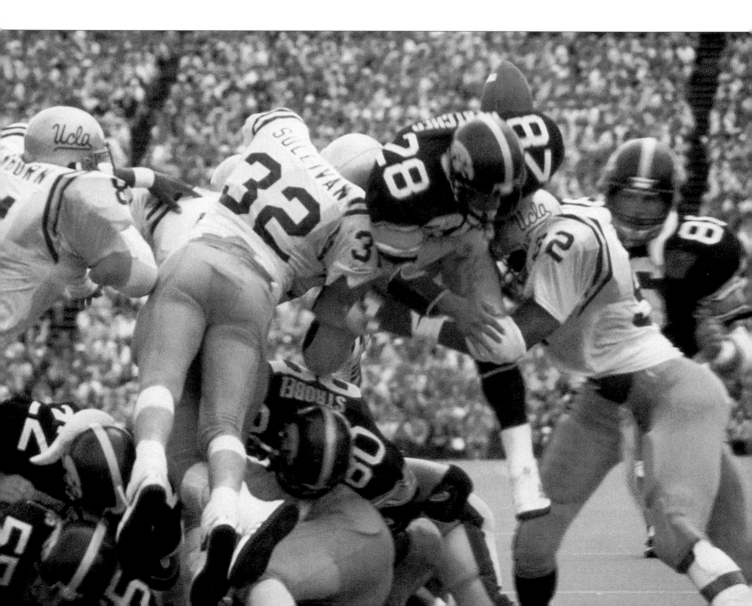

By Gus Schrader, The Gazette

Hey, Hayden, maybe it's time for other schools to lighten their football schedules by dropping Iowa.

Especially those coming to Kinnick Stadium while rated sixth or seventh in the nation.

It was UCLA's turn to land in the Fry pan here Saturday, and a capacity crowd of 60,004 delirious fans whooped it up for a brutal Hawkeye defense that held the vaunted, versatile Bruins to 35 yards rushing, 4 in the second half, and scored a resounding 20-7 upset.

At least the rambunctious students waited until the game was over this time. Then they spilled onto the field, bent both goal posts to the ground and helped Iowa players carry Fry on their shoulders.

"We were completely dominated in every phase of the game by Iowa today," said Terry Donahue, UCLA coach. "I don't remember ever in my coaching career being as ineffective with the running game as today.

"When we ran up the middle they stacked us up. When we tried to go outside they ran us down. And when we went back to pass they sacked us."

Wow! Seven sacks for 19 yards.

The Iowa offense wasn't bad, either. With Gordy Bohannon filling in admirably after starting quarterback Pete Gales suffered a hand injury, the Hawks outgained the ruined Bruins 336 to 121 in total offense.

"I've never been happier in my life," exulted Coach Hayden Fry, "and not just because this was my 100th coaching victory. How sweet it is!

"We were so embarrassed last week with our play at Iowa State, but our coaches and players put it all back together

Phil Blatcher, a senior, who filled in for injured running back Eddie Phillips, carried for 113 yards on 36 carries against the UCLA Bruins.

today. I never dreamed we could shut them down that much. The defense was just superb. I think we'd have shut them out if we hadn't given them the ball on our 20-yard line with that fumble.

"This was bigger than Nebraska. This was No. 100 for old John Hayden, and the team gave me the game ball."

There were some notes of sadness in the sweet symphony of success. Lon Olejniczak, the outstanding wide receiver, punter and placekicker from Decorah, suffered a broken leg and will miss the rest of the season.

Fry said he hoped the Big Ten would grant Oleo, a junior, an extra season of eligibility to replace this one.

He said several other Hawks were injured — Gales and running back Eddie Phillips most notable — but refused to speculate on whether they would be ready when the Hawks open the Big Ten season at Northwestern next Saturday.

Iowa displayed a freshman who seemed admirably qualified to take over Olejniczak's share of the kicking. Indeed, Tom Nichol of Green Bay, Wis., won the hearts of the home fans with the way he used his soccer-style to boot two field goals in three tries, convert an extra point and kick off with at least one amazing result.

The Hawks also got a marvelous performance out of a bench-warming halfback. Phil Blatcher, often-injured senior who had gained only 34 yards in 13 carries previously this season, spurted for 113 yards in 36 trips Saturday after Phillips was hurt midway in the first quarter.

Gales got Iowa's first touchdown on a 16-yard sprint off the option play. UCLA matched that on quarterback Tom Ramsey's 1-yard sneak with 10:47 left in the half.

The Hawks' second touchdown was, appropriately enough, achieved by the defense alone. Dave (Fat Daddy) Browne, junior-college transfer who took over for ailing Jim Pekar at defensive right tackle, knocked the ball loose from Ramsey and Mark Bortz recovered for his second touchdown in two years.

That score was merely a bonus for the defense, as Nichol provided all the margin needed on a 35-yard field goal with

SCORE BY QUARTERS					
Iowa City, Sept. 26, 1981					
IOWA	7	0	3	10	— 20
UCLA	0	7	0	0	— 7

Hayden Fry huddles with wide receivers Ivory Webb (25) and Jeff Brown (27) on the sidelines. The victory over UCLA was Hayden Fry's 100th career win.

"That Tom Nichol is phenomenal! He never gives up."

Coach Hayden Fry

9:48 left in the third quarter, and a 43-yarder with 6:24 remaining in the fourth period.

"That Tom Nichol is phenomenal!" chuckled Fry. "He never gives up. After he missed that first field goal (a 50-yarder just before the half) by inches from way out in the pea patch, he told me he'd get the next one for sure.

"Then he pulled that strange kickoff. We weren't trying to onside-kick, but Nichol hooked it low, and it hit a big UCLA linemen with our guys (Zane Corbin) recovering."

Pat Dean, the big senior noseguard, was the standout on a bristling defense that overran the Buins like a rolling ball of butcher knives. He had 10 solo tackles and two assists. Three of his stops were for seven yards in losses.

Browne had two sacks for minus-five yards, and Bryan Skradis and Andre Tippett also had a sack each.

Iowa's passing produced only 57 yards. Gales hit 3 of 6 passes for 28 yards, and Bohannon 4 of 11 for 29 yards. Iowa still hasn't passed for a touchdown this year.

But both Gales and Bo startled the UCLA defense with their running. Gales wound up with 28 yards on two scampers, and Bo was the No. 2 rusher with 72 yards in 13 tries. He had Iowa's longest rush of the day, a 25-yarder that set up Nichols' last field goal.

Reggie Roby added five-hundredths of a yard to his nation-leading punting average. He had averaged 54.09 in his first two games, and he boosted that to 54.14 Saturday. He had boots of 54, 45 and 64 yards. On another one, he kicked out of bounds for 53 yards, but it was negated when UCLA was penalized for roughing him after he barely got the kick away.

The Hawkeye defense also came up with three pass interceptions. Bobby Stoops, Jim Erb and Lou King made the thefts.

Herky the Hawk stirs up the Hawkeye fans during the unforgettable upset over UCLA.

Mighty Michigan Is No Match For Inspired Iowa

By Don Doxsie, The Gazette

SCORE BY QUARTERS						
Ann Arbor, Mich., Oct. 17, 1981						
IOWA	6	0	3	0	—	9
MICHIGAN	0	7	0	0	—	7

Before the current college football season began, many Iowa fans no doubt hoped their team would have a winning season.

But, those fans really underestimated "Hayden's Heroes."

Make no mistake about it, the Iowa Hawkeyes have arrived not just as a team with a winning record, but as a full-blown powerhouse in the world of Big Ten football.

Any last doubters were almost certainly swayed Saturday as Coach Hayden Fry's Hawks recorded perhaps their biggest victory in the last 20 years, stifling traditional heavyweight Michigan, 9-7, before a sardined-in crowd of 105,951 at Michigan Stadium.

The crowd, which was the largest ever to see an Iowa football game and the third-largest in Michigan history, also included representatives from six different bowl games, and they no doubt returned to their individual areas of the country very impressed.

Iowa used a conservative ball-control offense, a big-play defense and the talented foot of freshman Tom Nichol to record a victory over a team ranked among the top half-dozen

in the nation for the third time this season.

The win also moved the Hawks into undisputed possession of first place in the Big Ten as Wisconsin lost to Michigan State, 33-14. Iowa is now 3-0 in league play (5-1 overall) while Wisconsin is 3-1 and Ohio State is 2-1.

"Man, that was one great football game," exclaimed an ecstatic Fry in a postgame press conference. "I thought I fouled up a jillion times by playing it too close to the vest. But we put a lot of faith in our defense.

"Nobody expected us to win this football game except those guys over there in the next room. Nobody's heard of Iowa football for 20 years."

The Hawkeyes stunned both Nebraska and UCLA in nonconference games earlier in the season when those clubs were ranked No. 6 in the nation in both wire service polls, but Fry didn't hesitate to point out that they were sixth in the *Sports Illustrated* rankings.

But this victory was much, much sweeter than the conquests of UCLA and Nebraska, according to Fry. Perhaps it was because this one came on the road. Perhaps it was because this one counted in the league standings. Or perhaps it was because the Hawks had to scramble back from a halftime deficit to win this one.

Iowa trailed by a single point before Nichol's third field goal of the game a 30-yarder with 2:40 to go in the third quarter gave the Hawks a 9-7 cushion.

The field goal came at the end of a 5½-minute, 67-yard drive following a interception by Iowa's Mel Cole in the end zone.

Seventeen minutes and 40 seconds later, the score was still 9-7 as the Hawks chewed up much of the intervening time with a methodical, one-first-down-at-a-time approach. Under the guidance of senior quarterback Gordy Bohannon, the visitors had possession of the ball for almost 14 minutes more than Michigan over the course of the game.

"That was our game plan to hold the ball," added Fry. "We stuck to our guns. I'm kind of proud of ol' John Hayden. I

Quarterback Gordy Bohannon (11) had possession of the ball for nearly 14 minutes more than Michigan during the game.

really wanted to go back and throw the bomb but we stuck to the game plan."

And of course the defense, which has ranked at the top of the Big Ten most of the season, did its job again. There were three crucial points in the second half when the Hawks rose up to stop the Wolverines. Cole's interception on a deflected pass with 8:19 to go in the third quarter was the first. A fourth-down stop by tackle Mark Bortz on flanker Anthony Carter early in the fourth quarter was the second. And, an Andre Tippett-influenced incomplete pass with 31 seconds left was the third, marking the end of the Wolverines' hopes.

After that, Bohannon fell on the ball twice to run out the clock.

The Hawks took a 3-0 lead in their first possession of the game with the help of a fumbled punt. Dave Strobel jumped on Evan Cooper's fumble at the Michigan 38-yard line and a 25-yard completion from Bohannon to Ivory Webb moved Iowa to the 11. The drive stalled at the 4 and Nichol came in to kick a 20-yard field goal.

Nichol got another field goal, from 36 yards out, later in the fist quarter, capping a 57-yard march.

"My kicking was pretty shaky all week long," admitted Nichol, "with a new holder and a new center and everything. They had a really good rush on us today, too, but we did OK."

Michigan jumped in front, 7-6, on a 17-yard touchdown pass from Steve Smith to Carter with 6:30 to go in the second quarter. The 68-yard drive was helped by a personal-foul penalty against Iowa.

"One of our key mistakes was giving up that touchdown to Carter," said Fry. "However, I knew they were going to call that play before they even ran it and even though we defended against it properly, they still were able to score. That's just a tribute to Carter's ability as a receiver."

Carter caught five passes for 91 yards in the contest but the Wolverines completed just one other pass all day. Smith was the home squad's leading rusher with 60 yards while tailback Butch Woolfok was held under 100 yards for the first time all season. He netted 56 in 14 carries.

Norm Granger led a balanced Hawkeye ground attack with 44 yards. Bohannon rushed for 34 yards and also completed 10 of 19 passes for 127 yards.

California's Calling as Iowa Earns Rose Bowl Bid

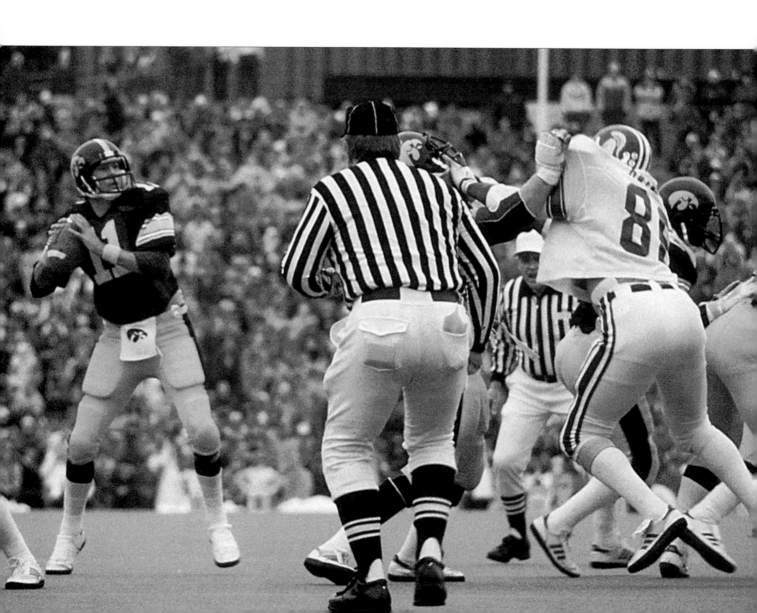

By Gus Schrader, The Gazette

Start packing! California, here they come! Pasadena or bust!

Rose Bowl, how sweet it is! How do we get tickets?

Or, as Coach Hayden Fry said, "How 'bout those Hawks? Yaaahooo!"

Who would have guessed it three months ago? Or two months ago after the Hawkeyes were upset at Iowa State? Or a month ago when Iowa lost two straight, to Minnesota and Illinois?

Or even a few hours ago, when an incredible two-game Big Ten parlay had to come home Saturday? But Iowa's 36-7 triumph over Michigan State, coupled with Ohio State's 14-9 upset of Michigan, turned the Rose Bowl key.

It's true, no matter what the odds were, and Jan. 1 the Hawkeyes will be playing Washington's Huskies before 103,000 people in Pasadena's Rose Bowl with most of the world watching on television.

Yes, Iowa's Cinderella team that was picked by nobody to win the Big Ten, Saturday finished in a title tie with Ohio State, which ironically earned little but the right to play Navy in the Liberty Bowl at Memphis.

The Hawks will play a Washington team that earned its third Rose Bowl berth in the last five seasons. The Huskies, coached by Don James, beat Michigan, 27-20, on Jan. 1, 1978, and last New Year's Day lost a 23-6 decision to Michigan.

"I think Iowa will be a great team to represent the Big Ten in the Rose Bowl," said Muddy Waters, the Michigan State coach who was a gallant and generous loser.

"I don't care who we play in the Rose Bowl," said an ecstatic Fry, who came into the interview room carrying a long-stemmed rose and wearing a Rose Bowl patch stuck on his forehead. "Shoot, except for the money, I'd go out to

Gordy Bohannon (11) ran for 34 yards, mostly on quarterback draws, and completed 8 of 16 passes.

Pasadena tomorrow if they'd let me, but I guess our team will probably go out Dec. 22 or 23.

"Yes, we finally came of age, and I'm ready to admit this is a pretty good football team.

"About all our team has accomplished since the game ended — besides hug each other — was to give thanks to the good Lord, who certainly smiled on us today. We're the chosen people. I'm no preacher, but I want to thank the Lord for giving me the privilege of being associated with this group of fine young men."

Fry was asked if he really expected Ohio State to upend Michigan.

"Hey, apparently there were a lot of folks listening to that game on their radios in the stands," the coach replied. "We could hear our crowd roar every once in a while, but I didn't know if all the drunks had got together or what.

"I finally got hold of a man with a radio. He said the score was 14-9, but he was so uptight he couldn't even tell me who was ahead. So I asked him how much time was left, and he said about a minute. I asked who had the ball, and he said, "The team that's ahead."

SCORE BY QUARTERS						
Iowa City, Nov. 21, 1981						
MICHIGAN STATE	0	7	0	0	—	7
IOWA	16	0	20	0	—	36

"Well, I believe that Art Schilchter (Ohio State QB) when he said they were going to beat Michigan, and heard on that last touchdown he wasn't to be denied. But Schilchter also said Ohio State was going to the Rose Bowl, and I didn't believe that.

"I guess you can tell Mr. (Bo) Schembechler (Michigan coach) that there was another game in the Big Ten today. I read my team what he said about it coming down to the same old story of Michigan and Ohio State being the Big Two and fighting for the Rose Bowl again."

Fry passed out praise to his team, his staff, the long-suffering Iowa fans, even the news media. As soon as all the Hawks were dressed, he broke his three-year policy by letting reporters invade the Hawkeye dressing room to interview everyone at will.

The press never saw so many roses. The dressing room looked like a gangster's funeral.

Almost every Hawkeye had at least one long-stemmed

rose. Somebody bought 'em by the gross.

"Yes, I got the game ball," smiled Phil Blatcher, the explosive tailback who gained a whopping 247 yards in 27 carries as the Hawks piled up almost 400 yards net on the ground.

"That's the game ball over there in my locker, along with the roses," said the shy senior from New Orleans. "Eddie Phillips gave the ball to me. He presented it, and everybody said it was mine.

"I had no idea of how many yards I had. Hmm, 247. No, I never gained that many in a game before, not even in high school. All I knew was I was awful cold and my feet were freezing.

"Yes, I took myself out in the first half. I got hit and I didn't feel it, so I figured it was time to get out of there."

The Iowa fans didn't seem to mind the cold. After Iowa had assembled its 36-7 lead with 2:49 to play, rambunctious celebrants began gathering in both end zones.

It's the custom of the cheerleaders to do as many pushups as the Hawkeyes have points after each score. So literally hundreds of fans got into the prone position and did pushups right with 'em. Greatest thing for mass physical education in years!

The scamps couldn't wait until the game ended, even though booed by more mature fans.

With two minutes left, a few put a serious list to the south goal post by grabbing the crossbar.

As the final minute ticked away, first the south goal post was bent asunder, and then the north one. With 12 seconds left, a horde of loyalists charged out onto the field, engulfing the players. The officials looked nervously at the final seconds on the clock, then wisely tucked their caps under their arms and hustled to their dressing room.

It was a scene that hadn't taken place in Iowa's Kinnick Stadium since Coach Forest Evashevski's Hawks did it in both the 1956 and '58 seasons.

The players finally escaped from the clutches of their admirers and reached the locker room. Still the fans milled around, replaying the game, reliving the thrill of experiencing a "double-header" — watching Iowa in person and listening to Michigan's downfall on radio.

A few fans admitted they were crying with happiness. At the northeast corner of the stadium, a man had fallen and his friends used their bodies as shields to keep him from

Phil Blatcher (28) outraces the Spartan defense. Blatcher exploded for 247 yards on 27 carries as the Hawkeyes piled up nearly 400 yards on the ground.

being trampled. The air carried strong whiffs of alcohol. Outside the stadium, a young man threw up with great, heaving sobs.

The sober ones talked of "Hayden's Heroes," and there were many.

One had to be Tracy Crocker, the tough senior cornerback from Cedar Rapids Kennedy.

It was his interception that turned the tide when Michigan State, trailing 16-7, was striking toward another touchdown early in the third quarter.

Bryan Clark, Michigan State's quarterback, had led the Spartans to Iowa's 6-yard line.

Although Fry claimed his confidence in his team never wavered, many felt something slipping when the Rose Bowl was so close at hand.

Clark hurled a pass into the end zone, intended for Daryl Turner, but Crocker snatched the ball and ran it out to the Iowa 16. The Hawks immediately marched down and got a field goal — the first of two by freshman Tom Nichol — and suddenly the gates were open to California.

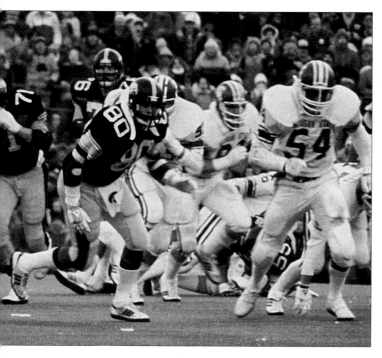

"Michigan State had been hurting us with timing patterns all along," Crocker explained.

"Clark would throw when his receivers weren't even turned around because they were counting on knowing when the pass would be there.

"I read this one right, and the ball came right to me. When an interception happens, the credit should go to 10 other guys, because that's the end result of good defense. We're not the type of team that big-play an opponent to death. So we have to keep doing our jobs until we get a break."

Crocker admitted he was feeling like wearing a goat's horns instead of a halo a few minutes earlier. He was charged with hitting MSU's Ted Jones after a line play was over, and Iowa was penalized 15 yards.

"Yes, that was stupid of me," he admitted. "But No. 21 (Jones) had been hitting us all along, and later he got kicked out for it. But I shouldn't have hit back.

"Then, a couple of plays later, Clark completed that 30-yard pass on us. You can put the blame on which ever one of us you want to, but Bobby Stoops and I messed up on our coverage, and he (receiver Otis Grant) got behind us. Yes, I was feeling like a goat when that interception came along."

That was Crocker's first pass theft of the year. The Hawks stole two others, both by Lou King, who tied immortal Nile Kinnick's school record for a season with eight.

The Hawks made their first big break of the game on another theft, but it was ruled a fumble recovery and runback instead of an interception. Doesn't matter, they count, too.

Michigan State, playing without its two leading rushers — halfbacks Aaron Roberts and Lance Hawkins stayed home because of injuries — coughed up the ball on its very first play.

Clark threw a pass to tight end Al Kimichik in the right flat. Strong safety Bobby Stoops popped Kimichik so hard the ball zipped away like a melon seed. End Andre Tippett came up with it and was credited with an 8-yard return.

The Hawks scored on two 9-yard bolts by Blatcher, and only 1:01 had ticked away.

The defense treated the offense to another score midway in the first quarter. Wellman's James Erb knifed through and blocked Ralf Mojsiejenko's punt, and the ball bounced clear through the end zone for a safety.

Now it was the offense's turn. Glenn (Lightning) Buggs returned the kickoff after the safety 29 yards, and the Hawks went the 54 yards in 12 plays. Biggest gains were Eddie Phillips' 9-yard run and his 12-yard gain on a pass from Gordy Bohannon. Phillips plowed over for the final yards, and it was 16-0 after Nichol's kick.

The second quarter was scoreless until the Spartans got their only points with 1:20 to go.

Reggie Roby, who averaged "only" 40.5 yards on two punts, kicked 44 yards, but Iowa was penalized to its own 44 for a personal foul. Showing respect for Iowa's rushing defense, Clark passed one yard to James Hodo for the touchdown. Denmark's Morten Andersen kicked the extra point, giving him a perfect 28 for his senior season.

This happened after the Hawks and their fans knew about Ohio State's victory.

"I told our guys at the half to forget all the stuff about bowls and start playing just as if our score was 0-0," said Fry.

The Hawks didn't get the hang of it again, though, until after Crocker's theft stymied the Spartans. Then Nichol kicked his 26-yard field goal. Later he got a 23-yarder.

Blatcher's devastating runs his longest was 46 yards behind merciless blocking blew the game open. When Blatcher tired, Phillips came in. He got 76 yards with 16 his longest.

Blatcher got two TDs, Phillips one.

Iowa's Tricks on Offe

By Mark Dukes, The Gazette

Iowa's defense corked "Champaign" Tony Eason and Coach Hayden Fry allowed a bit more of his offense out of the bottle Saturday afternoon.

Both of which left Fry bubbling with enthusiasm after the Hawkeyes roared into a tie for second place in the Big Ten football race with a thrilling, 14-13 triumph over Eason and Illinois.

On the eve of Halloween, Fry's tricks turned out to be quite a treat for the 59,922 fans at Kinnick Stadium and the millions of other who watched on regional television.

"Illinois is something else, but they're not as good as the Hawks — at least not today," Fry crowed. "I don't care if we didn't win a game the rest of the season, we can already look back on what we accomplished.

SCORE BY QUARTERS					
Iowa City, Oct. 30, 1982					
ILLINOIS	10	0	0	3	— 13
IOWA	7	0	7	0	— 14

"I've got the most beautiful players in the world. They're not the best, but they just don't quit. I think Billy Graham could get a lot of people in his mission from around here. This game was a true measuring stick of our character."

Iowa, which plays at Purdue on Saturday, is tied with Ohio State for second place at 4-1 behind undefeated Michigan in the Big Ten. The Hawks hike their overall record to 5-3 with their fifth victory in the last six games, undoubtedly impressing scouts from the Liberty and Tangerine bowls. Illinois, which hosts Michigan on Saturday, slipped to 5-2 in the Big Ten and 6-3 overall.

Mike Hufford (86), Mark Bortz (63) and Iowa held off Illinois in the fourth quarter to improve to 5-3 overall, 4-1 in the Big Ten.

nse No Treat for Illini

Eddie Phillips (22) had 27 carries for 158 yards, his second straight 100-yard game.

Fry unveiled several "exotics" in an attempt to keep Illinois off balance, but the rushing game was Iowa's most effective weapon. Junior Eddie Phillips sparked a Hawkeye running attack that produced 259 yards, notching his second straight 100-yard game with 158 in 27 carries.

Phillips, who ran 2 yards for Iowa's first-quarter touchdown, said he dedicated the game to his late older brother. Napolean Phillips was slain eight years ago in a gang-related assault in Chicago.

"I never dedicated a game to my brother, just like I never told him I loved him before he died," said Phillips, who gained a career-high 198 yards last week at Minnesota. "I have a lot more determination, and I figured that sooner or

late my time would come." The deciding touchdown came on an 8-yard pass from Chuck Long to Ronnie Harmon with 10 seconds left in the third quarter. Tom Nichol's second conversion kick put Iowa in front, 14-10.

Mike Bass kicked a 45-yard field goal with 11:29 remaining, but Iowa shut down the Illini from there. Bass also made a 52-yarder in the first quarter and now is 20-of-23 for the season, including 10-of-12 from 40 yards and beyond.

Eason, who hit 31-of-46 passes for 292 yards, was poised to rally Illinois in the waning minutes. But the Hawkeyes, despite four penalties, erased more than six minutes off the clock after gaining possession with 6:47 remaining.

The most crucial play came on third-and-29 from the Iowa 32-yard line. With the Illini expecting the pass, Phillips was sent through the left side. Aided by guard Jon Roehlk's open-field block, Phillips darted 30 yards for a first down.

Iowa eventually was forced to punt from the Illinois 44, but Nichol angled the ball perfectly inside the Illini 1. Eason threw four incompletions out of desperation.

"With 99 and ⁹/₁₀ yards to go, there was nothing much we could do," Illinois Coach Mike White said. "It was a great punt, a great punt.

"It was really a painful experience. Iowa made the crucial first downs when they had to and Illinois didn't. It's that simple. You have to give Iowa credit because they did what they had to do and they did a great job."

Although the Hawks trailed, 10-7, at halftime, Fry brushed off his playbook in the first half by using the following:

■ Halfback passes by Phillips and J.C. Love Jordan that yielded a total of 63 yards.

■ A fake field goal by second-string quarterback Tom Grogan, which netted 14 yards and a first down.

■ A left-handed shovel pass by Long to Phillips for 9 yards and a first down.

■ A reverse run-pass option by receiver Ronnie Harmon, who rolled 26 yards to set up Phillips' touchdown. Fry used two other reverses with Harmon, although one lost 14 yards.

"We've been saving those plays for a day like this," Fry confided. "We had to throw them off balance because they have a tremendous blitz. We had to gamble, but mainly I like to dance with the gal who brung me."

Behind Phillips' running, Iowa moved 53 yards in 11 plays on its first possession of the game before Long's pass intended for tight end Mike Hufford was intercepted by Mike Heaven at the Illinois 16.

Eason wasted little time in putting Illinois on the board, heaving a 47-yard bomb to Oliver Williams on the sixth play after Heaven's theft. Williams' TD, achieved by beating cornerback Keith Hunter, and Bass' conversion put Illinois on top 7-0 with 7:44 left in the first quarter.

Phillips whipped a left-handed halfback pass to Harmon for 36 yards on the first play after the kickoff. Four plays later, Harmon ran 26 yards on what appeared to be an option off a reverse, giving Iowa first-and-goal at the

Illinois 4.

Phillips twice gained 2 yards, scoring on the second run by breaking a tackle at the 5 and veering left into the end zone. Nichol's kick tied the game, 7-7, with 5:49 left in the first quarter.

Eason, who completed the first seven passes he attempted, marched the Illini into scoring position by hitting five passes for 41 yards. Bass capped the 10-play, 46-yard series with his 52-yard field goal from a right-to-left angle.

With 12:09 left in the half, Iowa began a lengthy drive that consumed 7 ½ minutes off the clock. The series included Love-Jordan's 27-yard halfback pass to Dave Moritz, Long's shovel pass to Phillips and Grogan's run off the fake field goal.

Grogan's 14-yard dash through Illinois' midsection gave Iowa a first-and-goal at the 8. But a procedure penalty and Harmon's 14-yard loss on a reverse set the Hawkeyes back.

On third down from the 25, Long was sacked for a 13-yard loss and fumbled to Illinois' Dan Gregus.

Starting at his 38, Eason marched Illinois quickly into Hawk territory. But the drive stalled when the Illini were cited for a clipping penalty at the Iowa 10 and sophomore defensive tackle George Little followed with an 11-yard sack of Eason.

On Iowa's first series of the second half, Nichol barely missed to the left on a 43-yard field-goal attempt at the 10:33 mark. Long had hit Moritz twice for gains of 7 and 27 yards, and found Love Jordan once for 10.

Eason hit seven passes on Illinois' next series and had two completions nullified. But the 10-play drive was stopped when Iowa stacked up an Eason sneak for no gain on fourth-and-1 from the Iowa 18.

Long's winning touchdown pass to Harmon in the back of the end zone came on only the fourth play of a 69-yard series. The other three were long gainers, a 20-yard pass from Long to Moritz, a 24-yard run by Phillips and a 17-yard burst by fullback Owen Gill.

Gill added 60 yards rushing on eight carries, while Moritz topped Iowa receivers with five for 89 yards. Defending national punting champion Reggie Roby kicked three times for a 50.3 average, including a 63 yarder.

Iowa Just Peachy Ag

inst Vols

By Gus Schrader, The Gazette

Just as the new song predicted, when the New Year was greeted here Friday night, "Iowa was waltzin' and Tennessee was singin' the blues."

Iowa's unsung offense waltzed plenty in the first three quarters, rolling up a 28-19 lead on the passing arm of Chuck Long and the sticky fingers of Dave Moritz. But again it was the old, reliable defense that made Tennessee sing the blues with some savage play in the final minutes that preserved a 28-22 victory.

Although the 15th annual Peach Bowl had been listed as a virtual sellout, only 50,134 showed up on a cold, windy day that turned into New Year's Eve in a hurry. Most of the enthralled spectators were still on hand at 6:15 p.m. Eastern time when senior end Straun Joseph sacked Tennessee's bril-

SCORE BY QUARTERS
Atlanta, Dec. 31, 1982

IOWA	0	21	7	0	—	28
TENNESSEE	7	0	12	3	—	22

liant quarterback, Alan Cockrell, the final time.

"It was just a super game," Iowa Coach Hayden Fry said. "I have never seen a defense rise up on the goal line and sack the quarterback like that. We were very tough when we had to be."

Fry was overjoyed at "redeeming ourselves for the 28-0 embarrassment in the Rose Bowl." The Hawkeyes scored their first touchdowns in a bowl game since Jan. 1, 1959. Indeed, they didn't even cross Washington's 29-yard line in last year's game at Pasadena, but they quickly atoned for that omission.

Singin' the blues? Well, not Johnny Majors, the former Iowa State coach who had directed the Volunteers to a 6-4-1 record coming here. He gave Iowa full credit, and even admitted the

Iowa, which didn't get past Washington's 29-yard line in the 1981 Rose Bowl, scored its first touchdown in a bowl game since Jan. 1, 1959. "It was just a super game," Coach Hayden Fry said.

Iowa quarterback Chuck Long completed 19 of 26 passes for a Peach Bowl-record 304 yards and three touchdowns — a 57-yarder to Dave Moritz, and two to Ronnie Harmon of 18 and 8 yards. Iowa led, 21-7, at halftime.

Hawkeyes surprised him on a few things.

"Iowa did a heck of a job," Majors said. "They execute very well, especially in the first half. Sure, we made mistakes, but Iowa is very strong. I'm not surprised Iowa passed on us that much, but their quarterback did a good job of throwing, especially on that deep one for their first touchdown."

You see, Iowa came into this contest with the reputation of being a run-oriented pass-when-you-got-to type of team that would stick to the ground as much as General William Tecumseth Sherman's armies did in the battle of Atlanta in 1864.

Sherman didn't have an air arm to match that of Long's. The Hawkeye sophomore completed his first 11 passes to break his own school record of nine in a row set against Northwestern earlier in 1982. He ended up 19-for-26 for a Peach Bowl-record 304 yards and three touchdowns — a 57 yard thing-of-beauty to Mortiz and two to freshman Ronnie Harmon of 18 and 8 yards.

That gave Iowa a 21-7 halftime lead. After Tennessee pulled to 21-13, the Hawkeyes got their only land-based score. Eddie Phillips, who returned to action after recovering from a knee injury, scored what proved the clincher on a 2-yard burst with 8:29 to go in the third quarter. Phillips gained 34 yards in 10 carries, finishing second to starter Owen Gill, who had 70 yards in 16 trips. Gill also caught three passes for 39 yards to expand his offensive role.

Iowa's Fry admitted he had been worried about the speed of this Volunteer team, especially their wide receivers headed by "the world's fastest football player," Willie Gault.

It would be wrong to say Gault was a goat, but those thousands of Tennessee fans waving orange pompons couldn't understand why whizzing Willie caught only one pass all afternoon — the 19-yarder for his team's final touchdown. He did return four kickoffs, but the swarming Hawkeyes limited him to a total of 60 yards on them. His longest was a mere 23 yards.

And Reggie Roby, who lost the punting duel to Tennessee's

Jimmy Colquitt, saw to it that Willie didn't get to run back a single punt. True, it cost Roby some precious yardage, but he kicked out of bounds for the team's sake. He showed what he could do on the final one, and Tennessee's Majors admitted it might have been the key to the game. Roby sailed the ball 52 yards and it went out of bounds on the Tennessee 35 with 1:56 to play.

Tennessee struck first and Iowa frittered away two possessions on the Volunteers' 31- and 34-yard lines. It seemed like the Rose Bowl revisited at that stage, especially when Gill fumbled on first down at the 50. Tennessee moved, going 36 yards on Chuck Coleman's stunning reverse. Cockrell then sped the final 6 yards on a quarterback option, a play that was to backfire late in the fourth quarter.

The Hawkeyes got the next three touchdowns on Long's passing. Coleman whittled the gap to 21-13 on a 10-yard run, but then Iowa's Nate Creer came through with an unexpected play. Fuad Reveiz, who had kicked 20 straight extra points this season, got a low snap from center, and Creer rushed in to block it.

Gault's touchdown left Iowa's lead at 28-19, and this time Cockrell's pass for two points went over the end zone.

Reveiz, one of the nation's most feared field-goal kickers, finally got his chance with 10:05 left in the final quarter. He kicked a 27-yarder: 28-22, and you could hear the 20,000 Iowans sucking in their breath and figuring what another Vol-

unteer touchdown would do.

Then the old defense took over for the Hawkeyes. Tennessee got the ball twice more, and the finish was one of the most exciting in Peach Bowl history.

Cockrell, who broke the Peach Bowl record with 22 completions, led his team to Iowa's 6-yard line. It was fourth down and 1 yard. Everyone expected to see fullback Dough Furnas high-diving for the first down, as he had done on three previous occasions in the second half.

Tennessee's strategy board might have outsmarted itself. Cockrell was told to work the quarterback option instead. Iowa's James Erb came shooting into the gap, grabbed Cockrell by the by shirt and threw him down at least 1-yard short. The clock showed 3:29 at that point, and Iowa couldn't gain. Even after Roby's splendid punt, Tennessee had one last gasp. But Mount Vernon's Paul Hufford belted Cockrell lose from the ball on third down, leaving Tennessee with a fourth-and-25 situation. This time it was Joseph, a senior from Newton, who came storming in to sack Cockrell the final time.

The Peach Bowl people were still adding up records tied or broken in the darkness of the stadium press box, and at last count they reached a figure of 18.

Meanwhile, the horde of happy Hawkeye fans moved from the stadium parking lots to downtown Atlanta to greet the new year in hilarious style. Even General Sherman's soldiers never felt this good.

"It was just a super game. I have never seen a defense rise up on the goal line and sack the quarterback like that. We were very tough when we had to be."

Coach Hayden Fry

Iowa Out-powers

Penn State

By Don Doxsie, The Gazette

About 84,628 football fans got their money's worth here Saturday afternoon. And then some.

Oh sure, many of them no doubt went home pouting, frustrated that their Penn State Nittany Lions had gone down to a 42-34 defeat at the hands of the 13th-ranked Iowa Hawkeyes.

But they'd also seen a game that featured more twists and turns and thrills and offense (with a capital O) than almost any game anyone could remember.

"They'll be talking about this one for a long, long time," said Iowa Coach Hayden Fry, who was almost whimsical after handing the defending national champions their third straight loss.

SCORE BY QUARTERS						
University Park, Pa., Sept. 17, 1983						
IOWA	14	0	21	7	—	42
PENN STATE	7	14	7	6	—	34

"This has got to be one of the longest football games in history. And it's probably one of the most exciting and best games ever played, too."

Among other things, the game proved Iowa quarterback Chuck Long really can throw long, that Iowa's offensive explosion against Iowa State last week was no fluke, that Penn State does indeed has an offense of its own, and that the Hawkeyes, heading into next week's Big Ten clash with Ohio State, really do rate among the nation's elite teams.

"We executed when we had to to win the game," said Fry, "but it wasn't pretty as far as our defense is concerned. They (the Lions) really executed against us. They picked us like chickens."

The Iowa defense wasn't the only one that went afoul, though.

Iowa running back Owen Gill (33) got his fifth touchdown of the season on a 4-yard run in the first quarter to give the Hawkeyes a 14-7 lead. The touchdown capped a 72-yard drive.

"It was the poorest tackling by a team that I've ever been associated with. In a lot of ways it was a good football game. In spots we just didn't make the plays we should make."

Penn State Coach Joe Paterno

"It was the poorest tackling by a team that I've ever been associated with," said Penn State Coach Joe Paterno. "In a lot of ways it was a good football game. In spots we just didn't make the plays we should make."

You could play the numbers game with this one all day.

Iowa rolled up 587 yards, the sixth-highest figure in its history, and probably will lead the nation this week in total offense (561 yards per game) and scoring (46.5 points per game).

Long set Iowa and Beaver Stadium records with his 345 yards passing. The 599 yards in the air by both teams and 1,079 total yards are also stadium standards. Add to that the 254 yards passing by Penn State's Doug Strang, 131 yards rushing by Iowa's Owen Gill, 104 yards by Lions freshman D. J. Dozier and 119 yards receiving by Hawkeye Dave Moritz, and you begin to get some idea of what kind of game it was.

Yet it was a trio of third-quarter fumble recoveries by the Iowa defense which ultimately turned the tide in the Hawks' favor.

The Nittany Lions had a 28-21 lead and the football midway through the quarter when a Hawkeye gang tack-

le jarred loose the second of the fumbles from Dozier. Paul Hufford fell on it and the Hawks then turned to the tactic which played a major role in their last three touchdowns: The long (or Long) pass.

After Hufford's recovery, Moritz beat Lion cornerback Mark Fruehan down the middle, making a lunging grab for a 46-yard gain. Long carried it into the end zone from 5-yards out and Tom Nichol's extra-point kick made it 28-28.

In a turnaround typical of the day, Penn State charged back downfield, moving to the Iowa 21 before the defense put in another appearance.

Tackle George Little, a Pennsylvania native, roared into the backfield and leveled Strang and popped the ball onto the turf, where linebacker Mike Yacullo retrieved it.

Again, the Hawks struck swiftly and efficiently. Long hit Gill up the right sideline for a 38-yard gain and Norm Granger split the Penn State defense on a perfectly executed trap play, juking out two defenders while going 23 yards for the go-ahead TD.

The Hawks produced one more bomb with about eight minutes remaining in the game. On the first play after a Lions punt, Long fired to Ronnie Harmon streaking down the left side.

Harmon leaped for the underthrown toss, snared it over the top of Fruehan, spun in the air, landed and sprinted the last 35 yards into the end zone.

The 77-yard play was the longest Iowa pass completion since 1973.

"Their cornerbacks were playing real tight," Long said. "We kept looking for that play and looking for it all day and finally got it. Ronnie made a great catch."

The Lions, down, 42-28, still didn't quit. Strang drove them 72 yards in nine plays with Skeeter Nichols scoring from 7-yards out with 5:37 to go. Strang's pass for the two-point conversion was dropped by normally reliable Kenny Jackson.

It turned out to be Penn State's final gasp.

The first half had a comparable number of momentum shifts plus a little controversy. The way things started out, it looked like the Hawks might fare about as well against the Lions as the Christians of ancient Rome.

Long was called for intentional grounding on the first play, backing Iowa up to its 4-yard line. Fry elected to use a quick kick on third down (Tom Grogan doing the booting) in an attempt to get out of the hole, but the Lions got the ball at the

Iowa's Owen Gill (33) raced past Penn State for 131 yards and one touchdown. The Hawkeyes gained 587 total yards, the sixth-highest total in school history. Quarterback Chuck Long set an Iowa record with 345 yards passing.

Iowa 33. Strang threw a 9-yard scoring pass to Dean DiMidio five plays later.

The Hawks didn't bat an eye. They marched 80 yards back the other way, chewing up half that distance on an impromptu scrambling 40-yard completion to Moritz. Eddie Phillips plunged into the end zone from 1-yard out.

The Hawks stampeded 72 yards to make it 14-7 the next time they had the ball, Gill notching his fifth TD of the season on a 4-yard run.

At one point early in the second quarter, the Hawks had accumulated 227 yards to 54 for the home squad.

But nothing stayed the same for very long in this game. After being pinned back at their own 11 by a punt. Penn State launched perhaps its best drive of the game, rolling 89 yards in 14 plays. Strang threw to a diving Jackson in the corner of the end zone for the score.

A controversial fumble by Long plus an unsportsmanlike conduct penalty against Fry for protesting the call set up the third Penn State TD late in the half. Strang capped the 33-yard drive with a 1-yard sneak, making it 21-13.

The Hawks opened the second half by recovering the first of the three fumbles. Long evaded a heavy rush to sling a sidearm, 26-yard TD pass to Phillips moments later, creating a 21-21 deadlock.

Penn State bounced back with a 57-yard dash by Dozier, setting up an 18-yard Strang-to-Kevin Baugh TD pass which made it 28-21.

"Penn State just played a tremendous game," said Fry, whose team will take an 2-0 record into its home opener against Ohio State.

"That just makes our victory that much more valuable because we beat a great team that played very well."

Iowa goes Long way to rip Texas in Freedom Bowl

By Mark Dukes, The Gazette

TEXAS	0	17	0	0	—	17
IOWA	14	10	31	0	—	55

T
ake that, Texas!

Iowa's offense sizzled in the Southern California drizzle Wednesday night as the Hawkeyes rolled to a record-breaking 55-17 rout of Texas in the first Freedom Bowl.

Quarterback Chuck Long, perhaps playing his final football game for Iowa, led the onslaught with school passing records of 29 completions, 461 yards and six touchdowns. His scoring passes also tied the Big Ten record set by Illinois' Dave Wilson in 1980.

Long was a landslide winner of the game's most valuable player award. The 6-foot-4 junior helped Iowa deal the Longhorns their worst loss in 80 years. The University of Chicago beat Texas, 68-0, in 1904.

The victory was a most satisfying one for a native Texan named Hayden Fry. The Iowa coach had a 2-1 career record against Texas. It also was Fry's fourth straight season of eight victories or more, as the Hawkeyes finished 8-4-1.

Chuck Long broke Iowa records for completions (29), passing yards (461) and touchdown passes (six). "It wasn't easy because it was a great challenge to throw against Texas," he said.

"This is definitely the biggest win of my career," Fry said. "Being from Texas, you don't get the chance to beat the U of T very often. I have never had a victory more meaningful to me.

"It was a great victory and one that the coaching staff, especially myself, wanted very badly. We never dreamed we could throw that well on them, let alone score 55 points."

It was Texas' worst loss under Coach Fred Akers and the most lopsided Longhorn setback since losing to Oklahoma, 52-13, in 1973. Akers is 2-6 in bowl games.

"Iowa did a great job, as perfect as I've seen," Akers said "Chuck Long was everything we saw on film, and more."

A meager crowd of 24,093 weathered the game-long rain at the Big A and was rewarded with an unexpected offensive show.

The game had been regarded as a tossup, mostly because of the two top-20 defenses. But it became an offensive bonanza for Iowa very early.

Iowa, scoring the most points ever in six bowl appearances, padded a 24-17 lead with 31 points in the third quarter. Four of Long's scoring passes occurred in the third quarter alone.

Long, who has yet to announce his decision on returning to Iowa or turning pro, used five different receivers for his six scoring passes: Jonathan Hayes (twice), Mike Flagg, Bill Happel, Robert Smith and Scott Helverson.

The previous Iowa record was five TD passes by Fred Riddle against Indiana in 1963. Long also broke the completion mark of 26 set by Mike Cilek in 1967 and bettered his single-game yardage total of 420 set last year at Northwestern.

Asked if it was his best game at Iowa, Long replied, "Oh, yeah., it must have been. It wasn't easy because it was a great challenge to throw against Texas. But they used so much man- to-man coverage that we caught 'em."

The weather conditions and performances by Long and the Iowa team were similar to the Hawkeyes' 40-3 win at Purdue on Oct. 13. Despite a steady rain that day in West Lafayette, Ind., Long completed 17 of 21 passes for 369 yards and four touchdowns against man-to-man coverage.

The Iowa offense rolled up 560 total yards and 28 first downs against the Longhorns.

Texas, which finished 7-4-1, had just 300 total yards.

Long played nearly the entire game, but Fry had an explanation.

"We had put Long back in (the fourth quarter) because the backup broke his finger," said Fry, referring to second-string quarterback Mark Vlasic. "Fred Akers is a great man and a great coach and I apologize for the score being too high."

Long missed his first three pass attempts of the first half, but then caught fire. He completed his last nine passes and 14 of his last 15 attempts, sparking Iowa to a seven-point lead at intermission.

Texas, which had 46 turnovers during the regular season, gave up the ball twice in its first six plays and had five turnovers for the game.

On the Longhorns' sixth play, Mike Stoops gave Iowa brilliant field position when he snared his third interception of the season. He darted in front of receiver Rob Moerschell and picked off Todd Dodge's pass, returning the ball 18 yards to the Texas 19.

Iowa caught Texas off guard by scoring 31 points in the third quarter. The Hawkeyes totaled 560 yards and 28 first downs against the Longhorns.

A first-down draw play with Owen Gill gained 13 yards. Two plays later, Long found a wide-open Hayes in the end zone for a 6-yard scoring pass.

The Hawkeyes increased their lead to 14-0 when Long tossed an 11-yard touchdown pass to Flagg, a Cedar Falls freshman. A 41-yard reception by Flagg on third-and-3 set up the score.

Texas finally got its offense untracked on its next possession, driving 80 yards in 12 plays. Bill Boy Bryant made a diving catch of Dodge's pass in the front corner of the end zone. Jeff Ward's kick reduced Iowa's lead to 14-7 with 13:35 left in the half.

The Longhorn drive didn't faze Iowa's offense, though, as it drove 77 yards in 10 plays for another touchdown. Fred Bush scored the first touchdown of his career, blasting in from 1-yard out with 10:14 left in the half.

Long was 4 of 5 during the drive for 66 yards, including a 29-yarder to Helverson that put Iowa in Texas territory.

The seesaw scoring continued, as Texas rambled 80 yards in 11 plays. The Longhorns cut the lead to 21-13 when Dodge hit tight end William Harris on a fourth-down, 1-yard TD pass.

A big play in their drive was a 28-yard pass from Dodge to Bryant when Iowa had the Longhorns facing a third-and-17.

Texas, recovering a fumbled Iowa snap at the Hawkeye 27, tightened the game even more when Ward drilled a 46-yard field goal with 2:23 left in the half.

Ward had missed a 51-yard try to the left on the previous play, but Iowa's Keith Hunter was whistled for roughing.

Iowa extended its lead when Tom Nichol hit a 27-yard field goal on the last play of the half.

The Hawkeye offense continued to click in the third period, gaining a whopping 301 yards on just 23 plays.

Iowa was whistled for clipping on the second-half kickoff, but that was merely a temporary setback. Long rifled a first-down pass to Hayes over the middle and the talented tight end turned it into a 49-yard gain, rambling to the Texas 39.

Long hit Happel for a 10-yard gainer and a face mask penalty on Texas tacked on another 5, putting Iowa at the Longhorn 24.

Long's string of consecutive completions ended at 11 and the Hawkeyes settled for a 35-yard Nichol field goal.

On Texas' second play after the kickoff, linebacker Larry Station stripped the ball from Jerome Johnson and nose guard Hap Peterson recovered for Iowa at the Longhorn 33.

Long seized the opportunity immediately, lofting a beautiful 33-yard scoring pass to Happel. The Cedar Rapids junior roared past Tony Griffin at the line of scrimmage,

raced down the sideline and gathered in Long's toss in the end zone.

The rout was on.

Smith, the speedster from Dallas, was the next beneficiary of Long's arm. Smith leaped over the shoulder of cornerback James Lott and waltzed into the end zone. The 49-yard scoring pass and Nichol's kick put Iowa in front 41-17.

Long tied Riddle's record at the 4:53 mark of the third period, hitting Helverson on a 4-yard scoring strike to make it 48-17.

Jeff Drost's recovery of a Terry Orr fumble at the Iowa 35 stopped a Longhorn threat.

Smith's 31-yard pass reception put Iowa at the Texas 23. Long followed with an 8-yarder to Happel and a 15-yarder to Hayes, the latter breaking Riddle's record. With 2:19 still left in the third period, the scoring was completed.

Happel was Iowa's leading receiver with eight catches for 104 yards. Smith had four receptions for 115 yards, Flagg five for 71, Hayes three for 70 and Helverson four for 66.

Iowa consistently opened holes big enough to drive a truck through. The Hawkeyes handed Texas its worst loss since a 68-0 defeat to the University of Chicago in 1904.

Long's Great Fake Fo

ols State, Lifts Hawks

By Mike Hlas, The Gazette

Great quarterback. Hell of a football game. The Iowa Hawkeyes allowed 31 points and 580 yards of total offense. They might have coughed up their No. 1 national ranking. Were they downcast after a hard-earned victory over unheralded Michigan State on Saturday afternoon? No.

They were euphoric.

Chuck Long's 2-yard touchdown run with 27 seconds left gave Iowa a 35-31 victory over the Spartans before 66,044 screaming fans at Kinnick Stadium. A national-television audience saw more twists and turns than in 40 miles of bad road, but the final twist turned a very possible Hawkeye loss into victory.

SCORE BY QUARTERS					
Iowa City, Oct. 5, 1985					
MICHIGAN STATE	0	10	14	7 —	31
IOWA	7	6	15	7 —	35

Iowa had a third-and-1 at the MSU 2-yard line with 31 seconds left in the game and the Spartans ahead, 31-28. Long faked a handoff to Ronnie Harmon, and almost everyone in Johnson County bought the fake as Harmon tried to leap through the line.

But Long still had the ball.

He sprinted around the right end with absolutely no one breathing down his neck, danced into the right corner of the end zone and hugged a teammate or two.

Tight end Mike Flagg (86) caught two of the four touchdowns thrown by Chuck Long, who completed 30 of 39 passes for 380 yards. The 30 completions broke a school record, held by Long.

"That might have been the greatest fake of all time in college football," Iowa Coach Hayden Fry said. "I believe I could have scored on that one, and I'm really slow.

"Chuck's not all that fast. I noticed he hoisted the ball over his head at the 3- or 4-yard line, and I was about to have a heart attack."

Had Long not scored on the play, Iowa would have been confronted with a fourth down and no time-outs remaining.

"I probably shouldn't say this," Fry said, "but we already called the next play. We were going to put our field-goal players on the field and fake it instead of going for the tie. Thank gosh we didn't have to.

"We were going for it all the way. I didn't want a tie in our first game in the Big Ten."

"It was a gutsy call by Coach Fry because I either had to get in (the end zone) or get out of bounds," Long said.

But that's neither here nor there. Iowa is 4-0 and in a five-way tie for the Big Ten lead with a 1-0 mark. Michigan State is 2-2.

"I think today our team learned a lesson about life," Fry said. "If you keep the faith, hang in there and keep executing, you'll be real successful. It's something you can't learn in a textbook."

Iowa's victory was a bit of a payback for the Spartans' 17-16 win at Kinnick last fall that virtually knocked the Hawks out of the Rose Bowl.

"Certainly we hadn't forgot about that," said Fry.

Long's touchdown run capped a 12-play, 79-yard drive that began with 4:01 left. He completed six of seven passes to get the Hawks to the MSU 11. Harmon then ran 7 yards off tackle to the 4. Harmon ran around the end for 2 more, but couldn't get out of bounds, so Iowa spent its last time-out. Then Long scored.

Michigan State returned Marv Cook's kickoff to its 38 with 20 seconds left. Two plays gained 23 yards. But on the finale, Iowa safety Devon Mitchell tipped a Bobby McAllister pass away from flanker Mark Ingram in the end zone, and the deed was done.

Iowa's offense didn't wait for the game's close to make hay. Long completed 30 of 39 passes for four touchdowns and 380 yards. The 30 completions improved his school record by one. He was 29-of-39 against Texas in last December's Freedom Bowl.

A packed crowd at Kinnick Stadium watches Iowa rally from a 31-28 deficit to defeat Michigan State and improve to 4-0 overall. It was the Big Ten opener for the Hawkeyes.

Hawkeye receiver Scott Helverson grabbed nine of Long's throws for 102 yards. Tight end Mike Flagg and Robert Smith caught two touchdowns apiece.

The individual glory was shared by the two teams. MSU sophomore tailback Lorenzo White was brilliant. White didn't carry the ball in the game's last nine minutes, but still managed 39 rushes for 226 yards and two touchdowns.

White left the field with an ankle injury after a 16-yard run to start the fourth-quarter. He came back for one more rush on MSU's last possession, then yielded to freshman Craig Johnson.

"That might have been the greatest fake of all time in college football. I believe I could have scored on that one, and I'm really slow."

Coach Hayden Fry

"Bobby did a better job and that allowed our running game to work so well." Iowa's defense opened the day leading the nation in total defense (154.3 yards a game) and rushing defense (17.7 yards).

Kiss those babies goodbye.

Michigan State had 25 plays in which they gained 10 or more yards. Nine of those were carries by White, 11 were McAllister completions.

"Obviously, our defense didn't play too well," Fry said. "They (the Spartans) all did a great job. They hadn't shown hardly any of those things they did out there, and we had to adjust during the game. They did something we hadn't prepared for. They had a great game plan and executed extremely well.

"And obviously some of our players didn't tackle too well."

"They were mentally prepared for us," Iowa defensive tackle Jon Vrieze said. "It seemed like they knew the defense we were in before they ever snapped the ball.

"Lorenzo is such a good back. I can't say enough about him."

The game had the early appearance of a fourth consecutive Iowa romp. Long fired a 60-yard touchdown strike down the right sideline to a streaking Smith for a 7-0 lead five minute into the game.

Flagg carried half the MSU defense into the end zone with him on a 17-yard reception that made it 13-0.

Johnson was a day at the beach for a weary Iowa defense. He toted the ball eight times on that final drive, including a 25-yard touchdown run that put the Spartans ahead. Johnson had 89 yards in 10 attempts.

If Michigan State's 305 yards of rushing weren't enough, how about almost the same amount in passing?

Spartan quarterback McAllister, a red-shirt freshman, wasn't supposed to do harm with his arm In two previous starts in place of injure Dave Yarema, McAllister completed only 10 of 32 passes for 99 yards. MSU beat Western Michigan the week before by the measly score of 7-3.

Saturday, McAllister was 18 of 27 for 275 yards and no interceptions. He ran the Michigan State offense masterfully.

"We felt coming into the game that we could run," MSU Coach George Perles said.

Houghtlin's Prayer Answered as Late FG Dooms U-M

Iowa quarterback Chuck Long completed 26 of 39 passes for 297 yards, bolstering his chances for the Heisman Trophy.

By Gus Schrader, The Gazette

In all the classic fang-and-claw struggles between No. 1 and No. 2 in college football, there might never have been a more dramatic finish than Iowa's 12-10 victory over Michigan on Saturday.

Thousands of delirious fans from the Kinnick Stadium record crowd of 55,350 poured onto the field after Rob Houghtlin's 29-yard field goal split the uprights on the final play.

And what was Houghtlin thinking as he knelt over the kicking tee before the fate-filled kick?

"I was praying," the slender junior from Glenview, Ill., replied. "I was praying to the Lord, asking for a little strength and direction."

As soon as Houghtlin's kick was in the air, he and his holder, Mark Vlasic, leaped with arms raised, pre-empting the call by the officials.

SCORE BY QUARTERS					
Iowa City, Oct. 19, 1985					
MICHIGAN	0	7	0	3 —	10
IOWA	0	6	0	6 —	12

And what was Coach Hayden Fry's first reaction"

"Praise the Lord!" the Iowa mentor told the CBS interviewer after he and Michigan's Bo Schembechler exchanged kind words at midfield. Before shaking hands with Fry, Schembechler looked at Iowa running back Ronnie Harmon and congratulated him. Harmon put an affectionate arm around the Wolverine coach.

Then the landslide of Iowa fans onto the field became an avalanche. A little later, some of the more rambunctious ones succeeded in tearing down the north goal posts, through which the last two of Houghtlin's four successful field goals had passed.

Michigan's vaunted defense, which still has given up only one touchdown in six games and led the nation by allowing its first five foes an average of 4.2 points a game, did succeed in holding Chuck Long without a touchdown pass.

But Long feathered his nest with the Heisman Trophy voters by completing 26 of 39 passes for 297 yards and one interception. Bill Happel caught nine of them for the second time this season.

"Long is a magnificent quarterback," said Schembechler after recovering from his near-apoplexy demonstrations on the sideline. "If it were just Long or just Harmon, we could handle either of them. But with both in there, it's just about impossible."

Harmon dented Michigan's reputation of being so tough against the run by gaining 120 yards in 32 darts, dashes and divergent dipsy-dos. He also hauled in six of Long's passes for 72 yards.

Scott Helverson came up with five grabs for 60 yards. Most of the crowd and undoubtedly many of the millions watching on CBS nearly nationwide TV audience thought another of Helverson's remarkable catches should have counted, that one for a touchdown. It might have made the Hawkeyes' victory easier, and not so dramatic.

Get this: Iowa ran 84 rushing and passing plays to Michigan's 41. The Hawkeyes won the yardage battle, 422-182. And they had ball possession 38:05 to Michigan's 21:55.

After a scoreless first quarter, Iowa was on the march with its first possession in the second period. With Long launching and Harmon harpooning, the Hawks penetrated to the Michigan 18. On third down, Long scrambled away from Michigan's tacklers and hurried the ball deep into the end zone.

Helverson leaped above Michigan's highly regarded defenders, caught the ball and fell to the sneaking artificial surface. An official finally ruled the catch no good, indicating they thought Helverson had landed on the line before touching either foot inbounds.

"I don't think I had one foot inbounds," Helverson said later. "I was sure I had my whole body inbounds."

CBS-TV instant replays made the official ruling look wrong, but it stood. So Houghtlin was summoned to kick a 35-yard field goal and Iowa was on the board first, 3-0.

The Hawkeyes tried a new kickoff man, Mike Kennon, a junior from Stanton, Iowa., who had never appeared in a college game before. Kennon's kickoff was taken by Michigan's Tom Wilcher on the 8-yard line and returned 60 yards.

The Wolverines proceeded to score the games' only TD, but it also was marred by controversy. Michigan quarterback Jim Harbaugh several times asked for and received permission from referee Jerry Hendrickson to walk away from his center and halt the 25-second count because of "excessive crowd noise."

On third-and-goal from Iowa's 5, Harbaugh scrambled away from pursuit and shoveled a little pass to his fullback, Gerald White, who scored. Mike Gillette, one of Michigan's two barefoot kickers, booted the extra point to make it 7-3.

That score held up until the final play of the half. Again, Iowa probed deep into Michigan territory but came up dry on touchdowns. So Houghtlin kicked a 27-yard field goal.

The third quarter also was scoreless, but Iowa inched ahead, 9-7, with 14:20 to play on Houghtlin's third three-pointer. This was a 36-yarder and gave him 10 in a row over five games.

Again, Iowa's kickoff game proved shaky, as White returned Kennon's short boot 17 yards to his 37. With Bob Perryman running for 17 yards and Jamie Morris for 24, the Wolverines reached the Iowa 23.

On fourth down, Gillette kicked a 40-yard field goal to put Michigan on top, 10-9, with 10:55 to go.

Now it was the Hawkeye defense's turn to bare its teeth. Richard Pryor and Hap Peterson tackled Morris and Per-

Wild scene follows Fry's biggest victory

By Mark Dukes, The Gazette

Moments after Rob Houghtlin's memorable kick sailed neatly through the uprights Saturday, the floor of Kinnick Stadium felt electric as hundreds of stampeding fans celebrated the close of a classic football game.

The wet turf was artificial and the lighting was artificial, but the fan reaction was very real.

It was spontaneous reaction by emotionally spent fans, energized one last time by the dramatic ending.

Near the tunnel leading to the Iowa locker room, Iowa defensive back Jay Norvell was crying, hugging everyone in sight. Offensive guard Bob Kratch also had wet eyes, happy eyes, as he made his way through the mob of fans.

From sideline to sideline, hundreds of yellow Styrofoam hands — index fingers extended — were thrust in the air as the band played In Heaven, There is No Beer.

Fans remained on the field or in the stands several minutes after Iowa's 12-10 win over Michigan. Governor Terry Branstad was ushered to the Iowa locker room without much commotion, but Hayden Fry was escorted off the field by three state troopers, who threw elbows at will just to clear a path for the coach.

It was an extraordinary scene following an extraordinary game.

"The locker room was bananas," Iowa quarterback Chuck Long said. "It was maybe the loudest, rowdiest locker room since I've been here."

Added wide receiver Scott Helverson, "I've never seen so much hugging and kissing in all my life."

Fry brought his coordinators, Bill Snyder (offense) and Bill Brashier (defense), to the jam-packed postgame interview session to be questioned. But Fry, who said he hadn't voted Iowa No. 1 in previous weeks, quickly got into the discussion.

Asked if it was his greatest victory at Iowa, Fry said, "I don't even have to think about that. Yes, it is. In fact, I'm going to vote us No. 1 tomorrow. It's super great!

"I told (Michigan Coach) Bo Schembechler before the game that the only thing bad about this game was that one of us had to lose. After the game, I told him he had a great team. He said 'you have the greatest.' Bo even gave me a pack of chewing gum. I think I'll frame it."

The final drive to victory — from the Iowa 22-yard line to Michigan's 12 — was reminiscent of the Hawkeyes' come-from-behind, 35-31 triumph over Michigan State

ryman, respectively, for 4-yard gains. On third-and-two, All-America Larry Station knifed through and nailed Morris for a 2-yard loss. It was his ninth tackle of the day. Fellow linebacker George Davis was credited with 10.

Happel fielded Monte Robbins' 45-yard punt with a fair catch on the Iowa 22, and the tense offense began again with 5:27 to play. Same script: Long and Harmon, Harmon and Long. Twice Long converted on third down by passing to Mike Flagg. Another hairy third-down situation arose at the Michigan 22, but David Hudson solved it neatly with a 6-yard run.

All eyes were on the clock as Harmon slashed through for 4 yards to the Michigan 12.

two weeks earlier. In that one, Long scored the clinching touchdown with 27 seconds remaining.

"I had the exact feeling I had in the Michigan State game during the last drive," said Iowa offensive tackle Mike Haight. "I just felt deep down that we were going to win.

"In the huddle before Rob's kick, we were telling each other to block like crazy because Michigan would be coming 100 miles an hour. There must have been a pile-up four feet high. I looked up just as the ball was going through the uprights and my knees felt weak."

Houghtlin admitted he was nervous before the kick. Iowa's time-out with two seconds left was followed by one charged to Michigan.

Larry Station (36) and Iowa recorded thrilling victories against the University of Michigan and Michigan State.

Fry instructed the Hawkeyes to call their final time-out, and they did it with two seconds showing, almost causing heart failure for thousands.

Houghtlin went onto the field to set up his tee, but Fry called him over to the sideline to quiet his nerves. When the teams lined up again, Michigan did the expected and called another time-out.

"Yes, I was nervous," Houghtlin said. "However, as soon as I hit it, I knew it was good I had the feeling we would score a touchdown on our final drive, but after the clock got down to the final minute I knew it was going to come around to my kick attempt."

"Yeah, I was nervous," Houghtlin admitted. "I knew I hit it good but I don't remember it.

"I thought we were going to score a touchdown. We'd been close all day and I really thought we were going to score. But with a minute, 24 seconds left, I had an itchy feeling It'd come down to a kick without much time left.

"Coach Fry asked me if we were close enough and I said, 'Yes.' Coach called me back over tot he sideline after Michigan took time-out and said just what he says every time: 'Concentrate and hit it straight.' "

Iowa trailed, 7-6, at halftime, but many felt the Hawkeyes were denied a touchdown before Houghtlin put Iowa ahead, 3-0, with a 35-yard field goal. Helverson caught a pass from Long deep in the end zone, but officials said he was out of bounds. Television replays clearly showed he had one foot in bounds.

"I was screaming at the official, "Whattaya mean I'm not in," Helverson explained. "I just assumed he (the official) was out of position. That's the first time I was robbed like that. It hurt, because I felt I had one taken away last week by the goal post." Helverson dropped a ball in the end zone last week at Wisconsin when he ran into the goal post.

Iowa gained 422 yards on a Michigan defense that was allowing only 220 per game. Long completed 26 of 39 passes for 297 yards.

Hawkeyes Take Fight Out of Illini With 59-0 Rout

By Mark Dukes, The Gazette

....

SCORE BY QUARTERS
Iowa City, No. 9, 1985

ILLINOIS	0	0	0	—	0
IOWA	35	14	0	10	—	59

This was one skunk that smelled awfully sweet. Iowa rebounded from last week's "embarrassing" loss to Ohio State with a thorough White-washing of Illinois, 59-0, allowing the Hawkeyes to retain a share of the Big Ten Conference football lead.

The sixth-ranked Hawkeyes roared to a 35-0 lead after 15 minutes, upped it to 49-0 at halftime and coasted to their eighth victory in nine games. Iowa, which plays at Purdue on Saturday, is a 5-1 in the Big Ten and tied for first with Ohio State.

Iowa was favored to win this 50th meeting in the series, but no one expected such a rout.

A crowd of 66,120 saw 13 school, Big Ten or stadium records set. It was Iowa's most lopsided victory over Illinois, topping the 58-0 win in 1899. It also marked the first time a Mike White-coached Illini team had been shut out since he arrived in Champaign in 1980, and the first time Illinois had been shut out in 80 games.

"To shut them out and score 59 points you just don't see that happening that often," a delighted Iowa Coach Hayden Fry said. "Whether we're that good or Illinois was off, I

don't know. This probably wouldn't happen again in 100 contests with them. To do what we did was phenomenal.

"We were embarrassed on national TV last week at Ohio State and knocked out of No. 1. You have to realize that we've got a lot of pride. We may have lost one of the battles, but we're not going to lose the war.

"Like I told our president, Dr. (James) Freedman, this is something you can't learn in a textbook. We were tested in front of the public eye to see if we could come back. You have to experience that in combat."

Bowl scouts lined up to congratulate Fry after the game. Orange Bowl officials met him in the tunnel after the game, then scouts from the Sugar, Cotton and Fiesta greeted him later.

Illinois, 4-4-1 overall and 3-2-1 in the league, previously posted a win over Ohio State and a tie with Michigan. But on this day, the Illini were out of it shortly after the opening kickoff. Iowa's 49-point half shattered the school record, which lasted only a short time. The Hawkeyes scored 44 in the second half against Drake in the season opener.

"There's not a lot to say," White said. "We got beat in every phase of the game. Iowa certainly bounced back from their loss last week. We'd like to have an explanation, but we certainly don't offer any excuses. We disappointed ourselves and we disappointed our fans. We're very unhappy."

Heroes were numerous on the Iowa side.

Chuck Long: The Iowa quarterback threw four interceptions in last week's loss to Ohio State, but rebounded with a brilliant performance; 22 completions in 30 attempts, 289 yards and four touchdowns. He had 256 of his yards and all four TD passes in the first half.

Asked if it put Long back into the thick of the Heisman Trophy hunt, Fry responded, "I don't think he was ever out of it."

Long, who didn't play the final 20 minutes, increased his career touchdown passing total to 72, breaking by one the previous record by Purdue's Mark Herrmann. His 25 TD passes this season are school and conference records.

"You can't beat 59-0, especially when it's against Illinois," said Long, whose home is Wheaton, Ill. "It was hard to forget the 33-0 loss we had at Illinois a couple of years ago. The first half was one of the best I've ever played in and one of the best I've ever seen anywhere. You just can't get any better than that."

Robert Smith: The fleet Texan burned Illinois defenders twice in the first 7 ½ minutes, scoring on passes of 49 and 43 yards from Long. He has seven TD receptions this season and 13 for his career, both Iowa records. Jack Dittmer's career record had stood since 1949.

Smith, defensive end George Millett, nose guard Hap Peterson and safety Devon Mitchell all were injured in the first half and did not return. In addition, linebacker Larry Station played only sparingly.

Fullback David Hudson, a freshman from Waxahachie, Tex., rushed for 66 yards and two touchdowns.

BROKEN RECORDS

INDIVIDUAL RECORDS

PATS, GAME
8 by Rob Houghtlin
(ties Marcos Melendez vs. Northwestern, 1968; Tom Nichol vs. Northwestern, 1981; Nichol vs. Iowa State, 1984)
Also tied a Kinnick Stadium record.

TOUCHDOWN PASSES SEASON
25 by Chuck Long (old record 22 by Long in 1984)

TOUCHDOWN RECEPTIONS, SEASON
7 by Robert Smith
(ties Bill Happel's mark, also set this season)

TOUCHDOWN RECEPTIONS, CAREER
13 by Smith (ties Jack Dittmer, 1946-1949).

TEAM RECORDS

PATS, GAME
8 (ties vs. Utah State in 1957, vs. Northwestern in 1968 and 1981, vs. Iowa State in 1984). Also tied a Kinnick Stadium record.

TOUCHDOWN PASSES, SEASON
28 (23 in 1984).

BIG TEN RECORDS

TOUCHDOWN PASSES, SEASON
25 by Long
(23 by Mark Herrmann and Mike Phipps of Purdue).
TOUCHDOWN PASSES, CAREER
72 by Long (71 by Herrmann)

KINNICK STADIUM RECORDS

PASS ATTEMPTS
58 by Illinois (50 by Iowa vs. Purdue in 1964).
PASS COMPLETIONS
30 by Illinois (29 by Northwestern in 1983).
POINTS IN HALF
49 by Iowa (44 by Iowa vs. Drake in 1985).

Robert Smith scored two touchdowns on passes of 49-and 43-yards in the first quarter.

David Hudson: The freshman fullback from Texas rushed for 66 yards and scored two touchdowns. "After last week, we had to play mad," he said. "We took it out on 'em pretty good."

The Iowa defense: The Hawkeyes caused nine Illinois turnovers, including four interceptions of quarterback Jack Trudeau (one each by Jay Norvell, Rick Schmidt, Mitchell and Ken Sims). Trudeau had entered with an NCAA record of 214 passes without an interception and a string of 282 in Big Ten play. But Norvell picked off Trudeau's second attempt early in the first quarter.

The Iowa defenders, led by linebacker George Davis (14 tackles), allowed Illinois only 5 yards rushing. The Illini had minus-7 yards at halftime.

"We wanted to make up for last week," cornerback Nate Creer said. "We read that Trudeau had that NCAA record so we figured we owed it to our offense to break that record.

"We wanted these guys because of the way they act out

"We wanted these guys because of the way they act out there, hot doggin' it."

Cornerback Nate Creer

there, hot-doggin' it."

The game was only three minutes old when Smith whipped Illinois cornerback Todd Avery and gathered in a 49-yard TD pass from Long. Rob Houghtlin kicked the first

of his eight extra points. That total tied school and stadium records.

David Williams, who became the Big Ten career leader in receiving yards (70 yards on 10 receptions broke Anthony Carter's record of 3,076 by 5 yards), was used on a reverse on Illinois' first play. But Williams was tackled 9 yards behind the line of scrimmage, the ball popped loose, and Iowa's Hap Peterson recovered at the Illinois 19-yard line.

A 15-yard Long-to-Happel pass put the Hawkeyes at the 4. Three plays later, Hudson dove into the end zone to give Iowa a 14-0 lead with 10:16 left in the first period.

Norvell picked off his seventh pass of the year three plays after the kickoff, ending Trudeau's streaks. Four plays later, Smith faked Craig Swoope silly and gathered in a 43-yard scoring strike from Long.

The rout was on.

"Whether we're that good or Illinois was off, I don't know," said Iowa Coach Hayden Fry.

Iowa Maintains Its Rosy Outlook, Rallies Past Purdue

By Mark Dukes, The Gazette

I t was the drive that kept everything alive: national-championship dreams, Rose Bowl hopes and Chuck Long's quest for the Heisman Trophy.

Those dreams and hopes and quests hung in the balance in the fourth quarter at Ross-Ade Stadium on Saturday, but Iowa's football team passed the test once again.

In a drive reminiscent of ones constructed in come-from-behind wins over Michigan and Michigan State earlier this year, Long masterfully marched Iowa 64 yards in 12 plays to the winning points. Rob Houghtlin's heroic, 25-yard field goal capped a 5:22 march that gave Iowa a 27-24 Big Ten football triumph.

"It wasn't a great kick but it got the job done," said Houghtlin, whose 29-yarder beat Michigan a month ago, 12-10. "The offense has always come through and it always will."

Iowa began the final drive on its 28-yard line with 6:30 remaining and the score tied, 24-24.

"We all knew what we had to do, just like against Michigan and just like against Michigan State," said offensive tackle Mike Haight. "We'd been in that situation before. It turned out exactly like we wanted."

Freshman fullback David Hudson, who had a career-high 118 yards, gained 5 on first down, but that was lost when Iowa was whistled for illegal motion on the next play.

Hudson then gained 2, setting up third-and-8 at the Hawk-

Rob Houghtlin (7) helped Iowa defeat Purdue with a 25-yard field goal with 1:08 remaining in the game. The field goal capped a 12-play, 64-yard drive that took 5:22 off the clock.

eye 30. Not to worry, though, as Bill Happel, the reliable receiver from Cedar Rapids, gained 10 important yards on a pass from Long.

"It was a 5-yard route but I knew it was third down and I'd have to go upfield," explained Happel, whose second effort got the needed yardage. "When I caught the ball I looked at the first-down marker and knew I needed to go."

Long, who completed 3 of 4 passes for 40 yards during The Drive, connected with Quinn Early for a 15-yard gain to the Purdue 45. Hudson gained 1 on first down and Long threw incomplete on second, setting up third-and-9.

"We knew a tie wouldn't hurt us, but we didn't want a tie," Long said. "A tie is like losing."

This time, Long rifled a pass over the middle to Scott Helverson, whose catch was good for 25 yards to the 29.

"It was a basic 'in pattern' that we should've used more," Helverson said. "I knew it'd be open because we hadn't thrown it all game.

"It was a great time for it. The ball was a little low, but perfect. It was a tough day for upsets and we didn't want to be one, so my only thought was catching the ball and keeping things alive."

The Hawkeyes were within Houghtlin's range at that point, but they were able to expend 2½ more precious minutes off the clock.

Ronnie Harmon who had 122 yards rushing and 118 receiving on a gimpy ankle, bolted 14 yards to the Purdue 15, then ripped off 5 more to the 10. Harmon lost 3 on the next carry, but Hudson rushed for 5 to the 8. Purdue called time-out with 1:11 remaining before Houghtlin's field goal.

"Those were probably the two worst-kicking teams in the country facing each other," Purdue Coach Leon Burtnett said. "But their kid made that kick when he had to. The only thing not good about Iowa is their kicking game."

SCORE BY PERIODS						
West Lafayette, Ind., Nov. 16, 1985						
IOWA	7	17	0	3	—	27
PURDUE	7	10	0	7	—	24

"We knew a tie wouldn't hurt us, but we didn't want a tie. A tie is like losing."

Chuck Long

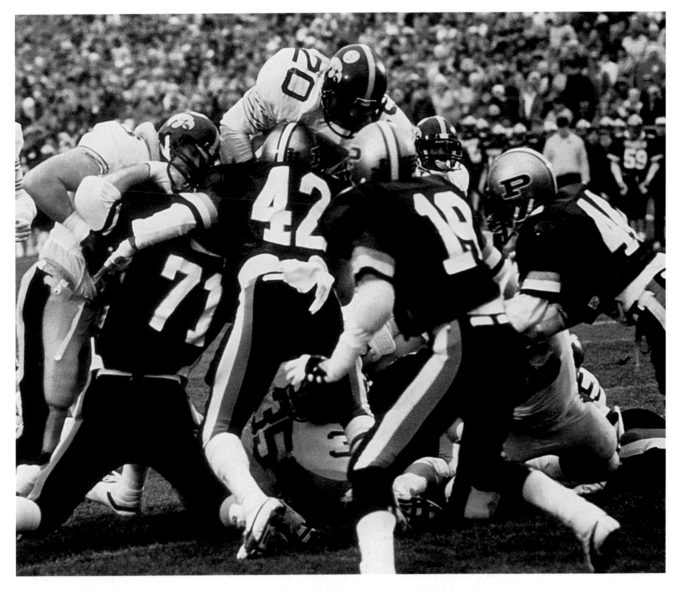

Fullback David Hudson had several key plays on Iowa's winning drive. After Ronnie Harmon gained 16 yards on three carries to the Purdue 13, Hudson rushed 5 yards to the 8 to set up Rob Houghtlin's winning field goal.

Iowa Coach Hayden Fry passed out the praise in equal helpings, saying "Chuck Long played super with some clutch passing, Ronnie Harmon had a great game and the development of David Hudson has to be the most enjoyable thing that's happened. Happel, Helverson and Early all had clutch catches in that drive, too.

"We wanted to win but we knew if we tied we still had a chance to go to the rose Bowl. So I wasn't that interested in scoring. All we wanted to do is run as much of the clock off as possible."

Iowa gained sole possession of first place in the Big Ten because Wisconsin knocked off Ohio State, which previously was tied for the top with the Hawkeyes.

Iowa players learned that Wisconsin defeated Ohio State at halftime. Because the public-address announcer refused to divulge the score until after the game, Iowa fans helped the Hawkeyes with an altered version of "taste great, less filling." They chanted, "Wisconsin 12, Ohio State 7."

"When we came in at halftime, I was nearly afraid to tell the players about Ohio State," Fry said. "I was afraid it was hearsay and I couldn't get anybody to confirm it. That kind of thing could have a good or bad effect. But this is a very mature group, and they didn't show much excitement."

On a CBS telecast to 80 percent of the country, Long at least keep pace with Auburn running back Bo Jackson in the Heisman race. Long completed 20 of 33 passes for 268 yards with one interception and no touchdowns. Jackson had 121 yards and two touchdowns on 19 carries in Auburn's win over Georgia.

"I don't know what Bo did today and I'm not worried about it right now," Long said. "I'll start thinking about the Heisman after the Minnesota game (Saturday)."

Most of the talk here outside the Iowa locker room was not of trying to avenge last year's 21-16 loss, but instead of savoring one more comeback.

"Coach Fry told us that good teams will be tested two or three times during the year and the real good teams will come out on top," Happel said. "I guess we have a pretty good football team."

Fullback David Hudson outraces Purdue defenders Kennedy Wilson (23), Kevin Sumlin (44) and Kevin Roy (46). The victory moved Iowa into sole possession of first place in the Big Ten.

Iowa quarterback Chuck Long kept pace with Auburn's Bo Jackson in the Heisman race. He completed 20 of 33 passes for 268 yards.

CHUCK LONG

Destiny played a hand in quarterback's storied career

By Mark Dukes

Destined for greatness? How could anyone possibly — especially so boldly — predict another's destiny?

A hunch? A true evaluation? A motivational tool? A wild idea? An off-the-cuff comment not meant to be taken seriously?

Chuck Long was a virtual nobody in late summer of 1982 — just another Iowa player competing for a job. He was lightly recruited out of North High School in Wheaton, Ill., and wasn't necessarily the favorite to win the starting job as Iowa's quarterback in 1982, the year after the school's first Rose Bowl appearance in 23 years.

Then in August before that season, Coach Hayden Fry made reporters sit up in their chairs at the fall kickoff media conference with an uncharacteristic pronouncement. "He's gifted. He's talented. He has great poise," Fry said. "He is destined for greatness."

Destined for greatness? Did he really say that? Rewind the tape and let's get it down, word for word. What did Hayden Fry know and why was he so sure of himself?

An old quarterback himself, Fry always felt a special kinship with his QBs. He always looked for those special qualities of leadership, poise and intelligence. Either Fry was a tremendous evaluator of talent or Long made him look like a psychic.

Whichever, Long WAS destined for greatness.

In four seasons as Iowa's starting quarterback, Long set 28 school, conference or national records for passing or total offense. In 44 games he started, Iowa won 34 and tied one. He finished his career as the Big Ten's career leader in total passing yards (10,461 yards), and in touchdown passes in a game, season and career.

In career passing efficiency, only Jim McMahon and Steve Young — two Brigham Young quarterbacks — ranked higher in the NCAA record book. His career passing yards was sixth in college football history, bettered only by the likes of Doug Flutie, McMahon and John Elway.

Sure, part of the Long's success was related to the system Fry employed, one that allowed quarterbacks to be productive in the passing game. But Long not only had the pinpoint accuracy from a three-quarter delivery, he had a tremendous supporting cast and some intangibles.

"There's just something about that quarterback. He's got fire in his eyes when you hit him," said Penn State tackle Joe Hines after Long riddled the Nittany Lions for 345 yards in 1983. "You figure when you really do hit him he's not really going to get up from that. No way. But he does."

At 6-foot-4 and 213 pounds, Long was sturdy enough to take a beating. But it takes a bit more than physical toughness sometimes.

"He's just unflappable," Fry said.

"There is a spark in there," his mother said.

There's more, according to Chuck.

"You step up to the line of scrimmage. You see a lot of guys moving, you hear a lot of shouting, and then you call the play, and there's this split-second of silence," Long told The Detroit Free Press in 1987. "It's right there. Just you. Center stage. You're in control. You're all alone. On an island. Make the decision. That's my favorite part."

Long wasn't always at center stage, but maybe that's why he got there.

As a seventh-grader at Franklin Junior High School in Wheaton, Long was beaten out for the starting quarterback job. He was good enough to play another position, split end, but Long still was crushed.

"I always regretted it and I always hated my coaches for it," he said. "I didn't like rejection. Not at all. Some kids could take it. I couldn't. I wanted to be the quarterback."

Long soon got his wish. He quarterbacked Wheaton North to the state championship in 1979, his junior season, and was named all-state as a senior. Under his direction, the team won 23 of 24 games in two seasons.

But there was one not-so-small problem. In his senior season, Long attempted only 92 passes. North was a running team and Long generated more than 1,000 yards in total offense as a senior. "You know how colleges are," he said. "They don't recognize you if you don't throw."

The number of major colleges that saw something in Long can be counted on one hand: Iowa, Northwestern and Northern Illinois. He chose the Hawkeyes after watching fans at a basketball game on his recruiting visit.

Long played only a few downs as an Iowa freshman but entered the 1982 season as a contender for the starting position with Tom Grogan. Long earned the season-opening start against Nebraska but the Cornhuskers buried him and the Hawkeyes, 42-7. Long lost his job to Grogan for the next game, against Iowa State. Grogan was ineffective in a 19-7 Iowa loss, so Long got the job back for a September 25 contest at Arizona.

A star was born. Against many odds — 90-degree heat, night game, grass field and nine-point underdog — Iowa rode Long's leadership to a 17-14 victory. The Hawkeyes had 431 yards in total offense,

> ## "There's just something about that quarterback. He's got fire in his eyes when you hit him. You figure when you really do hit him he's not really going to get up from that. No way. But he does."
>
> ### *Joe Hines, Penn State tackle*

"It boiled down to three reasons. I wanted to continue my education. Second, I wanted to be with a team that could be one of the most exciting in Iowa history. Most important, though, I'd like to have another chance to go to the Rose Bowl."

Chuck Long, on his return to Iowa for his senior season

with Long clicking for 187 and two touchdowns.

Iowa won seven of nine games after that, including a 28-22 triumph over Tennessee in the Peach Bowl. And three glorious years followed.

Iowa posted 9-3 and 8-4-1 records the next two seasons. Long, injured along with star running back Ronnie Harmon in a November tie against Wisconsin in 1984, finished the 1984 campaign in high fashion.

Against Texas, a team Fry dearly wanted to beat, Long exhibited one of the best performances in bowl game history with 461 passing yards and six touchdowns in a 55-17 rout at the Freedom Bowl in Anaheim, Calif.

Long could have finished his career after that game and gone down as one of Iowa's all-time greats. He set school records in 1984 for completion percentage (67.1) and passing yards (2,871), and set a NCAA record with 22 straight completions in a game against Indiana.

But because of a change in NCAA rules, Long was given the chance for another season of eligibility. He could have been eligible for the NFL draft and would have gone in an early round. Or he could wait a year and try to better his lot.

Two months passed after the Freedom Bowl, leaving Iowa fans — and Fry — on pins and needles as to Long's decision. Then near the college national letter-of-intent signing day in February, Long announced he'd return to

Iowa for his senior season.

"It boiled down to three reasons," Long said. "I wanted to continue my education. Second, I wanted to be with a team that could be one of the most exciting in Iowa history. Most important, though, I'd like to have another chance to go to the Rose Bowl."

The 1985 season, his "extra" season, defined Long's greatness. He led Iowa to the Big Ten championship and a No. 1 national ranking, and finished second to Auburn's Bo Jackson in the closest Heisman Trophy voting ever.

A few defining moments:

— After three lopsided victories to start the season, Iowa took the No. 1 rating into a game against high-powered Michigan State. The Spartans led, 24-13, in the third quarter and 31-28, late in the game. Long drove Iowa the length of the field in the final minutes, scoring himself on a magnificent bootleg for a 35-31 Iowa triumph. By the way, he completed 30 of 39 passes for 380 yards and four touchdowns.

— Two weeks later, Iowa topped Michigan in a battle of No. 1 and No. 2 teams, 12-10. Again, Long took the Hawkeyes on the winning drive, twice completing passes on third-and-8 for needed yardage. It set up a 29-yard winning field goal by Rob Houghtlin on the last play of the game. Long hit 26 of 39 passes for 297 yards against Michigan, then the nation's top-rated defense.

Hayden Fry huddles with his quarterbacks on the sidelines of the 1985 Michigan contest.

— The next week, as the nation's UNANIMOUS No. 1 team, Long set a Big Ten record with six TD passes in a rout of Northwestern.

— A week after suffering a 22-13 loss at Ohio State, Iowa responded with a 59-0 rout of Illinois behind Long's four TD passes. Later, Illinois tied Michigan, 3-3.

The season was stained by the loss to Ohio State, and a 45-28 setback to UCLA in the Rose Bowl. But in large part, Long achieved what he had set out to do.

Professional football didn't turn out so well, but it wasn't entirely Long's doing. Sure, he sat out 41 days of camp in a contract dispute after the Detroit Lions made him a No. 1 draft pick. That put Long way behind. After signing a four-year, $1.75 million contract, he spent most of his first season on the sideline.

But in late November, in mop-up duty against Tampa Bay, Long got his shot. And on his first pass attempt, he hurled a 34-yard TD pass to Leonard Thompson. Long got his first start in the next-to-last game of 1986 against the mighty Chicago Bears on Monday Night Football. Although the Lions lost, 16-13, Long completed 12 of 24 passes for 167 yards.

His greatest NFL performance was a 33-for-47 effort against Green Bay in 1987. But those games were too few. Long, victimized too often by a weak offensive line, finished his nine-year NFL career with 3,747 yards and 19 touchdown passes.

Ten years after his glorious season in 1985, Long returned to Iowa as a defensive backfield coach under Fry. And every time he's seen in Kinnick Stadium, fans remember how he became a Hawkeye football great.

Destined, or not.

Hawks Edge Gophers, 30-27; Earn Holiday Trip

By Mark Dukes, The Gazette

Rob Houghtlin's second-chance field goal with one second remaining capped a 30-point second half and gave Iowa a 30-27 Big Ten football victory over Minnesota Saturday night.

The Hawkeyes' brilliant comeback, sparked by quarterback Mark Vlasic, enabled them to keep Floyd of Rosedale and the Minnesota for third place in the Big Ten conference at 5-3.

Iowa, 8-3, accepted a bid after the game to play in the Holiday Bowl Dec. 30 against the Western Athletic Conference champion, Minnesota, 6-5, will play in the Liberty Bowl Dec. 29 against Tennessee.

"This is one of the greatest comebacks I can remember," Iowa coach Hayden Fry said. "Tonight's game was one of the most courageous games I've ever seen.

"It was a great feeling to come from behind, particularly with this bunch. We had seven guys who didn't practice this week. We're thrilled to death to receive an invitation to the Holiday Bowl. Other than the Rose Bowl, we're going exactly where we want to go."

Minnesota had tied the game, 27-27, on Chip Lohmiller's

SCORE BY QUARTERS
Minneapolis, Nov. 22, 1986

IOWA	0	0	13	17	—	30
MINNESOTA	7	10	7	3	—	27

49-yard field goal with 1:03 remaining after the Gophers faced a fourth-and-10 at the Iowa 32. Then with no time-outs, Iowa drove from its 20-yard line to the Gopher 34 in 53 seconds.

The march was engineered by Vlasic, who took over for starter Tom Poholsky at the start of the second half and completed 16 of 21 for 199 yards.

Vlasic completed a 25-yard pass to Quinn Early to midfield. Tight end Marv Cook caught a 5-yard pass and got out of bounds with 23 seconds left. An 11-yard pass from Vlasic to Jim Mauro moved the Hawkeyes to the Minnesota 34. An incomplete pass stopped the clock with 10 seconds remaining.

Houghtlin's 51-yard field goal sailed wide to the right, but the Gophers had 12 players on the field.

"Holy smoke! What a way to lose a game," Fry said. "I feel sorry for them. Whoever's the substitutes coach of Minnesota, I may send him a Christmas gift."

The 15-yard penalty allowed Houghtlin to try his game-winner from 37-yards.

"I got lucky didn't I?" Houghtlin said. "I went form goat to hero in a matter of a few minutes."

"If you want to feel the emotions, you should be a college football coach," Minnesota coach John Gutekunst said. "We played our hearts out against the defending Big Ten

Iowa recovered two fumbles on Minnesota kickoffs and returned them for touchdowns. The teams combined for 57 points, the most ever in the series' history.

champions."

Vlasic suffered a shoulder injury in the third game this season against Texas-El Paso, and has been slow to recover.

"I didn't feel 100 percent," Vlasic said. "I thought, 'What the heck. It's my last game and I've got nothing to lose.' "

Said Fry, "Evidently he (Vlasic) just forgot about his shoulder tonight. In the pregame, (offensive coordinator) Bill Snyder noticed he was throwing better than the has since he got injured.

"At halftime, I got rid of those clear glasses and got my shades out. I'm very superstitious, you know. They made me see things a little better. We took a chance and went with Mark. He was obviously the spark we needed."

A Metrodome record crowd of 65,018 fans watched the Gophers roll to a 17-0 halftime lead capped by Lohmiller's school-record 62-yard field goal as the first-half clock expired.

Running backs Darrell Thompson of Minnesota and Rick Bayless of Iowa reached milestones in the second period.

Bayless became the third player in Iowa history to gain 1,000 yards in a season. The Hugo, Minn., junior gained 78 yards on 19 carries hiking his total to 1,040.

Thompson won the Big Ten rushing championship, setting a Minnesota season record.

His total was 1,240 yards after gaining 104 on 23 attempts.

Lohmiller's kick fell one year short of the Big Ten mark. Michigan State's Morten Anderson kicked a 63-yarder against Ohio State in 1981.

Iowa appeared content to run the clock out in the first half, but the Hawkeyes called time-out with 21 seconds left before a third-and-4 play. Minnesota dropped Bayless for a one-yard loss and called timeout with 15 seconds remaining.

Roselle Richardson returned Gary Kostrubala's 44-yard punt to the Iowa 45. Lohmiller lined up for his kick with :04 showing.

Iowa stifled Minnesota's first scoring threat when nose guard Dave Haight recovered Kevin Wilson's fumble at the Hawkeye 20. The Gophers drove 57 yards in nine plays on their second possession, scoring on Ron Goetz's 6-yard run. Rickey Foggie's 18-yard pass to Craig Otto and Thompson's 17-yard run sparked the drive. Lohmiller's extra-point kick put Minnesota in front 7-0 with 3:50 left in the first.

Minnesota, which had the ball eight minutes longer than Iowa in the first half, marched 80 yards in 12 plays to its second score. Thompson took a pitch from Foggie and danced eight yards around right end. Lohmiller's kick gave the Gophers a 14-0 lead with 9:42 left in the half.

At that point, Minnesota had run 32 plays to Iowa's 12.

Iowa drove deep into Minnesota territory on its next two possessions, but failed to score each time.

A 54-yard pass from Poholsky to Mauro took the Hawkeyes to the Minnesota 11. But three plays later, Gopher linebacker Mark Dusbabek knocked the ball loose from Poholsky and nose guard Gary Hadd recovered at the Minnesota 12.

The Hawkeyes advanced to the Minnesota 14 on their next series. But Poholsky was sacked for a 9-yard loss, then intercepted in the end zone by Donovan Small on a pass over the head of Early.

"This is one of the greatest comebacks I can remember. Tonight's game was one of the most courageous games I've ever seen."

Coach Hayden Fry

Iowa senior quarterback Mark Vlasic passed for 199 yards against Minnesota in the second half.

Vlasic started the second half and got Iowa rolling immediately. He completed his first two passes, including a 35-yarder to Early.

That set up Houghtlin's longest field goal of the season, a 49-yarder with 12:56 left in the third.

Freshman Peter Marciano gave Iowa a huge lift when he returned Brent Herbel's punt 89 yards for a touchdown. Marciano picked up a wall in front of the Minnesota bench and followed blocks by Ken Sims and Anthony Wright into the end zone. Houghtlin's kick trimmed Minnesota's lead to 17-10 with 9:30 remaining in the third.

In Iowa's last trip to the Metrodome, Bill Happel had set an Iowa record with a 95-yard punt return for a touchdown.

Houghtlin's 38-yard field goal with 37 seconds left in the third cut the Gopher lead to 24-13. The 45-yard drive was helped by a pass interference call on Minnesota's Charles McCree on Early in the end zone. The pass was from tight end Mike Flagg, who had taken a lateral from Vlasic.

Vlasic was sharp early in the fourth when he drove Iowa to a touchdown. He completed passes of 18 yards to Mauro, 15 to Cook and 17 to Bayless. Two plays later, the faked into the line with Bayless and passed a yard to wide-open Flagg in the end zone.

Fry opted for a two point conversion try with 10:23 left. But Bayless was stopped on a pitch to the right way short of the goal line, leaving Minnesota's lead at 24-19.

After the Iowa defense stopped Minnesota on downs, Iowa's charge continued behind Vlasic's direction.

Bayless' dive into the end zone from the 1 put Iowa in front, 25-24 with 5:27 left. After the Hawkeyes took their third and final timeout. Vlasic passed to Kevin Harmon for two points to hike Iowa's lead to three points.

The drive started after Marciano's 14-yard punt return, which gave the Hawkeyes possession at their 42. Fullback Richard Bass gained nine yards on first down, then Vlasic rifled a 24-yard pass to Flagg. Bayless gained 8, then 5, and Bass ran 4 yards. Vlasic's 7-yard pass to Early took Iowa to the 1.

Minnesota went 39 yards in 11 plays to set up Lohmiller's tying field goal.

Aztecs In Ruins As Houghtlin Kicks Iowa to Win

By Mark Dukes, The Gazette

R ob Houghtlin pulled the plug on the "Cardiac Kids" Tuesday night, kicking a 41-yard field goal on the last play of the game to give Iowa a victory in the Holiday Bowl, 39-38.

Kevin Rahill's 21-yard field goal with 47 seconds left put San Diego State in front, 38-36.

It was set up by a 45-yard pass from Todd Santos to Alfred Jackson, who caught the ball between two Iowa defenders at the Iowa 9.

The Aztecs had won seven football games this year by a touchdown or less and had been dubbed the "Cardiac Kids."

Kevin Harmon returned the kickoff after Rahill's field goal 48 yards to the SDSU 37.

David Hudson ran 6 yards and, after an incomplete pass, Rick Bayless gained 7.

Iowa called time-out with four seconds remaining, and the Aztecs followed with another time-out.

Holder Chuck Hartlieb handled a high snap from center,

Rick Bayless (13) ran for 110 yards on 19 carries and scored his 11th touchdown of the season against the Aztecs.

but Houghtlin drilled the kick. He won the regular-season final over Minnesota with a field goal, and his kicks boosted the Hawkeyes to wins over Michigan and Purdue in 1985.

"Wasn't that fantastic?" Iowa Coach Hayden Fry said. "It was probably more exciting than the Minnesota game. I'd prefer to beat the Gophers, but this was more exciting because there was so much action in the last 10 minutes."

The game, witnessed by 59,473 fans in San Diego Jack Murphy Stadium and a national-television audience, was in true Holiday Bowl fashion. Eight of the nine games now have been decided by a touchdown or less.

"It was a great ballgame, but a horrible, horrible loss," San Diego State Coach Denny Stolz said. "It was an awfully hard game to lose."

Iowa finished 9-3, San Diego State 8-4.

Although Iowa was outgained, 415-363, the Hawkeyes got touchdowns from five different players and key performances by many more.

Santos tossed three first-half touchdown passes and

SCORE BY QUARTERS					
San Diego, Dec. 30, 1986					
IOWA	7	6	8	28	— 39
SAN DIEGO STATE	6	15	7	10	— 38

sparked the Aztecs to a 21-13 halftime lead. Santos threw three TD passes in a game only once this season, in the opener against Long Beach State.

Santos finished with 21 completions in 33 attempts for 298 yards and three TDs. His counterpart, Mark Vlasic, hit 15 of 28 for 222 yards and two TDs. They shared the game's Most Valuable Player honor.

It tied the most points Iowa had allowed in a half this season. Ohio State scored 21 second-quarter points Nov. 1 in a 31-10 victory.

San Diego State won the toss and elected to receive. Santos was sacked for a 9-yard loss on the first play, as Jeff Drost and Jon Vrieze stormed through the line. Two plays later, Wayne Ross punted 52 yards to the Hawkeye 20.

Iowa used the running game exclusively in its first series. Bayless ran six times for 55 yards, but the Hawkeye drive stalled and Houghtlin missed a 42-yard field goal wide to the right.

But on the next play, Santo's pass was intercepted at the SDSU 30 by Keaton Smiley, who ran to the Aztecs' 5. It was Smiley's fifth interception of the year.

Bayless, who finished with 110 yards on 19 carries, scored his 11th touchdown of the year, as he shrugged off a tackle at the 4 and bulled into the end zone. Houghtlin's kick gave Iowa a 7-0 lead with 8:10 left in the first. The Aztecs' defense, which paved the way to four straight season-ending victories, created SDSU's first scoring opportunity. Duane Pettit stormed in from his tackle position and knocked the ball loose from Vlasic. Milt Wilson recovered at the Iowa 8.

Three plays later, Chris Hardy caught a 6-yard scoring pass from Santos. However, Rahill's extra-point kick hit the left upright. Iowa had a 7-6 lead with 4:52 remaining in the first.

Robert Smith's 37-yard kickoff return put Iowa at the SDSU 49. The Hawkeyes moved to the Aztecs' 5 in seven plays, sparked by a 19-yard pass from Vlasic to Quinn Early. An illegal-procedure penalty put Iowa back at the 10 and on third-and-6 at the SDSU 7, Aztec cornerback Mario Mitchell intercepted Vlasic's pass intended for Early at the 2.

San Diego State took its first lead with 6:38 left in the half,

Mark Vlasic completed 15 of 28 passes for 222 yards and 2 TDs. He shared the game's MVP honors with Todd Santos.

as Jackson got wide open behind the Iowa defense and caught a 44-yard scoring strike from Santos. Hardy hiked the Aztecs' lead to 14-7, running for a two-point conversion.

Jackson, who switched from defensive back to wide receiver this season, had four TDs among his 18 receptions during the regular season.

Vlasic scored on a 1-yard sneak with 2:22 left in the half, but Houghtlin failed to tie the score when his kick sailed wide of the uprights. Bayless' 5-yard run on fourth-and-1 and Mike Flagg's 31-yard gain with a pass from Vlasic sparked the drive.

The series started after linebacker J.J. Puk of Cedar Rapids got his first career interception, picking off Santos' pass at the Aztecs' 49.

But SDSU wasn't satisfied with a one-point halftime lead. Fullback Corey Gilmore gained 10 and 9 yards to put the Aztecs at midfield. Santos followed with a 23-yard strike to Monty Gilbreath, which put SDSU at the Iowa 28.

Gilbreath, a freshman who caught only four balls during the regular season, caught a Santos pass over the middle and weaved his way into the end zone. The 28-yard scoring play, and Rahill's extra point, put SDSU in front 21-13 with 39 seconds left in the half.

The half ended when Houghtlin's 58-yard field-goal attempt fell 10 yards short. Santos completed 10 of 19 passes for 143 yards in the fist half, Vlasic 7 of 15 for 102. Bayless had 72 yards rushing on 13 carries.

The Aztecs sacked Vlasic twice on the opening series of the second half, each time for 9-yard losses. SDSU got possession after Iowa's punt at the Hawkeye 45.

Santos drove SDSU to its fourth touchdown in nine plays, as Tilmore dove over the right side of the line on fourth-and-1. Rahill's kick put the Aztecs ahead, 28-13, with 7:52 left in the third.

A key play in that series was a 23-yard pass play from

IOWA HAWKEYES VS. SDSU AZTECS
SAN DIEGO JACK MURPHY STADIUM • DECEMBER 30TH, 1986 • $4.00

Santos to tight end Rob Awalt on third-and-6. It moved SDSU to Iowa's 5.

Harmon's 34-yard kickoff return went to the Aztecs' 47. Seven plays later, Hudson jumped into the end zone with 4:58 left in the third. Vlasic drilled a two-point conversion pass to Smith, trimming SDSU's lead to 28-21.

Bayless carried four times for 29 yards during the series. That put him over the 100-yard mark for the fifth time this season.

But the Aztecs responded with a 12-play, 68-yard scoring drive, which not only lengthened the lead but restored momentum for SDSU.

Hardy scored his second touchdown on a 6-yard, third-down run off the left end on the first play of the fourth quarter. Rahill's kick put SDSU ahead, 35-21.

During that series, SDSU faced a third-and-18 at its 44. But Santos passed 17 yards to Gilbreath and the Aztec coaches declined to punt on fourth down. Gilmore made 1 yard to keep the march going.

Iowa closed to 35-29 on Marv Cook's first career touchdown, a 29-yard reception from Vlasic on fourth-and-4, and Hartlieb's two-point conversion pass to Flagg.

Cook caught the pass on SDSU's 21 and raced into the end zone. Iowa lined up for a Houghtlin extra-point kick, but Hartlieb pulled up and fired into the end zone. The score occurred with 8:39 left.

Iowa's defense held the Aztecs on downs and got the ball with 7:03 to go at its 30 after a 52-yard punt.

Facing a third-and-10, Vlasic rifled a strike to Early for 18 yards. He followed with a 20-yarder to Early to the SDSU 32. Hudson dashed 12 yards to the 20.

Harmon gained 3, then turned a screen pass into a 14-yard gain to the Aztec 3.

Vlasic faked into the line then found a wide-open Flagg

Hawkeyes Cook OSU on TD With 16 Seconds Left

By Mark Neuzil, The Gazette

M arv Cook, now we know why they call you Marvelous.

Cook, the junior tight end, and quarterback Chuck Hartlieb teamed up on a miracle play, a 28-yard touchdown pass on fourth and forever, no time-outs with very little clock and nearly no Hawkeye hope left.

The play beat Ohio State, 29-27, on Saturday in sunny-but-surly Ohio Stadium.

It's historically significant because, before Saturday, Iowa defeated Ohio State only once in its last 20 attempts.

Further, you'll have to check back to 1959 to find the last Iowa win in Columbus. In 1959, Hawkeye Coach Hayden Fry was defensive coordinator at Baylor and Herbert Hoover was the most famous person to come from West Branch.

No more. Cook made his move to go one-up on the former President, at least in today's papers, by catching nine passes covering 159 yards and punting five times for a 43-yard average.

"To be honest with you, I don't even know the final

SCORE BY PERIODS						
Columbus, Ohio, Nov. 14, 1987						
IOWA	3	12	0	14	—	29
OHIO STATE	7	7	7	6	—	27

score," Cook said. "I know we won. That's all."

Fry, who has been trying to beat Ohio State since he became a head coach in 1962, was as happy as anyone has ever seen him.

"I think I'll just go ahead and retire right now," Fry said with a laugh.

The Hawkeye win might have hastened the retirement of Buckeye Coach Earle Bruce. His team lost its third straight Big Ten game, the first time since 1971 that's happened at Ohio State.

The Buckeyes are 5-4-1 overall and 3-4 in the Big Ten with the arch-rivalry at Michigan up next. A loss next week and Bruce could be saying goodbye, Columbus.

Iowa, 8-3 and 5-2, will choose between several bowl offers today after its fourth straight victory. Scouts from the Peach,

Iowa quarterback Chuck Hartlieb (8) completed 20 of 37 passes for 333 yards. He connected with Marv Cook on a 28-yard touchdown pass on fourth down with 16 seconds left.

Liberty, All-American, Bluebonnet, Hall of Fame, Freedom and Holiday bowl, were fighting for Fry's ear and seventh straight bowl appearance.

"Anybody listening, if you haven't called in about your bowl, please call in now," Fry said.

The winning points came after a 10-play, 64-yard drive marked with penalties, quarterback sacks and three Hartlieb-to-Cook passes.

Ohio State had taken a 27-22 lead on freshman tailback Carlos Snow's 14-yard run with 2:45 remaining.

Hartlieb, who finished 20-of-37 for 333 yards, went to work with short passes to Rick Bayless and Mike Flagg.

On the 14-yard pass to Flagg, the Buckeyes were flagged for 12 men on the field, tacking on another 15 yards to give Iowa the ball at the Ohio State 30.

But the Hawkeyes slipped into reverse. After a holding penalty, tackle Ray Holliman belted Hartlieb, whose fumble was recovered by fullback David Hudson for an 11-yard loss back into Iowa territory.

What do you call on second-and-31? A pass to Cook, which got back 27 to the OSU 24.

But Kevin Harmon, who gained 151 yards Saturday, was stopped short on third down. What do you call on fourth-and-3? Another pass to Cook in the left flat for 8 yards and a first down at the 15.

But this was Ohio State, not Northwestern or Kansas State or Wisconsin. Defensive end Eric Kumerow blindsided Hartlieb, sacking him for a minus-8, forcing Fry to use his final time-out with 47 seconds left.

Harmon lost 5 more yards on a sweep when Kumerow caught him. One incomplete pass later, Iowa was in trouble.

What do you call on fourth-and-23 with 16 seconds left? Yet another pass to Cook, who caught it inside the 10 and carried Sean Bell and Ray Jackson into the end zone. Barely.

"I didn't know for sure if he was in," Hartlieb said. "I was running downfield trying to get another play off."

If Cook doesn't score, the clock runs out and Iowa loses.

"I knew where I was and where I had to get," Cook said. "I was an inch over. It wasn't by much."

That pass play was installed especially for the Buckeyes this week.

Flanker Everett Ross (5) had two touchdown receptions from quarterback Tom Tupa to help Ohio State take a 14-3 lead. Ross' second touchdown catch went for 60 yards.

"He was well covered," Hartlieb said. "It took some luck. But for us not to win here in so long, they had to have some luck on their side. Maybe we had it today."

The Buckeyes elected to skip the blitz and drop back.

"We were playing three deep so they wouldn't get the big one," Bruce said. "But they hit in between the deep and underneath with the tight end. I thought we had him covered."

Famous last words.

"The tight end ran that play six or seven times," said Buckeye cornerback William White.

"We knew what they were going to do. They just made

the play and we didn't."

What's the name of that play, anyhow?

"It's called Marv Cook for a touchdown," Cook said.

Fry nearly sent Flagg in for Cook on the last play, but changed his mind and went with the smaller, faster Cook. "It was total chaos," Cook said.

"I was surprised at everything connected with that last play," Fry said.

It was the first touchdown pass the Ohio State defense had given up in 14 quarters. "We wanted this as badly as any game I've been in the last four years," Hartlieb said.

Midway through the second quarter, it looked like another Hawkeye loss.

Ohio State jumped out to a 14-3 lead on flanker Everett Ross' two touchdown receptions from quarterback Tom Tupa, the latter covering 60 yards.

Harmon scored on a nifty 50-yard run, the team's longest from scrimmage this year, to get Iowa back into the game. Rob Houghtlin kicked three first-half field goals, including a 22-yarder as the half ended to give his club a 15-14 lead in the locker room.

Houghtlin became Iowa's career scoring leader with 278 points, breaking Tom Nichol's record by one. The senior also broke his own mark for field goals in a season with 19.

"I'd rather win like that every game," Houghtlin said. "I'm not in it for the personal stuff."

Tupa found tight end Jeff Ellis for 6 to put the Buckeyes back in front, 21-15, with 6:14 to play in the third.

Ohio State wanted more, and might have gotten it if not for two disastrous penalties and a botched punt.

The Buckeyes had a first down inside the Iowa 30 called back because of a holding penalty. On the next play, an offensive pass-interference call pushed them back into their own territory.

Tupa's punt was rushed by a trio of Hawkeyes, with Marshal Cotton getting credit for a blocked kick.

Mike Burke covered the kick and stumbled to the Ohio State 37. Seven plays later, Hudson dove over from the 1.

Iowa's 22-21 lead was short-lived, though. Snow, who rushed for 96 yards in his second college start, finished off a 16-play drive with his touchdown.

"We got beat. What can I say?" were Bruce's final comments.

Defense, Kicking Win for Hawks

By Mark Neuzil, The Gazette

Iowa won five straight games with its offense. Wednesday night, the Hawkeye defense and special teams made it six in a row.

Iowa's 20-19 Holiday Bowl victory over Wyoming would not have been possible without three blocked kicks and an interception returned for a touchdown.

Safety Jay Hess returned a blocked punt for a touchdown. Cornerback Anthony Wright carried an interception back for a score.

Merton Hanks, who deflected the Hess TD, tipped Greg Worker's potential game-winning 52-yard field goal with 52 seconds left to cement the victory.

"It was a sweet victory," said Hawk Coach Hayden Fry. "It was ugly." Iowa's defense, maligned much of the season, played its best when it counted the most, shutting out Wyoming in the second half.

"Our defense and special teams came up with the big plays and really made the difference," Fry said. Paul Roach, who led the Cowboys to their first bowl game in 11 years in his debut season as head coach, was subdued.

"It was a really tough game to lose," Roach said. "In our opinion, we played a great defensive game but made two

Iowa kicker Rob Houghtlin missed a 30-yard field-goal attempt with 55 seconds left in the first half, but made up for it by making two key extra points.

SCORE BY QUARTERS
San Diego, Calif., Dec. 30, 1987

IOWA	0	7	0	13	—	20
WYOMING	12	7	0	0	—	19

errors that were obvious."

It was the second straight one-point Holiday Bowl triumph for Iowa, which beat San Diego State, 39-38, exactly one year earlier.

The exciting finish also followed the bowl game's 10-year tradition. Five of the matchups have been decided by a sin-

gle point. The crowd was listed as a bowl-record 61,892, although there were a few thousand no-shows on the clear, 50-degree evening.

The victory let 18th-ranked Iowa tie the school record for wins in a season with 10.

Wyoming, champions of the Western Athletic Conference, saw a nine-game joy ride come to an end.

Both teams finished the season with 10-3 records.

The Iowa offense, held in check most of the evening, scored the go-ahead touchdown on a one-yard run by fullback David Hudson with 7:33 left in the game.

Hudson's tally capped a 10-play, 86-yard drive, built

around a 48-yard completion from Chuck Hartlieb to a diving Travis Watkins at the Cowboy 20-yard line.

"The key play of the game was the long pass to Watkins," Hartlieb said. "They were taking chances defensively all night and we finally caught them."

But Wyoming, which won four games in the final two minutes this year, was not finished.

Quarterback Craig Burnett, the game's offensive MVP, marched the team to the Iowa 35 before throwing three straight incompletions. Worker's kick, which would have been the longest of his career, didn't have a chance as Hanks charged in from the left side to deflect it.

"We knew we had to dig in on that field-goal attempt, and I got through," Hanks said. "It was great getting my hands on the ball."

Burnett, a senior, attempted a Holiday Bowl-record 51 passes, completing 28 for 332 yards. Jim McMahon, playing for Brigham Young, threw 49 times in 1980.

Iowa's other cornerback, Wright, was named the game's most valuable defensive play.

He intercepted a Burnett pass in the third quarter and returned it 33 yards for a score to bring the Hawks within 19-14.

"I felt the interception was a little more devastating than the blocked punt," Roach said.

It was the first touchdown scored by the Iowa defense this season.

Wyoming jumped out to a 12-0 lead in the first quarter on two Worker field goals and Burnett's 15-yard touchdown pass to James Loving.

The Cowboys took the opening kickoff and drove 43 yards, including a 19-yard pass to Scott Joseph and a 24-yarder to Loving, before the march was halted. Worker connected from 43 yards out.

The Wyoming defense, which held Iowa to one first down and 28 total yards in the first quarter, set up the next field goal. Dave Eden sacked Hartlieb for a 14-yard loss on the Iowa 14.

Marv Cook's short punt gave the Cowboys the ball on the Hawkeye 44. Burnett hit Loving for 7 and Anthony Sar-

gent for 14, setting up Worker's 38-yard field goal to give the Cowboys a 6-0 lead.

On their next possession, the Cowboys peeled off a 63-yard, eight play drive. Burnett, who moved into second place on the career passing charts at Wyoming, threw for 58 yards on the march, including a 13-yarder to tight end Bill Hoffman and 24 yards to Sargent.

Hoffman, a first-team All-Western Athletic Conference pick and the team's leading receiver, suffered a broken arm on his catch and was wheeled from the field on a stretcher.

Iowa, which was outgained 144-28 in the opening 15 minutes, finally got on the board when Hanks blocked a Tom Kilpatrick punt. Hess, starting in place of the suspended Dwight Sistrunk, fielded the ball at the Cowboy 10 and ran it in. Rob Houghtlin's PAT pulled Iowa within 12-7.

Kilpatrick, who had two punts blocked this year, was the leading punter in the WAC. Iowa had blocked only one kick in its 12 regular-season games.

"We may have had one return called all night," Fry said. "We saw their snapper was inconsistent and detected a flaw in their protection. The surprise was that we got the field goal blocked."

Wyoming wasted no time getting the Hess points back. Burnett, who hit 16-of-30 in the first half, led the team on another scoring drive, finished off by Gerald Abraham's 3-yard TD plunge to put the score at 19-7.

The big play on the drive was a 20-yard pass to freshman tight end Gordy Wood —

Chuck Hartlieb completed eight of 18 passes in the first half.

playing in place of the injured Hoffman — on third-and-10 at the Iowa 23.

Iowa trailed at halftime, 19-7, when Houghtlin missed a 30-yard field goal with 55 seconds to play.

Houghtlin's miss was the final play in a 13-play drive, the Hawks' only sustained march in the half.

"Wyoming was the best defensive team we've seen all year for one half," Fry said.

Hartlieb, who was 8-of-18 in the half, underthrew a wide-open Quinn Early and overthrew a lonely Wadkins on potential touchdown plays in the opening 30 minutes.

A Shootout, It Certainly Wasn't

By Mark Dukes, The Gazette

It was a classic case of false advertising.

The 10th Holiday Bowl on Wednesday night was billed strictly as a showcase for two of the top offensive teams in college football, Iowa and Wyoming.

It was supposed to be a high-scoring shoot-out in which, as Wyoming Coach Paul Roach predicted, both teams would score in the 20's.

They were supposed to mirror each other, pass for pass, bomb for bomb, touchdown for touchdown.

It didn't happen.

Instead, this one was decided by defense as Iowa beat the WAC by a whisker again. Last year, it was 39-38 over San Diego State on Rob Houghtlin's last-second field goal. This time, it was 20-19 in one of the great defensive efforts in a while by the Hawkeyes.

It was Merton Hanks, Anthony Wright and Jay Hess, a tremendous trio from Texas this night. And it was J.J. Puk, Dave Haight, Kerry Burt and Myron Keppy, Iowans one and all.

Defense, defense, defense. That's the way they play this game in the Big Ten, isn't it?

Not that anyone will rant and rave and ask for a refund because the offenses scored only three touchdowns. In the Holiday Bowl tradition, it was another nail-biter, one that went down to the wire. It was the third straight one-pointer and the ninth time in 10 years this game has been decided by a touchdown or less.

Iowa looked like it left its offense at Sea World for three quarters. Penalties, dropped passes, missed field goals, a nasty fumble, missed opportunities. The Hawkeyes couldn't seem to do anything right when they had the ball.

"We just weren't in the flow of the game," Iowa running back Kevin Harmon said. "We just weren't in sync. Coach didn't say a word to us at the half. We knew we were lucky to be in the game. We should've been blown out."

If not for a guy who went to Iowa to become a quarterback and offensive leader — one who would put points on the board — the Hawkeyes would have been shut out for three quarters. Hess, a former QB at Texas A&M in his first start for Iowa at free safety, scored after he scooped up a punt blocked by Hanks.

Iowa's offense was far more effective in the second half because it was centered on the tight ends. Marv Cook and Mike Flagg, certainly a dynamic duo, caught nine passes in the second half as the Hawkeyes worked the sidelines.

Still, the end zone was a rumor to the offense, Iowa sputtered once and Houghtlin missed a 30-yard field goal. Kevin Harmon was within inches of the goal line on a sweep, then fumbled out of the end zone as the ball was turned over to the Cowboys.

A little defense on Wyoming's part, let's say.

When the Cowboys' Reggie Berry tipped a pass away from Cook on a fourth-and-2 play at the Wyoming 5, the Western Athletic conference champions seemed destined to lug the winner's hardware back to Laramie.

But then came the Wright stuff. Anthony Wright picked off an overthrown Craig Burnett pass and showed his 4.45 speed in the 40-yard dash over 33 yards. A touchdown off a turnover that brought Iowa within five points of Wyoming.

"I thought the ball was right on line," Burnett said. "I thought it would hit (the receiver) right on the head, but it just sailed.

"In the second half, they were running a four-deep coverage that we hadn't seen on film."

Hawkeyes Give 18th Ranked MSU The Boot, 12-7

By Jim Ecker, The Gazette

J eff Skillett and the Iowa Hawkeyes can rest easy again.

The demons that haunted them the last two years are dead.

They died at Spartan Stadium Saturday afternoon as the Hawkeyes upset 18th-ranked Michigan State, 12-7, in a defensive football tussle.

Skillett, haunted by the memory of a missed field-goal attempt here two years ago in a 10-10 tie, made a pair of clutch three-pointers.

The Hawkeyes, haunted by a losing season a year ago, came up with a series of big defensive plays to deny the Spartans in the Big Ten opener for both clubs.

Iowa Coach Hayden Fry was a sweaty and happy guy.

"It's been a long, long time since we did the hokey-pokey in the locker room," Fry said.

"We save it for the big, big victories."

This was one of them. The Hawkeyes hadn't danced like this since their 29-27 victory at Ohio State in 1987 on that miracle pass play from Chuck Hartlieb to Marv Cook.

SCORE BY PERIODS
East Lansing, Mich., Oct. 6, 1990

IOWA	0	9	0	3	— 12
MICHIGAN STATE	0	0	0	7	— 7

This triumph was just as good. It gave Iowa a 3-1 mark heading into Saturday's home game with Wisconsin. It dropped MSU to 1-2-1 with Michigan next.

Fry, remarkably, hasn't lost here in 12 years as Iowa's top guy. He has five wins and a tie in six trips. His last victory over a team ranked in The Associated Press poll occurred here. In 1985, No. 11 Iowa defeated No. 17 Michigan State, 24-21.

"There's just something mystical about this field," he said with a fat, happy smile.

Melvin Foster and John Derby had big, big days at line-

backer. On offense, Paul Kujawa performed superbly at fullback as a replacement for Lew Montgomery, who hurt his collarbone early and might miss a month.

Kujawa, a walk-on who got a scholarship last spring, accounted for 55 yards, earned some big first downs and blocked well. "He played one of the gutsiest games I've ever seen," Fry said.

But this game belonged mostly to Skillet and Iowa's defense, which blanked the Spartans for more than 55 minutes before they finally scored with 4:06 left on a 6-yard run by Hyland Hickson to make it 9-7.

"Our defense was truly superb," Fry said. "I never dreamed we could shut out Michigan State until nearly five minutes were left in the ballgame, but we did."

And on offense, the Hawks scored just enough.

Skillett's 34-yard field goal with 41 seconds left made it 12-7, and the Hawkeyes held off a last-second scare to win.

A 32-yard pass from Dan Enos to James Bradley put MSU at Iowa's 31-yard line with 27 seconds left, but the threat ended there.

"As poorly as we played most of the game, we still had a chance to win," said MSU Coach George Perles. "That's the most important thing."

The game started poorly for Iowa, but finished in grand style.

The Spartans stuffed the ball down Iowa's throat on their first drive, with Tico Duckett doing most of the damage. But John Langeloh muffed a 19-yard field goal, and that set the tone for a long day for MSU.

Skillet gave Iowa a 3-0 lead with a 31-yard field goal midway through the second period.

Then came the play of the day for the Hawkeyes.

Foster's interception and 14-yard return of an Enos pass gave Iowa the ball at MSU's 44-yard line, and Fry reached into his bag of tricks to get the touchdown.

Faced with third-and-3 at the MSU 5-yard line, Fry had Kujawa and Mike Saunders shift out of the I-formation to become wide receivers. That gave Iowa four wide

Sophomore receiver Danan Hughes (3) and Iowa leaped past 18th-ranked Michigan State to help Hawkeyes Coach Hayden Fry improve to 5-0-1 at Spartan Stadium.

receivers and no running backs, and it worked.

Rodgers found Nick Bell, who lined up as a flanker, in the back of the end zone and the Hawkeyes led, 9-0.

Iowa had never run that play.

"Specially designed for Michigan State," Rodgers said. "It was one of our tricks."

Rodgers was supposed to hit Saunders, who was open, but Rodgers had a Spartan defender in his face before finding Bell for the touchdown. "He was the last possible choice," Rodgers said.

Skillet missed the extra point, but his three-pointers more than made amends.

For once, Iowa's kicking game was better than its opponent's. Skillet had a better day than Langeloh, who missed both of his short attempts. Jim Hujsak, who had struggled somewhat with his punts, boomed seven for a 43-yard average.

Duckett, who shredded Iowa for 175 yards in MSU's 17-14 victory last year in Iowa City, picked up 121. Hickson finished with 86. But neither could break the back-breaker.

"They were eating chunks up, but we kind of lulled them to sleep, too," Fry said.

When Iowa needed a big play on defense, he said, the

Iowa halfback Nick Bell (43) caught a five yard TD pass from Matt Rodgers to give the Hawkeyes a 9-0 lead.

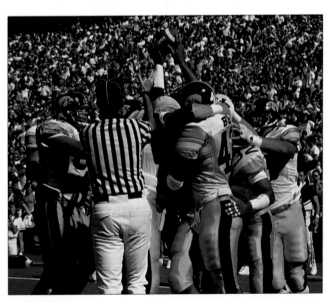

"They were eating chunks up, but we kind of lulled them to sleep, too."

Coach Hayden Fry

Hawkeyes knew where to look.

There were lots of big plays, perhaps none bigger than when Derby tackled Enos inches short of a first down at the MSU 29-yard line with less than two minutes left. That set up Skillett's clinching three-pointer and sent many of the 76,873 folks home early.

Derby finished with 11 tackles, and Foster was credited with 20, a phenomenal total that could make him the Big Ten defensive player of the week.

"He and Derby both were great," Fry said. "Some of those hits, those were pro hits."

Another vicious hit, this one by defensive end Moses Santos, flattened Enos late in the first half. Santos came from the blind side and belted the Spartan quarterback just as he threw the ball.

Enos finally got up, missed a few plays and returned for the second half. He hit 17 of 34 passes for 199 yards, well under his normal completion rate of 64 percent.

Enos sorely missed Courtney Hawkins, an All-Big Ten wide receiver who broke his collarbone last week. Spartan receivers dropped several balls.

Enos had passes picked off by Foster and Jason Olejniczak.

Rodgers clicked on 20 of 38 passes for 236 yards with no interceptions. And that came with Jon Filloon, one of his favorite receivers, on the sideline most of the game because of a leg injury that will be evaluated week by week.

Fumbles by Sean Smith and Tony Stewart following

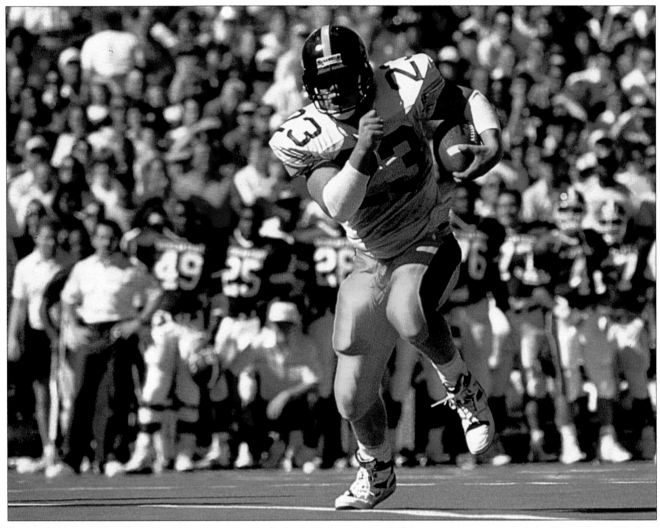

Paul Kujawa was filling in for Lew Montgomery, who had a broken collarbone. Kujawa, a walk-on, rushed for 55 yards and blocked well. "He played one of the gutsiest games I've ever seen," Coach Hayden Fry said.

pass receptions hurt Iowa's scoring chance. The Hawkeyes disputed both, thinking their people had hit the ground before fumbling.

In the final analysis, it did not matter.

Fry got a big hug after the game from one of his sons, Adrian, and looked very, very happy.

He likes beating the big boys and the Spartans are considered so in the Big Ten.

"Damn right," Fry said.

The victory will bring Iowa votes in the Top 25, and it could go a long way toward a winning season and a bowl bid.

Are the Hawkeyes back?

"For this game they were," said Fry.

This was the ninth straight time an Iowa-Michigan State game was decided by six points or fewer, and it squared the series record at 13-13-2.

It's been a great series, but won't be resumed until 1993, when Iowa makes a return trip. The Spartans drop off Iowa's schedule the next two years, with Indiana taking their place.

So long, old chum.

Iowa Tops U-M, Sitting in Driver's Seat in Big Ten

By Jim Ecker, The Gazette

I f you saw a delirious bunch of football players dancing their way into Iowa City Saturday night, don't be too alarmed.

They were only the Iowa Hawkeyes doing the hokey-pokey after their monumental 24-23 victory over the Michigan Wolverines.

Paul Kujawa's 1-yard plunge with 69 seconds left and Jeff Skillett's PAT gave Iowa a victory it will cherish for a long, long time and sent the Hawks dancing to their favorite dance again.

"Can you believe it!" said Iowa Coach Hayden Fry after he escaped the delirium in the U of I locker room. "Two wins in the state of Michigan in the same year. Woo-eee! First time ever."

Iowa whipped Michigan State, 12-7, two weeks ago in East Lansing, and on Saturday the Hawks were feeling mighty fine about the Big Ten race.

"We're sitting in the driver's seat," declared linebacker John

Eddie Polly and Iowa held Michigan's Jon Vaughn, the nation's leading rusher, to 96 yards. Vaughn did score on a 2-yard touchdown run in the first half.

SCORE BY QUARTERS
Ann Arbor, Mich., Oct. 20, 1990

IOWA	0	7	3	14	— 24
MICHIGAN	7	7	6	3	— 23

Derby, whose interception with 48 seconds left sealed the victory.

The 22nd-ranked Hawks stand 5-1 overall and 3-0 in the Big Ten, tied for the top spot with Illinois and Minnesota. Michigan, which was ranked No. 1 in the country just two weeks ago, fell to 3-3 and 1-2.

The Hawkeyes felt they didn't get any credit in the Detroit newspapers for their win at Michigan State, and they used that perceived slight to their advantage.

"Not one word of credit for the state of Iowa or the Hawkeyes," moaned Fry.

Even USA Today, he said, picked Saturday's Michigan State-Illinois game as the key to the Big Ten race, neglecting the Hawks.

"Oh well," said Fry. "It helped us. Thank you."

Iowa, a 13-point underdog, executed a beautiful 85-yard drive to the winning touchdown in the final minutes as Matt Rodgers picked the Wolverines apart.

Rodgers completed 5 of 6 passes for 67 yards on the march,

none bigger than a 12-yarder to Tony Stewart, who made a twisting catch for a first down at the 1. Kujawa scored on the next play and the Hawks went nuts.

Rodgers enjoyed a big afternoon before 105,517 fans and a national cable audience on ESPN. He hit 27 of 37 passes for 276 yards and a 4-yard touchdown to Danan Hughes, and did not throw any interceptions.

"We played about as close to perfect as we can," said Rodgers. "And it's tough to beat any team when you play perfectly." For a while, it looked like Rodgers might be the goat. Iowa failed to call a time-out with 19 seconds left in the first half and the ball at Michigan's 1-yard line, and the half ended, with Marvin Lampkin stopped just short of the goal line on a running play.

Fry roared in Rodgers' face, but later learned a substitute messed up and never made it to the huddle. Rodgers never got

the message to call a time-out and said he confused the game clock with the 25-second clock.

"It was just a miscommunication," said Rodgers.

"I apologized to Matt and the team before we went out for the second half," said Fry.

Whatever he said worked.

Iowa's defense held Michigan to just three first downs in the second half, and the Hawks roared back from an eventual 20-10 deficit to win.

"I'm happier than if we won the Big Ten championship or a bowl game," crowed Fry.

"Just incredible."

Iowa quarterback Matt Rodgers completed 27 of 37 passes for 276 yards and one touchdown. He completed 5 of 6 for 67 yards on the winning touchdown drive in the fourth quarter.

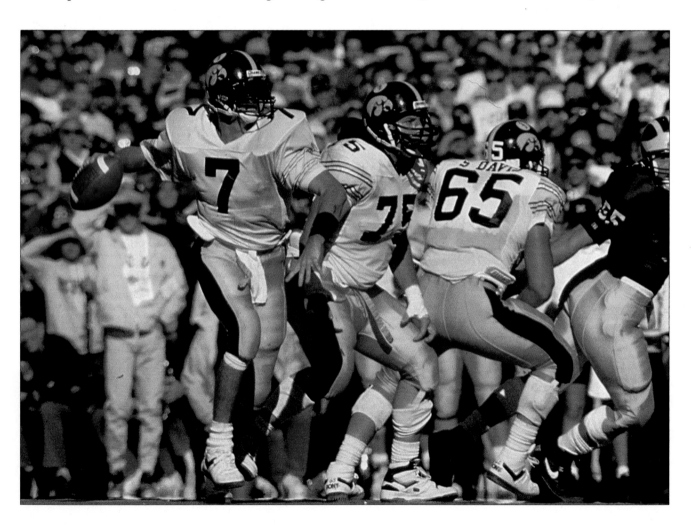

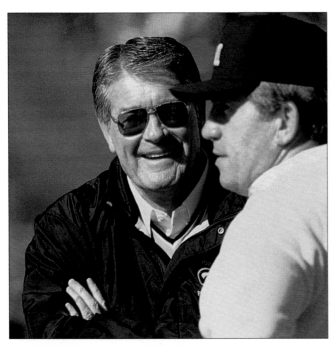

Iowa Coach Hayden Fry, left, had plenty to smile about after his team defeated Gary Moeller and Michigan.

But he said it was not his biggest win ever, not even his biggest in Ann Arbor.

"No, Lord, no!" he said "I remember one time we came up here and won, 9-7."

That was in 1981 and it propelled Iowa to the Rose Bowl. The Hawks think it could happen again.

Saturday's outcome ended two long Michigan streaks.

The Wolverines had won 22 straight Homecoming games dating to 1968. They hadn't lost back-to-back Big Ten home games since 1967, when Bump Elliott was the U of M coach.

Gary Moeller calls the shots for Michigan now, and one call the Wolverines made in the third quarter could haunt him for a long, long time.

Dwayne Ware had just given Michigan a 20-10 lead when he recovered a blocked punt in the end zone for a touchdown, and the hosts tried to trick Iowa with a sneaky two-point conversion.

While the holder and kicker lined up for an apparent extra point, a quick snap went to Jarrod Bunch, who was stopped short. A kick would have made it 21-10, and it's that one point that cost the Wolverines a potential 24-24 tie.

"This is coaching," said Moeller. "I'll take all the blame."

Ken Sollom, Michigan's holder, has the option of calling the play if he thinks it will work.

He did, but it didn't.

"We should have kicked the ball," said Moeller. "It's my call."

Last week, a failed two-point conversion pass with six seconds left cost Michigan in a 28-27 loss to Michigan State when no official called pass interference.

Michigan looked good in the first half. Jon Vaughn ticked off sizeable runs and Elvis Grbac hit 70 percent of his passes.

A 35-yard punt return by Tripp Welborne led to Vaughn's 2-yard touchdown, and a 38-yard kickoff return by Derrick Alexander set up Allen Jefferson's 7-yard score.

But the Hawkeyes adjusted after trailing, 14-7, at halftime. Vaughn, the nation's leading rusher, finished with 86 yards and spent much of the fourth quarter on the bench after aggravating an ankle injury.

This victory was no fluke. Iowa beat Michigan in first downs (24-11), total yards (367-236) and time of possession (33:18-26:42).

For Iowa, the glory was spread around. Nine Hawks caught passes and everyone seemed to make at lest one big, big catch.

Kujawa caught six, Hughes five, Michael Titley four, Jon Filloon and Mike Saunders three each. Filloon, knocked out of action two weeks ago with a bad knee, made a 16-yard grab on Iowa's winning touchdown drive.

Trailing, 20-10, late in the third quarter, Rodgers took Iowa on a 67-yard drive that culminated with his 1-yard sneak early in the fourth quarter. Skillett's extra point made it 20-17.

J.D. Carlson booted a 47-yard field goal for Michigan with 4:27 left, but Iowa took the ball and moved swiftly to victory.

Seven bowl scouts attended, but they might have wasted their time as far as Iowa is concerned.

A scout from the Florida-Citrus bowl was impressed with Iowa, but maybe a little too much.

"They may be going a little farther west than us the way they're playing," he said. And that could be Pasadena, the site of the Rose Bowl.

There are still five games left, starting Saturday against Northwestern at Kinnick Stadium.

Looming on the horizon is a Nov. 3 trip to Illinois. Circle that date on your calendar.

Bell Helps Hawks Ring Up Another Key Road Victory

By Jim Ecker, The Gazette

SCORE BY QUARTERS					
Champaign, Ill., Nov. 3, 1990					
IOWA	21	14	9	10	— 54
ILLINOIS	0	14	0	14	— 28

Maybe the Rose Bowl won't be good enough for the Iowa Hawkeyes this year.

Is the Super Bowl booked yet? And how about the national championship? Has Notre Dame or some other pretender already staked its claim?

If not, step aside for Hayden Fry's dancing fools, who danced all over the fifth-ranked team in the country Saturday afternoon while turning in yet another impressive performance on the road in the Big Ten.

It was Iowa 54, Illinois 28, and who in their right mind believes it? Stunning. Fantastic.

Unbelievable. Incredible.

Pick a word.

"It was like a whirlwind, wasn't it?" marveled Fry. "Just chopped 'em up."

And now the Iowa Hawkeyes lead the Big Ten with their first 5-0 league record since 1958. Pasadena is getting a whole lot closer.

"We could go for the Rose Bowl. We could go beyond that," said quarterback Matt Rodgers. "If we win the next four games, it could be anything."

A national tittle? For a team that started the season in purgatory? For a club that began the day ranked 13th in the country?

Rodgers cautiously backed off that idea, not wanting to arouse an upcoming opponent, but he was thinking along those lines.

"I'm looking at Ohio State right now," he insisted.

Ah, the Buckeyes. They'll be at Kinnick Stadium next Saturday trying to derail the Rose Bowl express.

Right now, it's hard to picture.

John Derby, a force at linebacker again, thinks there's only one team that can stop Iowa now. "I really think ourselves," he said, "if we fall over and lay dead."

Not likely.

This was an awesome, awesome performance by a team that's been overlooked and underrated most of the year.

It was 21-0 in the first quarter, 35-7 in the second.

Rodgers threw two touchdown passes, Tony Stewart

Senior running back Nick Bell (43) rambled 44 yards on Iowa's first play from scrimmage and finished with 168 yards. The Hawkeyes totaled 540 yards in total offense to improve to 7-1 overall and 5-0 in the Big Ten.

threw a touchdown pass on an exotic play and Jim Hartlieb threw a touchdown pass on an exotic play.

But the big, big story was the running game. The young offensive line blew holes in one of the strongest defenses in the country, and when you give Nick Bell a foot he takes a mile.

The 255-pound senior shredded the Illini for 130 yards in the first quarter alone, and his 44-yard gallop on Iowa's first play from scrimmage set the tone.

He finished with 168 yards and Stewart got 101 for their fourth 100-100 day of the year.

The Illinois defense spent most of the afternoon clutching at straws, when it wasn't sitting stunned on the sidelines.

Iowa scored touchdowns on its first five possessions and finished the day with 540 yards of total offense.

"If they play that way they can definitely beat anyone, anytime, anywhere," remarked Illinois Coach John Mackovic.

The Hawkeyes (7-1, 5-0 in the Big Ten) hold a one-game lead over Illinois (6-2, 4-1 in the Big Ten) and Minnesota

(5-3, 4-1 in the Big Ten) with three weeks to play in the Big Ten campaign.

It could be a beautiful November if the Hawks keep playing like this.

"That was just unbelievable," said Fry. "The running and the blocking, and when we had to throw the ball, it was truly exceptional From the sideline it just appeared everything was going great."

Fry marveled at Bell, who had TD runs of 26 and 1 yards.

"I wonder if anybody has seen anybody like Nick Bell at the college level," he said. "I thought I knew everything about Nick Bell, until the first half. He was incredible."

Reporters were piled six-deep around Bell, who finally got the 100-yard game he craved against a quality opponent.

"It shows we're capable of doing anything," he said.

He made believers out of Illinois, which features five All-Big Ten players on defense, including an All-American in Moe Gardner.

"I honestly think they looked past us," said Bell. "I don't think they thought we would do the things we did today."

Pick a statistic and Iowa excelled: 335 yards rushing, 205 yards passing, 24 first downs, a 13½-minute advantage in time of possession, no turnovers for the third straight game. You name it.

Fry said he's only felt this good one other time in his football life.

"Yeah, when I got a 10-year contract," he said with a twinkle. "That's the only thing I can think of that big."

The good feelings were all around for Iowa.

"I feel better than I ever felt in my life," said Rodgers, who engineered a flawless game.

He had plenty of reasons to feel good. Remember those four interceptions when Illinois whacked the Hawks, 31-7, in Iowa City last year? Ancient history now.

He went 11-of-16 for 188 yards and two TDs this time, and not even a hint of an interception.

"This week we put it all together," he said. "If we play like that, there's not too many teams in the nation that can beat us."

The one saving grace for Illinois was Jason Verduzco. The 5-foot-9 quarterback completed 32 of 51 passes for 358 yards and four touchdowns, but he was throwing uphill.

Shawn Wax caught 11 passes for 136 yards and three

touchdowns.

Verduzco gamely peeled himself off the Memorial Stadium turf all afternoon. Sacked four times and whacked a number of others, he kept coming back.

"Man, he got tea-kettled time after time," said Fry. "I'd like to have that little guy on my team. But right now I'll have to stick with Matt Rodgers and Nick Bell and Tony Stewart and all those guys."

A throng of 72,714 packed Memorial Stadium on Homecoming to get a piece of the Hawkeyes, who aren't too popular in these parts because of Iowa's role in the NCAA investigation of the Illinois basketball program.

But when it was over, most of the Illini faithful had left, leaving the 5,000 or so Hawkeye fans in the southwest corner of the end zone free to celebrate with their loved ones.

The Hawkeyes, en masse with their coaches, went

"I honestly think they looked past us," said running back Nick Bell (43). "I don't think they thought we would do the things we did today." The Hawkeyes totaled 335 yards rushing.

straight for their bench to salute their fans in a love-fest that lasted several minutes after the game.

"Undefeated in the Big Ten and loving it!" Melvin Foster, Iowa's exuberant linebacker, told the bumblebee backers.

Iowa took control early and never let go.

Illinois fumbled on its second play of the game. Derby recovered. Bell ran for 44 yards and the show was on.

Mike Saunders caught a 5-yard TD pass from Rodgers.

Danan Hughes caught a 3-yard TD toss from Stewart on a halfback-option pass. Bell shed a linebacker at the line of scrimmage and dashed 26 yards for a touchdown.

It was a 21-0 at the quarter, that by a team that had scored 16 points in all its first quarters combined this year.

But wait.

Bell clobbered two Illini near the goal line and spun across for the score. 28-0.

Illinois scored on a 20-yard pass from Verduzco to Wax, but that was only a temporary setback.

Iowa lined up for a field goal, but Hartlieb spun away., spotted Matt Whitaker open in the end zone and lofted a 14-yard TD pass. 35-7.

Five possessions for Iowa, five touchdowns.

Perfection.

And that against a defense that had allowed one touchdown in the last three games, and against a defense that had allowed only two touchdown passes all season.

The 54 points were the most a John Mackovic team at Illinois had ever allowed, and the most points Iowa had scored in Champaign since spotting 58 way back in 1899 when this ancient series began.

Mackovic told Fry, "you did a masterful job of getting your team ready to play today."

"They took advantage of every single possibility," said Mackovic. "They forced turnovers, they ran the ball hard right at us, they passed the ball, they picked up the blitzes when we tried.

"They really didn't give us much of a chance to get started."

Iowa led, 35-14, at halftime, a nice cushion but still not enough against a potent team like Illinois.

So the Hawkeyes came out firing in the second half. Rodgers found Hughes with a perfect 17-yard strike for a touchdown, Jeff Skillett kicked a 29-yard field goal and it was 44-14 with 5:20 left in the third quarter.

And the Hawkeyes loved it.

"The whole game was fun," said Hughes. "We had a good time out there." And they didn't even dance the hokey-pokey. Iowa's being referred to as "dancing fools" in *Sports Illustrated* rankled Fry last week.

Hey, these upsets of ranked teams on the road are becoming commonplace.

First Michigan State, then Michigan, now Illinois.

The Hawkeyes are waiting to dance in Pasadena.

And Illinois? More bad news. The Illini visit Michigan next Saturday.

Saunders Saves Day For the Hawkeyes

By Jim Ecker, The Gazette

One of the worst days of his life turned out just fine for Matt Rodgers on Saturday.

Thank you, Mike Saunders.

And that's to all the Iowa Hawkeyes who play defense and defense and defense some more.

A frustrating day for Iowa ended in jubilation when Saunders turned a last-ditch toss from Rodgers into a 14-yard touchdown with 44 seconds to go as the Hawkeyes broke Wisconsin's hearts, 10-6.

The miracle at Camp Randall Stadium extended the "Iowa Jinx" over the Badgers to 15 years, but this one left the 75,053 spectators gasping for air at the end.

"That's the way football is supposed to be played," said Iowa Coach Hayden Fry.

Rodgers had four of his passes picked off, including one for a 65-yard touchdown by Troy Vincent that kept Wisconsin in the lead until the bitter end of this Big Ten struggle.

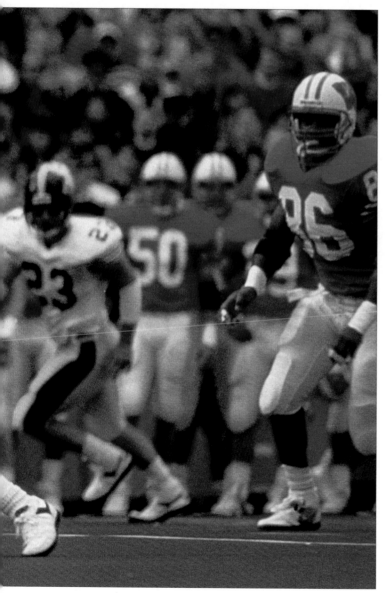

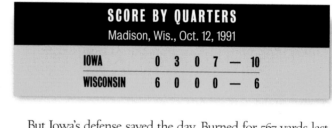

SCORE BY QUARTERS					
Madison, Wis., Oct. 12, 1991					
IOWA	0	3	0	7	— 10
WISCONSIN	6	0	0	0	— 6

But Iowa's defense saved the day. Burned for 567 yards last week against Michigan, the Hawkeyes absolutely stifled the young Badgers. Wisconsin collected four first downs and 82 yards all day, yet nearly pulled it out.

"Our defense played their hearts out," said Wisconsin Coach Barry Alvarez, who learned his lessons well at Fry's knee during eight years on the U of I staff.

"That's the hardest way to lose," said Alvarez. "Right now, they're down. You could have heard a pin drop in the locker room.

"Our kids played a Top-20 team nose to nose. It was like a 15-round heavyweight championship bout."

The Badgers had 17th-ranked Iowa staggering against the ropes, but Rodgers & Co. shrugged off the blows and finally delivered the knockout punch.

It came down to this: 50 seconds to go, Wisconsin leading 6-3, and Iowa faced with fourth-and-5 at the Badgers' 14-yard line.

The Hawkeyes surrounded Fry during a time-out.

"We were not going to go for the tie," Fry announced. "I already told everybody we're not going for the damn tie.

Iowa quarterback Matt Rodgers threw four interceptions, and one was returned for a touchdown. But he redeemed himself by throwing the winning score with 44 seconds remaining.

"I wasn't going to miss the trip if I had to drive up myself."

Mike Saunders, halfback

We're not going to kick a field goal. That kind of spiced everybody up."

Saunders, battling sore ribs, lined up as a wingback to the left. Rodgers hit him in stride, and the senior from Milton, Wis., slipped away from the Badgers' Reggie Holt and nosed into the end zone behind a block by Jon Filloon on Rafael Robinson.

The Hawkeyes squeezed Saunders in the end zone, making it even tougher for him to breathe. Saunders called the winning touchdown an isolation play.

"It was designed to get a first down," he said. "I was able to turn it up and get into the end zone."

Injured last week against Michigan, Iowa's No.1 tailback began the game on the bench but ended the afternoon in heaven.

"Just by luck we brought him along," said Fry. "If it hadn't been Wisconsin, we wouldn't have brought him along."

But there was no keeping Saunders out of his home state this day, cartilage problems or not.

"I wasn't going to miss the trip if I had to drive up myself," he said.

The Hawkeyes self-destructed all day against an inspired Wisconsin defensive unit that took its cue from Dan McCarney, the former U of I coach who is the Badgers' defensive coordinator.

Wisconsin Coach Barry Alvarez, right, was an assistant on Iowa Coach Hayden Fry's staff for eight seasons.

Vincent's 65-yard gallop to paydirt with an errant Rodgers pass in the first quarter was just the start of a long afternoon for the All-Big Ten quarterback.

Rodgers, who suffered 10 interceptions in 12 games last season, had three more picked off before the day was done.

Iowa intercepted one Wisconsin pass, but it was a doozy by Jason Olejniczak with 4:30 left in the game. It put the Hawks in business at the Badger 43-yard line, and this time the offense produced with everything on the line.

It looked bleak when Iowa faced 4th-and-8 at Wisconsin's 41 with 3:06 left, but Rodgers rifled an 11-yard sideline pass to Filloon for a first down.

It looked bad when the Hawks were looking at third-and-8 with 1:58 left at Wisconsin's 28, but Rodgers found Alan Cross for a 9-yard gain and another first down.

It looked nearly hopeless when the Hawks were left with fourth-and-5 at the Badger 14 with a mere 50 seconds to go.

Wisconsin came with a blitz, but Rodgers found Saunders in time on the left flank.

"They brought the house on the last play, and our line was able to pick it up," said Saunders.

Fry said he never considered

Because of injuries, junior fullback Lew Montgomery (34) started at tailback and gained 66 yards. Iowa, ranked 17th, struggled on offense for most of the game before pulling it out late in the fourth quarter.

yanking Rodgers in favor of Jim Hartlieb.

"Oh, no. You don't pull an All-Big Ten quarterback," said Fry. "You just give him time. He'll figure it out."

He did.

"A pro quarterback couldn't have thrown better strikes," said Fry of the winning drive.

"And he had to. Wisconsin was playing perfect defense."

Rodgers finished 23 of 37 for 180 yards. He refused to blame a sore hand for the four interceptions.

"I didn't play well today. I'll admit that," said Rodgers, who hurt his hand against a Michigan helmet last week.

"It's no big deal. We got the win and I'm happy."

Color all the Hawkeyes happy. With Saunders ailing and No. 2 tailback Marvin Lampkin home with a stress fracture in his leg, the Hawks went with fullback Lew

Montgomery at tailback and Montgomery responded with 66 yards.

With Rod Davis, Iowa's No. 1 middle guard, sidelined following arthroscopic knee surgery Friday, the Hawks got a solid game from Brett Bielema on the defensive line.

John Derby, the linebacker from Oconomowoc, Wis., led the charge with 12 tackles.

"Our defense was great," said Fry Freshman Jay Macias played most of the game at quarterback for Wisconsin, with senior Tony Lowery sidelined because of a bad thumb. Macias completed 5 of 16 passes for 22 yards.

But it was Jay Simala, the third-string quarterback who threw that ill-fated pass that Olejniczak intercepted in the fourth quarter.

Hawkeyes Beat Bucs in Thriller

By Jim Ecker, The Gazette

The Iowa Hawkeyes won this game for the grieving people back in Iowa City.

They won it for their loyal fans who followed them here.

And deep down, the Iowa Hawkeyes won this one for themselves. Justice prevailed Saturday as the Iowa Hawkeyes beat Ohio State, 16-9,

in a gripping Big Ten football game before a record crowd of 95,357 at Ohio Stadium. The Hawkeyes lost Matt Rodgers, their all-Big Ten quarterback, to a knee injury late in the third quarter, but held on behind another ferocious defensive effort.

"You're looking at the happiest man in the word right now," said Iowa Coach Hayden Fry. "What a tremendous victory."

But Fry wasn't happy just for himself, or just for his team.

"That tragedy back in Iowa City was so sad and so bad,

SCORE BY QUARTERS						
Columbus, Ohio, Nov. 2, 1991						
IOWA	0	13	3	0	—	16
OHIO STATE	0	9	0	0	—	9

I know it had something to do with us winning," he said soberly.

Nothing can ease the pain over those killed, he said, but at least for a few hours the Hawkeyes gave people a few hours of happiness.

"We won this for the University family," he said. "That's why this was so special."

When it ended — when Iowa had only its second win here in 30 years — the Hawkeyes shared victory with their jubilant fans in the northeast corner of the stadium.

Some of the Hawks jumped into the stands and traded hugs. Then, in the joy of their locker room, they danced the hokey-pokey.

Rodgers sprained his left knee late in the third quarter with the Hawks clinging to a 13-9 lead, but they closed ranks behind No. 2 quarterback Jim Hartlieb and kept OSU off the scoreboard.

"We came together and knew if we could keep them out of the end zone we'd win the game," said U of I linebacker John Derby. "We wanted to win it for Matt and we wanted to win it for the whole team."

Rodgers was enjoying a career day, hitting 20 of 27 passes for 258 yards and a 61-yard touchdown to Alan Cross

Lew Montgomery rambles for 43 yards against the Ohio State defense. He finished the contest with 71 yards rushing.

before he got bent over backward on a 3-yard run to the Buckeye 5 late in the third quarter.

Fry doubts Rodgers will play next Saturday against Indiana at Kinnick Stadium.

"It could go as many as four weeks," said Fry. "I don't think he'll be back this week, but he could be back in a couple of weeks.

"In the meantime, I'm confident Jim Hartlieb can do the job."

Jeff Skillett kicked a 30-yard field goal shortly after Rodgers got hurt, giving Iowa its 16-9 advantage. A 50-yard pass from Rodgers to Danan Hughes set it up.

And then Hartlieb and the U of I defense did what had to be done.

Hartlieb chewed some time off the clock and Iowa's "Sack Pack" took over.

Make that, Leroy Smith took over. The senior from Sicklerville, N.J. set a school record by sacking OSU's Kent Graham five times.

"We knew we were going to stop them," said Smith, a man of few words but many sacks.

The last time Iowa beat Ohio State here, the Hawkeyes wound up playing in the Holiday Bowl and the Buckeyes fired their coach. That was in 1987, and the same things could happen this year.

The 11th-ranked Hawkeyes (7-1, 4-1 in the Big Ten) are tied with Indiana (5-2-1, 4-1 in the Big Ten) for second place in the Big Ten, with the league runner-up heading to the Holiday Bowl in San Diego this season.

And OSU Coach John Cooper, under fire, might be running out of time here, just as Earle Bruce did after losing to the hawks 29-27 in 1987 on that miracle 28-yard pass from Chuck Hartlieb to Marv Cook with six seconds to go.

Nobody broached the subject with Cooper after the game.

"Give Iowa a lot of credit," he said.

"They played hard and deserved to win."

Jim Hartlieb, Chuck's younger brother, said he was thinking about Chuck and that dramatic game in 1987 during pregame warmups.

Iowa grabbed a 7-0 lead in the second period when Rodgers scored on a 1-yard keeper to cap an 84-yard, 13-play

Iowa Coach Hayden Fry was all smiles after the Hawkeye' victory, even though quarterback Matt Rodgers suffered a knee injury late in the third quarter.

drive. The Hawkeyes inserted two extra offensive linemen on the TD play, giving them a nine-man front with seven offensive linemen and two tight ends.

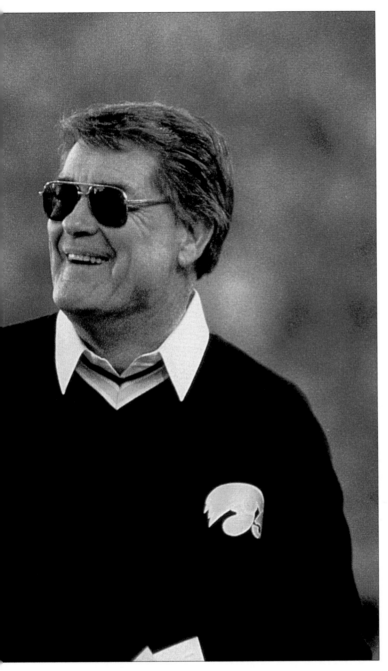

"That's what we call our 'Whale' formation," explained Fry, alluding to all the extra power up front.

Ohio State tied it, 7-7, with a sudden Snow-storm on a crisp day in the Old Horseshow.

Carlos Snow carried the ball nine straight times for OSU, finally scoring on a 2-yard run.

Snow accounted for every yard on the 50-yard drive as the Buckeyes blew gaping holes in Iowa's defense for one of the few times all day.

But the first-half thrills were far from over.

On third-and-2 from their 39, the Hawkeyes caught the Buckeyes in a blitz and made them pay. Cross was all alone and raced 61 yards with a soft toss from Rodgers.

"I was just hoping I didn't fall down on the way," said Cross, smiling.

That made it 13-7, but problems in the game struck again.

Skillett, who earlier missed a 32-yard field goal, had his PAT attempt blocked by OSU's Greg Smith, but that wasn't the end of it.

Ohio State's Jason Simmons picked up the bouncing ball and raced 85 yards for a two-point conversion for the defense, a gimmick adopted by the NCAA just a year ago.

So instead of leading 17-7 (if Skillett makes the field goal and PAT), the Hawks had only a 13-9 edge. And it stayed tense until the very end.

Ohio State, which beat Iowa, 27-26, with one second to go in Iowa City last year, tried for another dramatic finish.

Kent Graham lofted a 50-yard pass into the end zone toward Joey Galloway with 90 seconds left, but Iowa's Gary Clark batted it away.

A few plays later, Iowa's Love Fest '91 was happening in the stands in a replay of a 1990 celebration at Illinois.

The 13th-ranked Buckeyes fell to 6-2 overall and 3-2 in the Big Ten and were fairly lucky the game was as close as it was.

Iowa had a 2-to-1 advantage in total yards (443 to 221) and a 3-to-2 advantage in time of possession (36:01 to 23:59).

Ohio State, which led the Big Ten in rushing offense and rushing defense, got outdone in both areas, with the Hawks holding a 160-124 edge on the ground. Lew Montgomery collected 71 yards, including a 43-yarder, and Mike Saunders had 65.

Montgomery and Saunders also caught six passes apiece.

Fry raised his record against Ohio State to 3-7-1 with a victory for the ages.

"That's one I'll cherish for the rest of my life, for a lot of reasons," he said.

Iowa Remains Dean of Series Against Wisconsin

By Jim Ecker, The Gazette

P raise the Lord and strap on those dancing shoes.

There's a 63-year-old grandfather on the loose in Iowa City, and he's feeling mighty fine.

"Am I really 63, nearly 64, going through this?" Iowa Coach Hayden Fry wondered Saturday afternoon. "I feel like a young man."

"Man, I was hokey-pokeying and getting with it!"

The reason was Iowa's improbable, no, weird, no, crazy 23-22 Big Ten football victory over the hard-luck Wisconsin Badgers at Kinnick Stadium.

The Hawks won it with 55 seconds to go, when Jim Hartlieb and Anthony Dean seared their names into the hearts of Badger fans everywhere.

First came Hartlieb's 4-yard TD lob to Dean. That pulled the Hawks to 22-21.

Then came Hartlieb's two-point bullet to Dean for the lead and a big, big party in the end zone.

"At first I thought I was going to get myself hurt because everybody was jumping on top of me," said Dean, an unlikely hero.

SCORE BY QUARTERS					
Iowa City, Oct. 10, 1992					
WISCONSIN	0	6	6	10	— 22
IOWA	0	7	0	16	— 23

He was playing because Danan Hughes, who broke another career record Saturday with 2,052 receiving yards, had to retire early because of a sore ankle after passing Ronnie Harmon in the record book.

"We all had faith in A.D.," said Hartlieb.

And the Hawks had faith in each other.

It came down to this: Wisconsin leading 22-15 just 3:54 left in the game and the Hawks 80 yards away from the end zone.

"I just came in the huddle and told the guys it's our game to win if we want it," said Hartlieb. "We were in this position last year and we came through and we can do it again."

Last year, Matt Rodgers hit Mike Saunders with a 14-yard TD pass with 44 seconds left to beat the Badgers, 10-6, in Madison.

This time, the Hawks were kinder. This time they won it with 55 seconds to go.

"Hell, they're both tough," said Wisconsin Coach Barry Alvarez in sad defeat for the second year in a row.

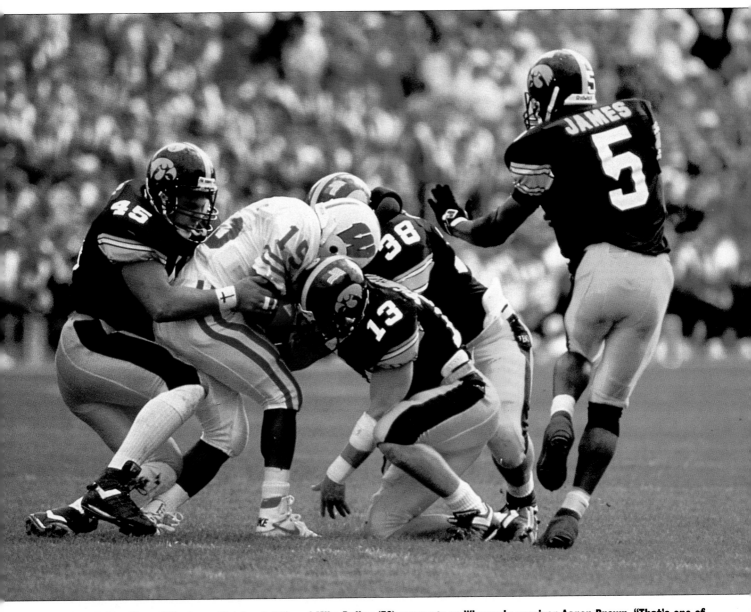

Iowa's Bobby Diaco (45), Jason Olejniczak (13) and Mike Dailey (38) converge on Wisconsin receiver Aaron Brown. "That's one of the most courageous victories I've ever been associated with," Hawkeyes Coach Hayden Fry said.

Hartlieb did it all on the winning 80-yard drive.

He passed 20 yards to Alan Cross. He passed 14 yards to Dean. He scrambled 17 yards for a big first down. He passed 33 yards to Marvin Lampkin, who scooted to the 3.

And then, on third-and-4, he waited and waited and waited and found Dean, who jumped and took the ball away from Wisconsin's Reggie Holt in the side of the end zone for six huge points.

"He did tip the ball," said Dean. "I was up in the air, and I bobbled it for a second.

"Once it hit my hands, I said I'm not going to drop this. This is staying in my hands."

Hartlieb took a little victory dance in the end zone after the ensuring two-point pass to Dean for the 23-22 lead, but it was far from over.

Wisconsin's Rich Thompson, blessed with a powerful leg,

lined up for a 53-yard field goal with six seconds left and 70,387 fans holding their breath for the outcome.

The snap came back on a hope, Thompson hesitated, then kicked it low and Iowa's Carlos James leaped and knocked it down.

"We felt that if we didn't block it, it was going to be good," said James, who was all smiles as he clutched the game ball.

Scott Plate, who recovered the blocked kick, gave James the pigskin for safekeeping.

"I'm keeping this with me all night," said James. "If you see me out, I'll have the ball."

Maybe he should have three, for the block and his two interceptions, one of which stopped a two-point conversion by Wisconsin in the third quarter. As it turned out, that was a big play, too.

But, the biggest news was Hartlieb, the oft-maligned quarterback who etched his name into Hawkeye lore in the fourth quarter.

"I've had a lot of great quarterbacks do a lot of great things, but that has to go right up there at the top," said Fry.

He put Hartlieb's name right up there with Chuck Long, Chuck Hartlieb, Mark Vlasic and Rodgers, the Hawkeye QBs of yesteryear who pulled a few chestnuts out of the fire during their years at Iowa.

Saturday's outcome left Iowa with a 2-4 overall record, but that's not the important number.

In this year of the Big One and Little Nine in the Big Ten, the Hawks are tied for second at 1-1, and did somebody say Citrus Bowl? That's where the Big Ten runner-up goes this year, and why not Iowa?

"We played the best," said Fry of losses to Miami, Michigan, Colorado and North Carolina State, "now win the rest. We've kind of taken up that motto."

The Hawks did the hokey-pokey Saturday, but there was no dancing at the other end of Kinnick.

"We're decimated," said Alvarez, who spent eight years on Fry's staff at Iowa. "Hell, nobody is up there partying. I'll guarantee you that."

This was a strange, strange game from the start.

Iowa kicked a field goal, then gave it back to try for a touchdown after Wisconsin roughed little Andy Kreider on the boot.

Oops. On the next play from the 9-yard line, Hartlieb tried a pitchout when he should have eaten the ball, and Wisconsin got the ball.

Later, the Hawks sacked Darrell Bevell on fourth down, which should have given Iowa the ball. But the Badgers were called for a dead-ball penalty before the snap, which nullified the sack and let Thompson kick a 44-yard field goal, pulling Wisconsin to 7-6.

Weird stuff.

The Badgers blocked a Kreider field-goal try late in the first half, then Kreider hit the upright on a 19-yard chip shot in the third quarter.

So the Hawks got to the 9-yard line and did not score. They got to the 19 and did not score. They got to the 2 and did not score. In other words, it didn't have to be that dramatic at the end.

Hartlieb completed 31 of 51 passes for 297 yards and two touchdowns. There was the big 4-yard TD to Dean and also an 11-yarder to Cross in the first half.

Hartlieb has passed for 605 yards and five TDs the last two weeks, which should stifle his critics.

"There are a lot of doubters out there," said Hartlieb. "I've heard different people saying he can't throw downfield, he's a running quarterback.

"I had kind of a goal to prove to people I'm a complete quarterback."

He got some help Saturday with nary a sack all day long.

The blocking was much better, with Scott Davis making a surprise return from the disabled list to lend a big hand at tackle after Bill Lange limped off in the second quarter.

The Hawks got Davis back but lost guard Ted Velicer to a knee injury.

That's why Fry was so moved after the game.

"That's one of the most courageous victories I've ever been associated with," he said.

"How we pulled it off, gentlemen, I just give credit to the Lord. And I'm sincere about that. I just don't know how else we could have won it."

The Hawks visit Illinois next Saturday in another big game, but now they know they can win.

"It's a huge, huge emotional boost for us right now," said Hartlieb.

Senior fullback Lew Montgomery (34) and Iowa defeated Wisconsin in the final minute for the second straight year. In 1991, Iowa won on a touchdown with 44 seconds remaining.

Iowa's Offense is Golden in Victory Over Gophers

By Jim Ecker, The Gazette

SCORE BY QUARTERS						
Minneapolis, Minn., Nov. 19, 1994						
IOWA	14	14	21	0	—	49
MINNESOTA	10	7	15	10	—	42

If you watched on TV, you probably didn't believe your eyes. If you were there, you had trouble catching your breath.

In a wild, crazy, nutty, unbelievable type of Big Ten football game, the Iowa Hawkeyes defeated Minnesota, 49-42, before 43,340 disbelieving fans Saturday night in the Metrodome.

How's this for nuttiness?

Tim Dwight, the fourth-string tailback, threw a touchdown pass to quarterback Matt Sherman for a 42-32 lead late in the third quarter.

Four seconds later, the Hawkeyes scored again when Bo Porter returned a fumbled kickoff 10 yards to the end zone for a 49-32 bulge.

And you know what? The game was far from over at that point.

Minnesota scored 10 points to close to 49-42 with 3:06 left and Iowa had to hold on for its life.

"Unbelievable," said Iowa Coach Hayden Fry.

In a game of wild offensive fireworks, it came down to a defensive stand by the Hawkeyes at the end of the night.

Parker Wildeman sacked Minnesota quarterback Tim Schade for an 8-yard loss at the Gopher 15-yard line with 1:25 left, then Bobby Diaco tackled Chuck Rios short of a first down on fourth-and-8.

Iowa (5-5-1, 3-4-1 in the Big Ten) ran out the clock and kept possession of Floyd of Rosedale.

"Thank gosh our guys sucked it up at the last," said Fry. "Otherwise they probably would have gone right down the field and scored again."

Minnesota (3-8, 1-7 in the Big Ten) finished last in the Big Ten after scoring its most points against Iowa since 1949.

"How you can have 562 yards of total offense, score 42 points and not win is beyond me," said Gopher Coach Jim Wacker.

It's simple. Demo Odems and Bo Porter recovered fumbled kicks for a pair of touchdowns, giving Iowa a 14-point edge in speciality teams. That offset all those fancy numbers by Minnesota.

Otherwise the game looked like something you'd see on a sandlot some Sunday afternoon, except with lots of polish.

"It was kind of a street fight there," said U of I guard Matt Purdy. "We scored, they scored, we scored. We knew we had to outscore them."

Odems and Sedrick Shaw, the distant cousins from Texas, scored twice apiece as Iowa finished the 1994 season in style.

"Sed told me to have a big game or he'd beat me up," joked Odems.

It was the second big game in a row for the Hawkeye offense: 49 points against Northwestern last week and 49 more against the Gophers.

"We've got a high-powered attack coming back next year," said Odems. "We're excited about it."

Sherman was the trigger man again, passing for 258 yards and two TDs in his second start.

"He's a dandy quarterback," said Wacker.

The Hawkeyes and Gophers have been tangling in this border skirmish since 1891. They never combined for this many points before. The previous high was 75, all by Minnesota in a 75-0 blowout in 1903.

The teams combined for 997 yards of total offense. Schade passed for 365 yards and Chris Darkins rushed for 188 yards and three TDs for the Gophers.

Hausia Fuahala (91) and the Hawkeyes maintained possession of Floyd of Rosedale.

The first half was jam-packed with spectacular plays and ended with Fry complaining about a bum call that cost Iowa its fifth touchdown of the half.

The Hawks settled for a 28-17 lead at intermission after an exhilarating 30 minutes of football.

It started early when Dwight separated Minnesota's Rodney Heath from a Nick Gallery punt at the goal line, with Odems recovering for a Hawkeye touchdown less than two minutes into the game.

That was just the opening salvo in a game-long brawl.

Darkins split a pair of Hawkeye defenders and raced 56 yards for a touchdown, tying the score at 7-7.

That happened less than three minutes into the game.

A few minutes later, Tavian Banks exploded around the right side of the Minnesota defense and scooted 25 yards for a TD. That made it 14-7 for the Hawkeyes.

The Gophers got a field goal and the first quarter ended with Iowa holding a 14-10 edge.

Minnesota took a 17-14 lead in the second period when Schade found Rios in the back of the end zone for an 8-yard TD, but the Hawks came storming back on a pair of sensational plays by Shaw.

The first one took several looks at the big-screen replay board at the Metrodome to believe.

The Hawkeyes picked up a blitz and Sherman hit Shaw in stride near the U of I sideline.

Shaw tip-toed to stay in bounds, then did a 360-degree spin to elude a Gopher defender before loping to the end zone for a 46-yard touchdown.

"It was just instincts," said Shaw.

Brion Hurley's PAT made it 21-17, but there was more to come.

Sherman passed 33 yards to Anthony Dean. Banks ran for 11. Kent Kahl banged for 22.

Banks ran for 9 more.

A penalty set them back, but Shaw took a straight handoff, cut and juked and high-stepped 17 yards for another Hawkeye score and a 28-17 advantage.

Iowa threatened again in the first half when Dwight fielded a punt, started to his right, stopped and circled left for a 42-yard return.

Sherman passed Iowa to the 6-yard line, where his fade pass to Dean appeared to give the Hawkeyes another score. The catch was ruled out-of-bounds and Fry complained as he left the field.

Hawkeyes' Shaw Badgers Wisconsin

By Jim Ecker, The Gazette

The Iowa Hawkeyes won it for Hayden.

With the 1995 college football season hanging in the balance Saturday, the Hawkeyes fought off Wisconsin in an emotional game dedicated to Coach Hayden Fry. Sedrick Shaw galloped for 214 yards and the defense survived an aerial onslaught by Wisconsin's Darrell Bevell to post a satisfying 33-20 victory before 78,907 fans at Camp Randall Stadium.

The victory kept Iowa's bowl hopes alive and extended its mastery over the Badgers and Coach Barry Alvarez for another year.

The Hawkeyes (6-4, 3-4 in the Big Ten) gave Fry the game ball out of respect and appreciation for his comments at Tuesday's press conference, when he scorched the media and some fair-weather fans.

"Coach Fry always takes the blame for us and is never going to put us in a bad situation," quarterback Matt Sherman

SCORE BY QUARTERS					
Madison, Wis., Nov. 18, 1995					
IOWA	7	17	0	9	— 33
WISCONSIN	0	7	7	6	— 20

explained. "We as players said, 'Let's do this for Coach Fry.' He's taken a lot of blame.

"This game was dedicated to him."

The Hawkeyes snapped a four-game losing streak and moved into serious contention for the Sun Bowl should they beat Minnesota this Saturday. There are other bowl possibilities as well if Iowa finishes 7-4.

Fry seemed touched by getting the game ball from his players. Captain Matt Purdy made the presentation in the locker room.

"First time I've ever gotten one from my players," Fry said. "I'm very appreciative of the intensity today.

"We obviously were on a mission this week, and we were successful."

Fry got his fourth straight win over Alvarez, one of his former assistants, and raised his record to 14-0-1 against the Badgers since becoming Iowa's head coach.

"I couldn't put into words how important this game was to the football team and the coaching staff, after what we've been through," he said. "Playing so hard against teams like Penn State and Northwestern and still losing the ballgames

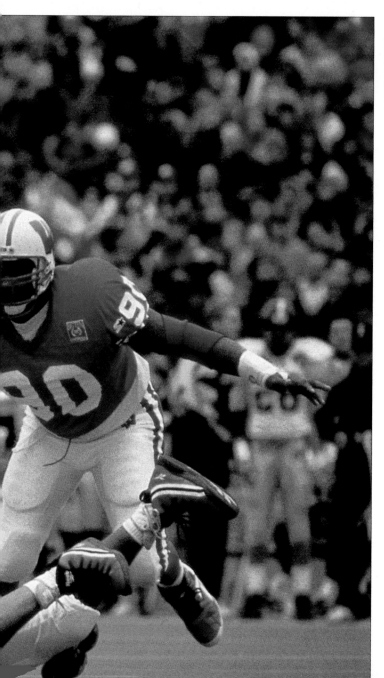

Iowa running back Sedrick Shaw set the school season record for rushing yards with 1,304. Dennis Mosley previously had 1,267 in 1979.

Jared DeVries and the Iowa defense gave Wisconsin little room to roam.

right at the end.

"I would have to classify this as one of my top-five victories of all time."

The Hawkeyes blasted to a 21-0 lead in the second quarter and had a 24-7 cushion at intermission, but Bevell made

them woozy in the second half with his antics.

The 25-year-old quarterback hit 19 of 21 passes for 207 yards in the third quarter alone as he rallied the Badgers within striking distance at 24-20.

The Hawkeyes bent but they did not break, thanks to four

Iowa's Sedrick Shaw (5) rushed for 214 yards and 3 touchdowns.

interceptions and another record-setting day by Shaw.

Bevell finished 35 of 51 for 352 yards and two touchdowns including two key picks by Damien Robinson that helped save the day.

Shaw, who set the U of I career rushing mark last week against Northwestern, snapped the single-season record Saturday with his 214-yard performance that included three touchdowns.

Shaw raised his season total to 1,304 yards, breaking the mark of 1,267 set by Dennis Mosley in 1979, but was seen limping to the locker room with a sore leg when it ended.

This raucous affair had more twists and turns than the picturesque roads through the Wisconsin countryside, and it all came down to the fourth quarter.

The Badgers (4-5-1, 3-4 in the Big Ten) stopped Iowa on fourth-and-goal from the 1-yard line with 10 minutes left in the game, keeping U-W within 24-20 and a shot at victory. Then things began to unravel.

Wisconsin offensive lineman Jamie Vanderveldt was caught holding Iowa's Jon LaFleur in the end zone for an automat-

ic safety, giving the Hawkeyes two points and a 26-20 lead with 10:20 remaining.

The teams traded turnovers, then Iowa put the game away with a 75-yard drive that ended with Shaw picking his way into the end zone from 4 yards away for his third TD.

Zach Bromert's 35-yard PAT after a celebration penalty made it 33-20 with 5:35 left and the Badgers could not recover.

"I thought Iowa was on the edge and we had all the momentum," Bevell said afterward.

The loss knocked Wisconsin out of contention for a bowl bid and extended its frustration level against Iowa to 19 years. The Hawkeyes are 16-0-1 against the Badgers since their last loss in 1976. The streak includes nine straight wins.

Fry beat Alvarez in 1990, '91, and '92 when Alvarez was getting his program started at Wisconsin, but they didn't meet in '93 when the Badgers went to the Rose Bowl or again in '94, when Wisconsin went to the Hall of Fame Bowl.

"I know we weren't very good the first three times we played," Alvarez said. "I don't know how good we are now."

Hawkeyes Bask in G

ow of Win in Sun

By Jim Ecker, The Gazette

The sun finally shone on the Iowa Hawkeyes in a bowl game. The Hawkeyes gave a dazzling performance in the 62nd Sun Bowl on Friday and dominated 20th-ranked Washington, 38-18, before 49,116 fans in El Paso.

The Hawks won their first bowl game since 1987, and they did it in style.

"That was a fine effort by a group of fine young men," Iowa Coach Hayden Fry said,

"And they whipped — and I put that in capital letters — a very, very fine Washington team that was co-champs of the Pac-10."

SCORE BY QUARTERS						
El Paso, Texas, Dec. 29, 1995						
IOWA	10	11	10	7	—	38
WASHINGTON	0	0	6	12	—	18

Fry had been 0-4 against Pac-10 teams in bowl games, including losses to Washington in the 1982 and '91 Rose Bowls, but he declined publicly to revel in getting that monkey off his back.

Don Patterson, his offensive coordinator, did the speaking on that topic.

"The Pac-10's kind of had our number," Patterson said. "It's nice to even it up. Not just even it up, but do it in a decisive way."

Iowa (8-4) jumped all over the mistake-prone Huskies from the start.

Hayden Fry had been 0-4 in bowl games against Pac-10 teams. That is, until Iowa trounced Washington, 38-18.

Tavian Banks (22), who missed half of the season because of a broken wrist, rushed for 122 yards.

It was 10-0 after one quarter, 21-0 at halftime and 38-6 early in the fourth quarter.

"They came out and royally kicked our butts," said Washington Coach Jim Lambright.

The Hawkeyes did everything right. Sedrick Shaw and Tavian Banks gave Iowa a pair of 100-yard rushers with big games. Kickers Brion Hurley and Zach Bromert broke school and bowl records by going 5-for-5 on field goals. The defense stuffed Washington and collected three turnovers in the first half. The offense turned those gifts into 13 points.

"I can't believe we just dominated the ballgame the way we did," said Fry, who got a victory ride from his players and a victory salute from the fans, who chanted "Hayden, Hayden, Hayden" as the seconds ticked away at Sun Bowl Stadium. Iowa had an awful experience on its last trip to Texas, losing 37-3 to California in the 1993 Alamo Bowl, but

this was a completely different story.

This day, the sixth-place team from the Big Ten was clearly superior to the co-champs from the Pac-10, who managed just three first downs and 90 yards of offense while the game was being decided in the first half.

Shaw, one of 17 Texans on the U of I roster, gave Iowa a 7-0 lead with a 58-yard burst less than two minutes into the game after Washington fumbled a punt.

Hurley made it 10-0 shortly after with a 49-yard field goal, the first of three long boots by the junior from Iowa City. That came after the Huskies (7-4-1) fumbled their first play from scrimmage.

"It was eight minutes into the game and we only had one play," moaned Washington quarterback Damon Huard, who was harassed by the Hawkeye defense all day until Lambright yanked him in the second half.

The game snowballed from there. Washington

snapped the ball out of the end zone in punt formation for a safety, making it 12-0. Bromert nailed a 33-yard field goal, making it 15-0. Bromert hit again from 34 yards, then Hurley drilled another from 47 and it was 21-0 at the half.

There was more to come. Hurley hit a 50-yard field goal that would have been good from 70. Banks turned a simple pitch into a 74-yard scamper, the longest of his career. Fullback Mike Burger plowed into the end zone for a pair of TDs.

"We got crushed," said Washington linebacker Jason Chorak. "I don't think anyone thought we'd lose this game."

The Hawkeyes thoroughly enjoyed their day in the sun.

"That was the best game of my life," Hurley said. "I thought we had a good chance to win, but I never thought we'd win so decisively."

Bill Ennis-Inge, a force at defensive end, spent the latter stages of the game singing with the Hawkeye fans and band as it celebrated the victory.

"We were almost flawless," he said: "We took advantage of their mistakes."

Washington played without injured All-America safety Lawyer Milloy and defensive lineman David Richie, which hindered their efforts.

"Replacing an All-American is impossible," said Hawkeye center Casey Wiegmann.

Lambright made no excuses. "We hurt ourselves, but they were good enough to take advantage," he said.

Shaw won the game MVP award after rushing for 135 yards on 21 attempts, giving the junior 1,477 yards for the year. He was happy to share the backfield with Banks, who missed half the season because of a broken wrist but made up for lost time with 122 yards on 13 tries.

"It's fun having Tavian back," Shaw said. "You can switch in and out and nobody can concentrate on one back."

Banks broke three tackles on his 74-yard run, which carried to the Washington 6. Burger scored two plays later for a 31-6 bulge midway through the third.

"It felt good," Banks said of his 74-yard jaunt. "I got my opportunity."

Iowa rushed for 286 yards, with Shaw and Banks com-

IOWA BOWLS WITH FRY

Hayden Fry's bowl record is 7-8-1 overall and 6-6-1 as the Hawkeye coach.

YEAR	BOWL	RESULT
1982	Rose	Washington 28, Iowa 0
1982	Peach	Iowa 28, Tennessee 22
1983	Gator	Florida 14, Iowa 6
1984	Freedom	Iowa 55, Texas 17
1986	Rose	UCLA 45, Iowa 28
1986	Holiday	Iowa 39, San Diego State 38
1987	Holiday	Iowa 20, Wyoming 19
1988	Peach	North Carolina State 28, Iowa 23
1991	Rose	Washington 46, Iowa 34
1991	Holiday	Iowa 13, Brigham Young 13
1993	Alamo	California 37, Iowa 3
1995	Sun	Iowa 38, Washington 18
1996	Alamo	Iowa 27, Texas Tech 0

bining for 257.

"Tavian's as quick as a cat," Patterson said. "His feet don't stay in one place too long."

Some of the Hawkeyes felt the Huskies looked down on them this week in El Paso. That made the victory taste twice as sweet.

"A lot of those Washington guys didn't respect us," cornerback Plez Atkins said. "The Big Ten was tough this year.

"We whipped their butts, just like they deserved."

Hurley won the MVP award for special teams players, and freshman defensive tackle Jared DeVries got the MVP award as the best lineman.

DeVries recovered one fumble and forced another, collected one of Iowa's four sacks and spent considerable time in the Huskies' backfield.

"I'm just happy," DeVries said about being named one of the MVPs. "I give that award to the entire team. The whole defense did a fine job with the scheme the coaches gave us."

Iowa broke an 11-game losing streak against ranked teams and ended an 0-3-1 string in bowl games since a 20-19 victory over Wyoming in the 1987 Holiday Bowl.

Hawkeyes Rally From 17 Down to Humble Spartans

By Jim Ecker, The Gazette

SCORE BY QUARTERS						
Iowa City, Oct. 6, 1996						
MICHIGAN STATE	17	6	7	0	—	30
IOWA	0	10	20	7	—	37

The boos began early in the first quarter Saturday but slowly turned to cheers as the Iowa Hawkeyes dusted themselves off.

By the time it ended, Coach Hayden Fry and the Hawkeyes were celebrating one of the biggest comebacks in school history and equaling the best comeback in the Fry era at Iowa.

The Hawkeyes went from bums to heroes in the space of one gorgeous afternoon with a wild 37-30 victory over Michigan State at sunny Kinnick Stadium.

The Hawkeyes trailed, 17-0, in the first quarter and the boobirds in the sellout crowd let them have it. Loud and clear.

Later, researchers combed the record books and found only one comeback victory bigger than this in the last 50 years: A 34-31 verdict over Oregon in 1949 afer trailing, 24-6. The rally matched one in 1986 at Minnesota, when Iowa trailed, 17-0, at halftime and won, 30-27, on a Rob Houghtlin field goal.

Fry and the Hawkeyes emerged from a happy locker room after winning their Big Ten opener by the skin of their teeth.

"We were slapping everybody on the back up there, the way they hung in there after getting off to a terrible start," Fry said.

"I'm extremely proud of our guys for keeping the faith and believing and doing whatever was necessary to come back and win the ballgame."

The Hawkeyes trailed, 23-10, at halftime, but junior Plez Atkins gave an impassioned speech to his teammates before they returned for the third period.

"We came out the second half and BAM!, it happened. We got right back in the ballgame," defensive tackle Jared DeVries said. "I think that sparked the team."

It went like this:

Tom Knight intercepted a pass and Matt Sherman hit Chris Knipper with a 9-yard touchdown pass, Knipper's second of the day.

Tim Dwight sped 46 yards with a punt return, shedding tacklers all the way to the MSU 5-yard line, and Sherman flipped a little pass to Sedrick Shaw for the score.

The Hawks, once given up for dead, suddenly had a 23-23 tie with 25 minutes remaining in this entertaining game.

Michigan State scored, Iowa countered, and they wheezed

Sedrick Shaw (5) dashes for daylight against the Spartan defense.

"We got ripped today. I could care less, as long as we win the ball-game. You guys are for stats, I'm for winning."

Coach Hayden Fry

Quarterback Matt Sherman, who passed for 177 yards and three touchdowns, visits with Coach Hayden Fry on the sideline.

into the fourth quarter, all knotted at 30-apiece.

Iowa took the lead on Michael Burger's 1-yard plunge into the end zone with 12:37 left, but nobody breathed easy until Damian Robinson intercepted a Michigan State pass in the end zone with less than 30 seconds to go.

"This is huge for us, especially coming from behind," said Sherman, who passed for 177 yards and three touchdowns. "We put a lot of points on the board. It was a good day." Michigan State (2-3, 1-1 in the Big Ten) nearly made it an awful day for the Hawkeyes (3-1, 1-0 in the Big Ten). The Spartans crammed the ball down Iowa's throat most of the afternoon with Sedrick Irvin and Duane Goulbourne scooting through holes created by big Flozell Adams, a 325-pound mountain of a man.

Adams dominated DeVries, Iowa's best defensive lineman who was one of the MVPs in the Sun Bowl last December.

"Yeah, it was rough," DeVries said. "He was a force. He's probably one of the best ones I'll go against all year. He did a heckuva job."

Irvin, a true freshman, slashed for 137 yards, and Goulbourne, a sixth-year senior, tacked on 109 of his own.

That wasn't all for the Spartans. Freshman quarterback Bill Burke caught Hawkeye defensive backs napping for a pair of first half touchdown passes. Add it up and Michigan State had all the ingredients for an upset victory.

"Obviously, we're very disappointed," MSU Coach Nick

Saban said. "We did a lot of good things, but Iowa has a very good football team. We gave up a couple of big plays and that had a big difference in the game."

Michigan State won most of the statistics: First downs

Iowa's Chris Knipper (81) caught two touchdown passes.

(24-15), yards rushing (236-138), total yards (399-315) and time of possession (34:32 to 25:28).

Iowa did not get untracked until Sherman and Demo Odems connected for a 54-yard gain on third-and-22 from the Hawkeyes' 10-yard line on the last play of the first quarter. That was Iowa's initial first down.

"We got ripped today," Fry acknowledged. "I could care less, as long as we win the ballgame.

"You guys are for stats, I'm for winning."

Brion Hurley helped Iowa win the ballgame with a 51-yard field goal and exquisitely placed kickoffs into the sun.

Three times Hurley arched a high kickoff into the sun near

the west sideline, and three times the Spartans fumbled the ball out of bounds.

Marvin Wright fumbled twice and Derrick Mason, one of the top kick-return men in NCAA history, dropped one near the sideline and another in open field.

Burke led the Spartans to Iowa's 20-yard line in the final seconds, where he faced fourth-and-3. He looked into the end zone for Gari Scott, but misfired. Robinson picked it off and the Hawks were out of trouble.

"It's a big win," DeVries said. "Any win is a big win. You don't want to start off the Big Ten season with a loss. It wasn't pretty, of course."

Happy Days for Hawkeyes After Happy Valley Win

By Jim Ecker, The Gazette

They were cold, wet, and tired, but it didn't matter. The Iowa Hawkeyes refused to leave the field.

They hugged. They danced. They celebrated with their fans. They raised their arms to the soggy skies above Beaver Stadium.

Finally, slowly, they retreated to the warmth and comfort of their locker room.

Then the chant began. "Hayden! Hayden! Hayden!"

The Hawkeyes must have repeated it a dozen times as they saluted coach Hayden Fry after their impressive 21-20 upset victory over 10th-ranked Penn State Saturday.

"What a happy group of young men," Fry said after leading the Hawkeyes in the hokey-pokey, their favorite victory dance. "Gee whiz. It makes coaching worthwhile."

The Hawkeyes danced in celebration of their first victory over a Top-10 opponent since 1990, when they dumped No. 5 Illinois and No. 8 Michigan on their way to Pasadena and the Rose Bowl.

"Big. Huge. The only words to explain it," said defensive tackle Jared DeVries. "We have confidence now. As soon as we step off the bus in Iowa City we're going to start thinking about Ohio State."

But not yet. The Hawkeyes were not done celebrating a rare victory in Happy Valley.

"This is Happy HAWKEYE Valley!" Fry announced.

Penn State Coach Joe Paterno owned a glossy 151-30 record in 31 years of home games at Beaver Stadium, but it's 151-31 now.

SCORE BY QUARTERS
State College, Pa., Oct. 19, 1996

IOWA	7	7	0	7	—	21
PENN STATE	10	10	0	0	—	20

The Nittany Lions were 10½-point favorites over Iowa, and why not? The Hawks could not beat Tulsa on the road, so why should they beat Penn State?

Too much to believe? Not necessarily.

"We knew we could do it," DeVries insisted. "It's not an upset in our eyes. Not at all. We knew we would win."

Quarterback Matt Sherman said the Hawkeyes had a great week of practice.

"We were excited coming over here," he said. "This is a great environment to play in."

Penn State embarrassed Iowa, 61-21, in their last meeting here in 1994, but the Hawks got even Saturday.

"This victory was very large," said free safety Damien Robinson, whose vicious tackling sparked the defense all day. "Penn State is considered one of the best teams in the Big Ten as well as the nation."

Running back Tavian Banks (22) and Iowa remained unbeaten in the Big Ten after upsetting No. 10 Penn State.

Fry said he felt it coming, even though he knew tailback Sedrick Shaw would be sidelined with bruised ribs.

"We showed a lot of heart today, a lot of character," Fry said. "Just super."

"Best feeling in the world," linebacker Matt Hughes remarked. "We knew the whole week we could play with these guys."

Iowa (5-1, 3-0 in the Big ten) stayed perfect in the Big Ten and knocked Penn State (6-2, 2-2 in the Big Ten) out of serious contention for the title.

Iowa's Tim Dwight scored on an 83-yard punt return and a 65-yard touchdown reception.

One of the Hawkeyes' Brightest Rainy Days Ever

By Mike Hlas, The Gazette

Blitzing Iowa safety Kerry Cooks blasted the football from Penn State quarterback Wally Richardson, and Hawkeye tackle Jared DeVries fell on it at the PSU 33-yard line.

Nittany Lions Coach Joe Paterno bit his lower lip hard enough to make his gums cry "No mas!" He had a beaten man's visage even though his team still held a 20-14 lead with more than 13 minutes left. The writing was on the Beaver Stadium wall, and Paterno knew it.

Two plays later — one a 25-yard pass from reserve tailback Rob Thein to wideout Demo Odems — Iowa led, 21-20. Penn State would not, could not threaten to score after that. It would not, could not muster any real second-half offense against Eleven Hungry Hawkeyes.

The 21-20 score lasted to the end. The 10th-ranked, sopping-wet, bone-chilled Lions departed the field in near-record time after the final play. The unranked, sopping-wet, bone-chilled Hawks wouldn't leave.

They formed a conga line of sorts to greet their pocket of fans in a stadium corner, jumping and dancing and whooping en masse, backs and tacklers, starters and scrubs.

"This is Happy Hawkeye Valley!" Iowa Coach Hayden Fry proclaimed later in a dry room underneath the stadium.

The Hawks left Happy Valley in high spirits because their defense got low-down mean and nasty in the second half. Maybe they decided that since they came all this way eastward just to slosh and shiver, they might as well get something for their troubles.

Those who make a living as motivational speakers should eavesdrop on Iowa's defensive coaches during their halftime talks to the defense. Two weeks earlier, Michigan State ran over the Hawks in building a 23-10 halftime lead. The Spartans got slowed in the third quarter and shut out in the fourth as Iowa won, 37-30.

The first 30 minutes of Saturday's game looked like the same old Penn State offense against Iowa. The Lions rushed for 186 yards in the first half. Fullback Aaron Harris had 108 of those on just six carries. Were the Hawks to win this day, it looked like it would

"I think Iowa is a darn good football team," Paterno said. "They sure were today."

Fry has 218 wins in his coaching career, but said this was extra special. "It's got to be one of the greatest, because we needed it," he said. "Joe Paterno and the tradition It's extremely difficult to win up here. And to win the way we did it. Just super."

Iowa trailed, 20-14, at halftime, but the second half belonged to the Hawks as their defense pitched a shutout.

The Hawkeyes held Penn State to 76 yards and four first downs in the entire second half after sprouting a few leaks in the first 30 minutes.

"I couldn't believe it," Hughes said. "In the second half, we were lights out."

Tim Dwight was the entire show for Iowa in the first half, scoring on an 83-yard punt return and racing under a 65-yard bomb from Matt Sherman to set up another TD.

But despite Dwight's heroics, the Hawks trailed by six at the half.

Both clubs slogged through an uneventful third quarter with Iowa still trailing, 20-14.

Then came the break they needed.

Kerry Cooks blitzed from his strong safety position and dumped Penn State quarterback Wally Richardson as the ball popped loose. DeVries recovered at the Nittany Lion 33 and the Hawks were in business.

have to be via a shoot-out.

Then came another intermission transformation.

"I don't know why," DeVries said. "We stick together and make adjustments. Our coaches do a good job at making adjustments at halftime. We never lose faith."

Fry agreed that his defensive coaches are correcting first-half sputters with their 20-minute halftime tune-ups, but added, "It looks like we might have played a little harder in the second half, too."

Penn State had four first downs and 76 total yards in the second half. Iowa's numbers weren't much better, but the Hawks got the ball in the end zone. Thanks to a set-up by the defense, of course.

"It can always get better," Iowa linebacker Matt Hughes said after his second straight outstanding game. He was the Big Ten's Defensive Player of the Week after helping the Hawks totally fluster Indiana the week before. He was in on 14 tackles and sacked Richardson twice Saturday.

But Matt, can it really get better than this outside of minor details?

"Realistically," Hughes admitted, "that was one of the best defensive performances I've ever seen."

Richardson became a sitting duck on the wet marsh, er, turf.

"It seemed like series after series we were going three-and-out," Lions flanker Joe Nastasi said. "I don't know what they did differently in the second half."

Neither did Richardson, who bore no resemblance to the fellow who fired two fourth-quarter touchdown passes in Penn State's 41-27 win in Iowa City last October. The offensive line that kept the Hawks at bay that day has moved on. The 1996 Lion blockers were overmatched against Iowa.

"It's especially disappointing when you lose real close because we should have beaten them," talented Penn State defensive end Brandon Short said.

Those words lacked substance. The Hawks took what the Lions had to give in the first half., stayed upright, then controlled the rest of the game.

"All we really needed was a big play," Short said. Yes, and all the announced crowd of 96,230 needed was sunshine to have felt more comfy as they shivered on the stadium's aluminum bleachers. That one big play was as far away as Mr. Blue Sky in the second half.

Has it been mentioned here that Iowa played great second-half defense? Well, it bears repeating. Senior free safety Damien Robinson left his calling card all over the field in the form of bruised and battered Nittany Lions. Not long ago, Robinson wasn't regarded as the most physical or most effective defensive backs on Iowa's roster. Now, he's a veritable hit man.

Iowa Maintains Dominance Over Badgers, Alvarez

By Jim Ecker, The Gazette

SCORE BY QUARTERS						
Iowa City, Nov. 16, 1996						
WISCONSIN	0	0	0	0	—	0
IOWA	10	14	7	0	—	31

Hayden Fry was one happy fella Saturday afternoon at Kinnick Stadium. Words like "tremendous" and "wonderful" and "fantastic" flowed from his lips in that Texas drawl.

He had words of praise for everyone.

He might have been the happiest 67-year-old coach in America after the unpredictable Hawkeyes defeated Wisconsin, 31-0, before 66,570 fans at Kinnick Stadium.

"Thirty-one to zip, to me, is unbelievable," Fry said. "I never dreamed we could do anything like that."

Fry had plenty to be happy about as Iowa collected its biggest victory over Wisconsin since a 41-0 whitewash in 1968.

The Hawkeyes (7-3, 5-2) climbed into a three-way tie for third place in the Big Ten and moved closer to their 13th bowl game in 16 years.

"One step closer," Fry said. "A big step."

The Outback, Alamo, Sun and Independence bowls are possibilities now with one game, a trip to Minnesota, left in the regular season.

Matt Sherman hushed critics with an impressive game at quarterback, Sedrick Shaw etched his name into the record book again and the Hawkeyes extended their mastery over the Badgers to 20 years.

Most of all, Fry was thrilled with the defensive performance that limited the big, bad Badgers to 128 yards and made 260-pound tailback Ron Dayne look like an ordinary freshman from New Jersey.

"Just fantastic," Fry said. "Just wonderful."

One statistic spoke volumes Saturday: Iowa led, 24-0, in the second quarter and at that point Wisconsin had zero net yards and zero first downs for the day.

"It seems unreal, huh?" defensive end Brett Chambers said. "Everything we did turned out well."

The Hawkeyes stuffed Wisconsin at the line of scrim-

Sedrick Shaw rushed for 143 yards and three touchdowns on runs of 39, 33 and 8 yards. He tied the school career record for touchdowns of 32, set by Ronnie Harmon from 1982-85.

Chris Knipper celebrates after catching an 8-yard touchdown pass from Matt Sherman. Iowa improved to 15-0-1 against Wisconsin under Coach Hayden Fry. Badgers Coach Barry Alvarez, an assistant under Fry, dropped to 0-5 against the Hawkeyes.

mage. Dayne, who rambled for 297 yards a week ago, had to hustle for 62 yards on Saturday as Iowa's front seven used its quickness to dodge all those 300-pounders trying to get in their face.

"It gave me an opportunity to sit back and watch," said free safety Damien Robinson, who had it quiet in the secondary.

Bill Ennis-Inge, one of 17 departing seniors, saved his best for last at Kinnick with a spectacular performance. He had four sacks (one shy of the school record), forced two fumbles and fell on a loose ball.

Just when you thought the Hawkeyes might be finished for the year — remember last week's 40-13 loss to Northwestern? — they came out and blew away a decent Big Ten team.

"We had to suck it up and regain our pride and self-respect," Ennis-Inge said.

Sherman came out hot, completing his first 10 passes as the Hawks raced away.

"I think he's symbolic of our football team," said Fry, now 15-0-1 against Wisconsin in 18 years at Iowa. "He can read, and he can hear. And I think all the experts that have written him off, had written bad articles or said bad things,

"I think (Matt Sherman is) symbolic of our football team. He can read, and he can hear. And I think all the experts that have written him off, had written bad articles or said bad things, motivated him to come front and center."

Coach Hayden Fry

motivated him to come front and center."

Sherman took short drops and completed quick passes, mostly to Tim Dwight and Demo Odems.

Those quick strikes kept Wisconsin off balance and moved the chains. It also created room for Shaw, the most prolific tailback in school history.

Shaw scooted for 143 yards and scored three times on runs of 39, 33 and 8 yards. The 8-yarder might have looked like a pass from Sherman, but was a lateral.

Shaw gave Dwight and Odems a chance to chop down some Badgers on his final TD, then waltzed merrily into the end zone for the 32nd touchdown of his career, tying the school record set by Ronnie Harmon (1982-85).

Sherman hit 12 of 17 passes for 99 yard and an 8-yard TD to Chris Knipper, who stretched the ball over the goal line.

Iowa converted 70 percent of its third-down plays in the first half and controlled the ball more than 60 percent of the game.

Sherman did not appear for postgame interviews. That's rare for him, win or lose.

Shaw spoke instead. He liked the way Sherman performed, considering all the criticism he's absorbed.

"I think that says a lot about his character," Shaw said. "I think people shouldn't pass judgement on any human being if you're not standing in his shoes. He's a great young man

and proved today that he's a competitor."

Defensive coordinator Bobby Elliott went home with the game ball after the Hawkeyes posted their first shutout since a 14-0 victory over Indiana in 1992.

Ennis-Inge set the tone early, ransacking quarterback Mike Samuel on Wisconsin's third play from scrimmage and knocking the ball loose for Jared DeVries, who was a terror on defense all day. That led to a field goal and 3-0 lead.

The Badgers went 1-2-3 punt, then Shaw quickly scored on a 29-yard burst. The Badgers went 1-2-3 punt again, then Sherman hit Knipper with a TD pass to cap a ball-control drive that took 7:43. Wisconsin went 1-2-3 punt again, and Shaw broke free for a 33-yard TD to finish a quick six-play drive.

"We've been able to establish the run most of the year," Wisconsin Coach Barry Alvarez said. "We just couldn't get it done today."

The Badgers committed five turnovers, with three fumbles and two interceptions. The Hawkeyes played a mistake-free game.

"We were beaten in every phase of the game," Alvarez said. "You have to take your hats off to Iowa."

Alvarez spent eight years at Iowa as one of Fry's assistants before leaving for Notre Dame and then Wisconsin. He hasn't beaten his old boss in five tries.

Shaw Emerges From Shadow to Spark Hawkeyes

By Jim Ecker, The Gazette

The Iowa Hawkeyes can remember the Alamo Bowl with fond memories now.

The 21st-ranked Hawkeyes threw a blanket over Byron Hanspard and Texas Tech Sunday night for a 27-0 victory before 55,677 fans in the fourth Alamo Bowl.

Hanspard rushed for 2,084 yards and won the Doak Walker Award this year as the nation's top running back, but he had 11 black-and-gold shadows in the Alamodome for the entire 60 minutes last night. He finished with a season-low 64 yards on 19 carries.

Sedrick Shaw, the "forgotten man" in all the pregame hubbub over Hanspard, emerged as the best tailback with an Alamo Bowl-record 113 yards and a sensational 20-yard touchdown.

Shaw was voted the game's Offensive MVP and Iowa's Jared DeVries garnered the MVP award on behalf of his defensive mates.

Shaw did the running, Matt Sherman and Tim Dwight did the pitching and catching, and the stout Hawkeye defense did the rest. The Hawkeyes (9-3) made amends for a poor performance in the first Alamo Bowl in 1993, when they gained only 90 yards in a 37-3 loss to California.

Iowa dedicated the game to teammate Mark Mitchell and his family following the death of his mother in a car accident Friday night.

Iowa's Sedrick Shaw (5) was overlooked leading up to the Alamo Bowl, but he was named the game's MVP after rushing for 113 yards against Texas Tech.

"We were thinking of him," DeVries said. "Our thoughts and prayers are with him and his family."

The Hawkeyes had the motivation and they had the method for stopping Hanspard.

Iowa took the Tiger Hawk emblem and gold stripe off their helmets in tribute to the Mitchell family.

"There just wasn't any way Texas Tech could beat us," Coach Hayden Fry said of the tragic circumstances surrounding the game. "Of course that's just talking, but they really felt that way."

The Hawkeyes played like a team on a mission.

"Like I said to the guys earlier today it's a great team with a purpose now," said wingback Tim Dwight, who set an Alamo Bowl record with six receptions.

"I could tell our guys were ready to go," said defensive coordinator Bob Elliott. "When we're playing right we're as good as anyone in the country."

Iowa held Texas Tech to just 206 yards and 13 first downs.

"The defense stole the show," Fry said.

The Hawkeyes made all the big plays in the first half and led, 17-0, at intermission before a highly partisan and highly disappointed Texas Tech crowd.

Shaw uncorked one of the best runs of his brilliant, record-setting career in the second quarter when he spun three times to elude tacklers and scored on a dazzling 20-yard maneuver.

Shaw celebrated too much in the end zone following his touchdown and drew a penalty for unsportsmanlike conduct, but the senior from Austin, Texas, enjoyed every minute of his trip.

Shaw drew a similar penalty in the Sun Bowl last year after a long TD run.

"His mama ran up to me after the game and gave me a

SCORE BY QUARTERS
San Antonio, Dec. 29, 1996

TEXAS TECH	0	0	0	0	—	0
IOWA	6	11	0	10	—	27

"When we're playing right we're as good as anyone in the country."

Bob Elliott

big hug and said, 'Don't say it, don't say it, you knew what we was gong to do,' " said Fry, laughing.

The Hawkeyes wanted to show everyone that Hanspard was not the only outstanding tailback in the game.

"He didn't have any respect down here the entire week," Sherman said. "Everything was about Hanspard. We had something to prove tonight."

Shaw had little to say about Hanspard and all the pregame publicity.

"That doesn't bother me," Shaw said. "He's a great back. He deserves all the credit he's gotten. He's a great man.

Sherman rolled right and found Chris Knipper for a two-point conversion after Shaw's TD, giving Iowa a 14-0 advantage.

The Hawkeyes made it 17-zip on the final play of the half when Zach Bromert, given a reprieve, nailed a 36-yard field goal. Bromert had just missed a 41-yarder when Ryan Driscoll had trouble with the snap, but an offsides penalty on Tech gave the Hawks a second chance.

The Hawks appeared to be sitting on their 14-0 lead late in the half when Sherman lofted a 51-yard pass to Dwight, setting a record for the longest pass completion in Alamo Bowl history.

Dwight caught five passes for 90 yards in the first half, returned two punts for 23 yards and made a diving tackle on punt coverage.

Iowa's defense established control of the first half on Tech's second play of the game.

Plez Atkins, from Bartlett, Texas, intercepted a pass by Tech's Zebbie Lethridge and returned 8 yards to the Red Raider 39.

Shaw, trapped in the backfield on a draw play, danced away from tacklers for 24 yards to the Tech 2-yard line. Sherman scored two plays later on a quarterback sneak for a 6-0 lead.

The snap from center Bill Reardon sailed way over Driscoll's head, following the PAT. Bromert booted a 25-yard field goal in the fourth quarter for a 20-0 bulge with 10:36 left.

Iowa polished off the Red Raiders in the final period with an impressive 14-play, 99-yard drive that consumed 7:36. Rodney Filer finished the march with an 11-yard score.

The victory squared Fry's bowl record with Iowa at 6-6-1.

"Coach Fry did a better job getting his players prepared than I did," Texas Tech Coach Spike Dykes said. "You have to blame someone and you have to start from the top. That means me."

Tech's deepest penetration in the first half was the Iowa 22. Trailing 14-0, Tech went for the first down on fourth-and-2, but the Hawks stopped Hanspard for a 1-yard gain.

Tech earlier reached the Iowa 25, but Jaret Greaser missed a 42-yard field goal.

The Hawkeyes paid a price for their victory in the third quarter when defensive backs Tommy Knight and Eric Thigpen were both hurt in the span of three plays.

Thigpen, the nickel back on passing downs, suffered a concussion. Then Knight, an all-Big Ten cornerback, hurt his left leg. He was taken to the sideline, where he suffered a mild seizure due to dehydration and collapsed.

Both players were taken to the locker room on a motorized cart for medical exams.

Neither was seriously hurt, according to U of I assistant coach Chuck Long. Texas Tech (7-5) had not suffered a shutout since a 31-0 loss to Arkansas in 1987.

Punter Nick Gallery tied an Alamo record with a 59-yard punt. Gallery also broke Reggie Roby's school record for most career punting yards.

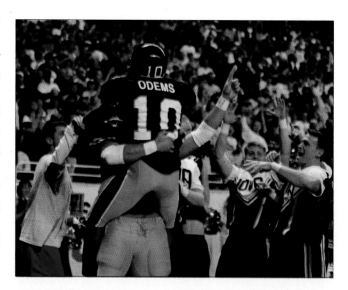

Demo Odems and Hawkeye fans had plenty to cheer about after toppling Texas Tech.

Defense Keys Hawks' Rout

By Jim Ecker, The Gazette

Bob Elliott left the press box and made his way to the field Sunday night in the final seconds of Iowa's 27-0 victory over Texas Tech in the Alamo Bowl.

Elliott, the defensive coordinator and architect of the impressive shutout, was looking for some hugs.

He found John Austin, the defensive line coach, and gave him a warm embrace.

Then he found Bret Bielema, the linebackers coach, and wrapped a big bear hug on Bielema that might have bruised a few ribs.

Then he found the players, the real heroes of last night's victory. Elliott saved the best for them. The coaches told Damien Robinson, their free safety, to shadow Texas Tech tailback Byron Hanspard as much a possible to slow the Red Raider attack. Robinson did his job from the secondary, and his teammates took care of the rest up front.

"We did what we expected to do," said Robinson, one of 17 Texans on the U of I roster.

"Like any other back we played this year, we knew what we had to do."

Sophomore tackle Jared DeVries was voted the outstanding defensive player of the game, but he'd gladly melt the award down and split the trophy 11 ways.

"If I could I would," he said. "It was a total team effort. Unbelievable."

Hanspard rushed for 2,084 yards this season and averaged 6.1 yards per carry. He eclipsed 200 yards in five games this year, but had nowhere to run tonight."

"They played a physical, fast defense," said Hanspard, who averaged only 3.6 yards on 18 carries. "We didn't execute our offense like we were supposed to."

Blame Iowa.

The Hawkeyes chased him all over the field. They did the same to Tech quarterback Zebbie Lethridge, a speedy option runner who finished with minus-four yards.

"We couldn't let them outside because they were going to outrun us," DeVries said. "The coaches had a great game plan. It was a lot of fun."

DeVries is 2-for-2 in the awards category at bowl games. He was honored at the 1995 Sun Bowl after Iowa's 38-18 victory over Washington.

Linebackers Vernon Rollins and Matt Hughes topped the defensive charts. Rollins made 10 tackles and Hughes nine. The Hawkeyes sacked Lethridge five times, with DeVries doing the honors twice.

Bill Ennis-Inge, Jon LaFleur, Robinson and Jon Ortlieb also played well.

Texas Tech scored 323 points and averaged 29.3 points this season, but the Red Raiders did not fire a shot against Iowa.

"This was a great defensive game," Texas Tech Coach Spike Dykes said.

"We couldn't let them outside because they were going to outrun us."

Sophomore tackle Jared DeVries

HAYDEN FRY

A Hero to Hawkeyes Found His Treasure in Iowa City

BY MARK DUKES

n a chilly December morning in 1978, the University of Iowa went through yet another exercise of introducing a new football coach. For going on two decades, the school had welcomed and waved good-bye to four other men who thought they could win, even sometimes gave indications they could win but somehow couldn't deliver.

Jerry Burns, Ray Nagel, Frank Lauterbur and Bob Commings had tried and ultimately failed to give the Hawkeyes a contending football team. All had their moments but all fell short. The Iowa faithful were at best complacent, at worst angry and starved for a winner.

One non-winning season had turned into 17 in a row by 1978, when Iowa hired a 49-year-old Texan named Hayden Fry. He came equipped with a distinctive drawl, an innovative offensive repuation and more one-liners than your average amateur comedian. He sought "total commitment" from everyone — university president, team, fans, media — but promised nothing more than a colorful, tough and exciting team.

Fine. But could the Iowa Hawkeyes win? For one season, at least, could they win more games than they lose? Could they beat Michigan and Ohio State, Hayes and Schembechler? Could they restore a reputation lost two decades prior, when Forest Evashevski not only got Iowa to two Rose Bowls, but won them?

It all sounded good, but could Fry deliver?

Not immediately, but almost. With new uniforms, a new logo and a new attitude, Fry resurrected a football program that many had left for dead. In his first year, the Hawkeyes won three straight games for the first time in 15 seasons. In three years, he beat Michigan and put Iowa in the Rose Bowl. In five years, he beat Ohio State. In seven, he had a No. 1-ranked team and a serious Heisman Trophy candidate in Chuck Long.

Through 18 seasons and headed for the next millenium, he had done wonders: Three Big Ten championships, 13 bowl games and 14 first-division Big Ten Conference finishes.

Fry himself couldn't write a recipe for similar success else-where. Turns out that Iowa, a state devoid of a major-league franchise, yearned for a team to holler for and spend millions on.

"I was pleasantly surprised that the essentials for winning were already present at Iowa; the academics, the enthusiasm, the crowds, the athletic director," Fry said. "Once I knew I had the opportunity to win at Iowa, the first thing to do was change the environment."

Attitudes changed.

Many fans were thoroughly encouraged — and some even celebrated — when Iowa played Big Eight powers Oklahoma and Nebraska off their feet in 1979, Fry's first season. The Hawkeyes lost both games but an overwhelmingly good feeling prevailed. Fry would have nothing of it. He chastised everyone for being satisfied with his team playing a close game.

"I had to get into the mental side of things," he said. "Players were going to class after losing to Oklahoma, and classmates and professors were slapping them on the back, telling them what a good game they'd played. I had to get across that losing and looking good was not acceptable."

Appearance changed.

Fry scrapped the old uniforms, which featured the lovable Herky, and replaced them with a version resembling those of the Pittsburgh Steelers, who had just won the Super Bowl. He had the logo redesigned to a more ferocious animal called "The Tiger Hawk." He almost immediately started the Hawkeye Marketing Group, a business which sold more than 60 items — mostly clothing and souvenirs. Fans gobbled up item upon item. Fry phased out of the business in 1981, citing media "cheap shots" over his venture, but the public had been dressed in the colors he preferred.

"Those things are all psychological," he said. "A lot of people took shots at me over the Hawkeye Marketing Group, but I knew that going in. I wanted to create an environment like at Nebraska and Oklahoma, where you see red or orange everywhere you look. I wanted to establish a black-and-gold environment on game day."

He even changed the way Iowa entered the field before kickoffs. No longer was it a helter-skelter, let's-get-fired-up entrance. He arranged his players in a tightly-fit bunch, put them hand in hand and had them jog on to the field. "The

> "I was pleasantly surprised that the essentials for winning were already present at Iowa; the academics, the enthusiasm, the crowds, the athletic director. ..."
>
> *Coach Hayden Fry*

Swarm" is as distinctive as any pregame ritual seen in Ann Arbor or Columbus.

Looking for even intangible advantages, Fry went so far as to have the visitor's locker room at Kinnick Stadium painted pink. He said he believed it would have a passive effect on the opponent. And he had a few superstitions, the most noticable for fans being the fact that, for years, Fry wore white pants and at least a black windbreaker on game day. No matter if it was a 90-degree day.

As the program grew in the 1980's and more wins added leverage to his cause, he continued to seek that "total commitment." He campaigned nearly two years for an indoor practice facility, more than once saying he'd consider resigning if the first spade of dirt wasn't turned. Requesting a $3-million-plus facility in the mid-1980's wasn't the best political move for Fry, because Iowa farmers were wrought with low market prices and high surplus.

Despite the rural plight, money poured in. Iowa became the first Big Ten school to raise $3 million in athletic depart-

Chuck Long (16) helped Fry and the Hawkeyes reach the 1986 Rose Bowl.

ment contributions in 1984. In 1985, the indoor facility referred to as "The Bubble" was finished.

Fry didn't just "ride into town on a wagon-load of wood," as he noted all too often in his early days in Iowa City. No, to understand where Fry went, one must understand where he was.

Born in Eastland, Texas, Fry became a hero in Odessa, a booming oil town in the 1940's. He quarterbacked Odessa to a 14-0 record and the state championship in 1946. In the Odessa school annual, Fry noted his ambition was "to hunt treasures."

His father died when he was 14 years old, forcing him to work on the oil rigs and at other jobs. His mother went to work taking tickets at a movie theater. "We were all poor and we knew it," Fry said of his childhood. "We made our own fun."

At Baylor, Fry was a backup quarterback who had a thing for psychology, which became his major. He continued to explore the subject during his stint in the Marine Corps and

still finds it a fascinating subject, and useful tool.

Fry eventually gave up on the idea of becoming a psychologist (at least professionally) when he had the opportunity to become his hometown's high school coach. He was an assistant coach for a year at Baylor, then for another under Frank Broyles before he became head coach at Southern Methodist.

He took the Mustangs to three bowl games, winning two, and provided fans with exciting football. Against Ohio State in 1968, SMU attempted 76 passes. Perhaps most importantly to Fry, he broke the color barrier in the Southwest Conference when he recruited Jerry Levias. "As far as I'm concerned, that's the greatest thing I've ever done," Fry said.

But Fry encountered problems at SMU. He had run-ins with some pushy alumni who thought they knew better how run a college football program, and he didn't always see about eye to eye with some of his Southwest Conference coaching colleagues. Long after he had been fired in 1972, controversy arose as to the circumstances. A report by a

Hayden Fry, left, and Joe Paterno of Penn State are the Big Ten's most revered coaches.

committee of United Methodist Church bishops alleged that SMU President Paul Hardin fired Fry after major infractions were found. But Hardin later said, "As far as I know, Hayden was not cheating during the time I knew him at SMU. The fact was that he never won enough games to suit the boosters."

Fry always has maintained the firing was a mystery to him. "No reason was ever given," he said. "None. No one even told me who was responsible for firing me. After that happened, I learned that anything can happen to anybody."

Fry rebounded with a good tour at North Texas State, where he had a 40-23-3 record in six years and consecutive seasons of 10-1 and 9-2. But even then, Fry didn't have utopia.

"We had some damn good teams at SMU and North Texas, but no one knew it. Everyone was interested in the Cowboys or Texas or Texas A&M. Or something else," he said.

Two days after firing Bob Commings after a 2-9 season, Iowa Athletic Director Bump Elliott and university vice-president Ed Jennings traveled to Dallas for a private meeting with Fry. Fry expressed interest in the Iowa job and he immediately became the prime candidate. Elliott later said about 50 people were considered and seven were interviewed, but clearly Iowa officials had focused on Fry.

"We wanted a man who had coaching experience and who we felt could come on here and turn this program around," Elliott said. "I had known Hayden for years. My brother Pete, who was then the athletic director at Miami

(Fla.), had talked to him about a job down there a few years earlier, but the situation wasn't quite right."

Fry was given a five-year contract at $45,000 annually, plus some perks. They included a commitment from the university, and undying support from fans. Unlike his stops at Denton and Dallas, Fry found in Iowa a place where there was little competition for fan allegiance. Outside of Ames, where arch-rival Iowa State played in the Big Eight, much of Iowa was Hawkeye country.

On the eve of his debut against Indiana, 700 people turned out at 6:30 a.m. for a Johnson County I-Club breakfast at which Fry revved the troops. The breakfasts, held on the Friday morning before home games, rapidly became a tradition in the Fry era.

The opener, which drew a sellout crowd, didn't turn out quite so well. Iowa stormed to a 26-3 lead against Indiana, but lost 30-26 on a 66-yard touchdown pass with 58 seconds left.

One cannot be precise as to the exact Resurrection Day in Iowa football, but some candidates emerged quickly:

■ The first three Saturdays in 1979, with hard-fought games against the Hoosiers, Oklahoma and Nebraska.

■ The 1981 season opener against Nebraska. Iowa had been drilled by the Cornhuskers 12 months earlier, 57-0, but pulled off a stunning, 10-7 triumph over the No. 7 team in the land.

■ Two weeks later in '81. Iowa upset No. 6 UCLA, 20-7, in a game that was even more lopsided than the score.

Fry chats with ABC's Keith Jackson. Under Fry, Iowa is a regular on national TV.

■Mid-October in 1981. Tom Nichol's three field goals gave Iowa its first win at Michigan in 23 years, 9-7.

■The 1981 regular-season finale. Needing an Ohio State upset win over Michigan and a victory of its own over Michigan State, everything fell into place for Iowa. Art Schlichter-led Ohio State knocked off Michigan, 14-9, in a game that concluded about midway through the game at Kinnick. Iowa ended up blistering the Spartans, 36-7, and earned its first Rose Bowl berth in eons.

Although the Hawkeyes were hammered in the 1982 Rose Bowl by Washington, 28-0, Iowa football was well on its way back. Seven straight bowl games followed in the 1980's, one of the most storied decades in gridiron history for the school.

The pinnacle was in 1985 when Iowa, the woeful program of the 1960's and 1970's, made a strong bid for the national championship.

Coming off a 55-17 Freedom Bowl bombing of Texas in 1984, a victory Fry particularly relished, Iowa drew the No. 4 ranking in the 1985 Associated Press preseason poll.

Hayden Fry: "I wanted to create an environment like at Nebraska and Oklahoma, where you see red everywhere you look. I want to establish a black-and-gold environment on game day."

With lopsided victories over Drake, Northern Illinois and Iowa State, the Hawkeyes ascended to No. 1 in the land. They protected it with tough wins over Michigan State and Wisconsin, setting up an October 19 meeting in Iowa City with No. 2 Michigan.

There have been few more defining moments in Iowa football history.

Linebacker Larry Station's crushing tackle for a third-down loss got Iowa the ball late in the fourth period, and Chuck Long moved the Hawkeyes into field-goal position. On the last play of the game, Rob Houghtlin, a former walk-on, drilled a 29-year-old field goal that lifted Iowa to a 12-10 triumph.

Iowa suffered its first loss in 1985 two weeks later at Ohio State on a wet afternoon, 22-13, putting a serious damper on Fry's chance to win a national title. A 45-28 loss to UCLA

in the Rose Bowl sent Iowa plummeting to 10th in the final rankings.

By then, though, Fry had successfully and firmly put Iowa back on the college football map. The "Big Two, Little Eight" domination of Ohio State and Michigan long had been shattered and Iowa was battling them, and the rest, on equal footing. A solid regional and national recruiting base was well in place, one that — with exception of a couple bumps along the way — translated into consistently solid teams.

Some fans wondered, at least a couple times, if Fry was losing his touch. He lost some key coaches in the 1980's — Bill Snyder, Barry Alvarez, Dan McCarney and Bernie Wyatt, among others — and Iowa slipped to 6-4-3 and 5-6 in 1988 and '89.

But the Hawkeyes responded with another Big Ten championship in 1990 (although Fry lost his third Rose Bowl game, 46-34 to Washington), and followed that with a 10-1 regular season in 1991 and a tie with Brigham Young in the Holiday Bowl.

Consecutive 5-7, 6-6 and 5-5-1 campaigns (1992-94) renewed feelings that there might be cracks in the foundation and that Fry's coaching career might be a coming to a close. But the man in the cowboy boots and sunglasses bounced back again.

An up-and-down 1995 campaign ended in a surprisingly easy, 38-18, triumph over Washington in the Sun Bowl. And in a hard-to-figure 1996 season — an early season shocking loss to Tulsa, then a victory at Penn State — concluded with a convincing whitewash of Texas Tech in the Alamo Bowl, 27-0.

Fry showed that rebuilding wasn't so much necessary as reloading, so long as a few more speedy players were part of it. Headed for his 20th season in Iowa City, Fry showed no signs of letting up.

The man who long ago thought he'd like to "hunt treasures" found a jewel in the University of Iowa. "Just once, I wanted to know what it was like to be the coach at 'The University of someplace,' " he said. Fry certainly found his place, and his treasure.